# Sociolinguistic Aspects of
# Language Learning and Teaching

# Sociolinguistic Aspects of Language Learning and Teaching

J. B. Pride

Oxford University Press
1979

Oxford University Press
Walton Street, Oxford OX2 6DP

Oxford London Glasgow
New York Toronto Melbourne
Wellington Cape Town
Nairobi Dar es Salaam
Kuala Lumpur Singapore
Hong Kong Tokyo Delhi Bombay
Calcutta Madras Karachi

ISBN 0 19 437079 8

Set in Monotype Imprint

Printed and bound in Great Britain
by Morrison & Gibb Ltd
London and Edinburgh

# Contents

viii **Contents**

# Introduction

Sociolinguistics is the name most commonly given to the study of who speaks (or writes) to whom, when, where, how, and why. In other words it is the study of natural language in all its various social and cultural contexts. In many respects therefore it deals with a larger field of knowledge than what is currently taught in many academic courses bearing the title linguistics. Properly speaking, sociolinguistics *is* linguistics, but of a kind which invites methods, models, and theories from other disciplines as well. One should not confuse any discipline, especially one which has been called 'a big pool of knowledge', with where it gets insights.

That said, it can still be asserted that there are just two main focal points in the whole field. One has been termed 'communicative competence', a possession of the individual language user; the other is the 'speech community', comprising those larger groupings of language users who share 'rules', or norms, for their use of a language or languages. Communicative competence has to do then with the individual's achievement of appropriateness and effectiveness in his choice of language (and associated non-verbal behaviour), and in a very direct and obvious sense involves both teacher and learner alike. But communicative competence must necessarily be with respect to the various speech communities to which an individual belongs. These may be multilingual, or they may not, but they will always be characterized by their own special mix of both dialects and styles of language: dialects related to social distinctions of all kinds (socioeconomic, regional, ethnic, occupational, age- and sex-related, and the like), and stylistic varieties related in particular to socially important spheres of activity (sometimes called 'domains'), topics, inter-personal relationships (of relative status, familiarity, etc.), channels of communication (speech versus writing predominantly), and speech functions (the pragmatic purpose or purposes of the communication at the time).

Communicative competence and speech community come together in the notion of verbal (also non-verbal) repertoire, namely the total linguistic, dialectal, and stylistic range from which the individual language user makes his choice. Sociolinguistics is then in part the study of all those socially and culturally meaningful choices available to and made by language users. But more too is involved than mere observable choice. Sociolinguistics takes account of the subjective side of things as well, that is to say of both individual and community-wide attitudes, assumptions, perceptions, motivations, and so on, directed moreover not only to choice of language itself but also to those who make the choices. And it is here, in this composite view of related objective and subjective factors, that we can best begin to understand what so many of our everyday labels for languages, dialects, and indeed language users, etc., really mean. The language teacher especially needs to know for example where he stands when it comes to say 'standard' and 'non-standard' (or 'vernacular', or 'sub-standard'), 'native' and 'non-native' speakers, 'formal' and 'colloquial' styles, 'high' (and 'mid') and 'low', 'international' and 'national' (or 'auxiliary'), 'major' and 'minor', 'full' and 'reduced', 'creole' and 'pidgin', 'first' and 'second', 'lingua franca', 'diglossia', 'Classical', and all the rest. To shift the image from a 'big pool of knowledge', sociolinguistics simply deals with a very large part of the ever-present problem of seeing the wood for the trees.

To pass on now to the papers themselves, in Section One, Fillmore's paper sets the scene in characteristically readable fashion, treating communicative competence as inherent in and basic to the grammatical make-up of a language rather than as something external hence merely correlatable with it. Fillmore emphasizes the linguist's need to extend his horizons from the grammatical analysis of isolated sentences to the far broader questions of coherent discourse within a theory of conversation and relationships between form and function generally. What does it mean to 'know' a language well enough to be able to use it appropriately in real-life situations? Fillmore's answers to this question take one far beyond the normal limits of autonomous linguistics, and are full of relevance to the practising teacher.

So too is Rubin's stimulating discussion of what it takes to be a good language learner: 'we need to isolate what the good learner does—what his strategies are—and impart his knowledge to less successful learners ... many foreign language teachers are so concerned with finding the best method or with getting the correct answer that they fail to attend to the learning process'. As just one example, the good language learner is a 'willing and accurate guesser'. And guessing 'is based on what we know about the social relationship between the speakers, the setting, the event, the mood, the channel ... rules of speaking ... factual probability ... also but not exclusively on what we know about grammar and lexicon'; in other words, it amounts to a kind of resourcefulness which is closely related to Fillmore's very broad conception of what knowing a language means in any case. Rubin goes into this and other learning strategies, the question of motivation ('the good language learner seems to have a high motivation to communicate, no matter where he is'), and the factor of opportunity ('the good language learner takes and creates opportunities to practise what he has learned whereas the poorer learner passively does what is assigned him'), and does not neglect to ask what the teacher can do to help matters on.

Ervin-Tripp's topic is social dialect variation, again informed by a very broad conception of the scope of communicative competence. Her discussion ranges over such questions as dialectal code-switching, stylistic consistency, current linguistic notions of inherent variability, comprehension across dialect boundaries, subjective evaluations of dialect differences, and skills in language developed by children. There is much here for the teacher who seeks new perspectives in the business of 'enlarging language competence'.

With Section Two we shift from the individual to the wider speech community. After some initial remarks on the role of sociolinguistic surveys in the implementation of policy, Whiteley presents a 'socio-linguistic profile' of Kenya, discussing various language types and language functions and going on to display something of the range of sociolinguistic variables which contribute to the amount of use made of each language. Note in particular Whiteley's emphasis on social appropriateness as a factor determining choice of language, also his concluding treatment of the basic notion of the speech community as such. There are underlying theoretical questions here which will no doubt persist, and which in one way or another confront all who are engaged in language education.

The question of the practical usefulness of sociolinguistic surveys is further taken up by Ohannessian and Ansre, with special reference to national educational needs in sub-Saharan Africa. Many relevant topics are covered in this succinct paper, including for example: styles of learning prevalent in minority groups; choice of variety of second language as a target for teaching, and attitudinal factors involved; vernacular languages as potentially 'divisive elements in the work of nation-building'; educational implications of complementary patterns of language use in the community at large; problematical statuses of forms of speech as languages or as dialects; the linguistically very heterogenous character of many classrooms in the area and the need to predict trends; attitudes towards orthographical changes; the problems posed by early school dropouts possessing a variety of linguistic abilites; the preparation of teaching materials for a given language which is first language for some pupils but second language for others; the need for 'sustained, controlled, objective observation in carefully selected areas and classrooms'; and many other related questions.

Section Three explores more fully the facts of dialectical and stylistic variation in the language of learners. As prelude, however, Haugen strikes a more basic note, in arguing, with some personal feeling, for the recognition of bilingualism itself as an achievement, rather than as a mark of impoverishment of one sort or another. His claim is that whereas bilingual education programmes have been officially supported and funded in the United States specifically for the benefit of low-income families with limited English-speaking ability, the scope of such programmes should be much broader, and be seen to be so. Only when the majority take to learning and using the language of the minority will certain types of social inequality begin to be rectified. But there are both social and linguistic reasons for the often low regard held for bilingualism. Haugen's main theme becomes in fact the nature of bilingual competence as necessarily involving quite variable and intermediate systems ('bilingual norms'), displaying the mutual influence of one language upon another which always arises in situations of language contact. 'We need to get away from the notion of "interference" as somehow noxious and harmful to the languages. The bilingual finds that in communicating he is aided by the overlap between languages and he gets his message across by whatever devices are available to him at the moment of speaking.' Haugen, like Rubin, is concerned with natural processes of language learning which have been all too often misunderstood.

Richards pursues further the theme of bilingual norms, and makes much use of Selinker's now well known theory of learners' 'inter-languages'. This notion is effectively applied in turn to immigrant varieties of English, indigenous-minority varieties of English, pidgini-zation and creolization, local varieties of English, and English as a foreign language. The reader who follows up the lead to Selinker may however find himself asking how much there is in his passing comment that learner strategies may be 'culture-bound'; and indeed whether the same question does not apply to another of Selinker's five processes, namely 'strategies of second-language communication'. There may, correspondingly, be a distinct cultural component in the remaining three processes, not least in that labelled 'language transfer'. Further-more, what is transferred may be not only cultural meanings associated with or inherent in the native languages of the learners themselves but also strategies of learning and communication associated with the native way of life generally. Selinker, one feels, is dealing with processes which are in fact as much sociolinguistic as they are psycholinguistic.

The remaining two papers in this section throw further light on the presence of code diversification in situations of language contact. Ma and Herasimchuk, introducing their report of linguistic behaviour in a Puerto Rican community in New York, claim that in such a community 'bilinguals interact and communicate with each other, using both languages, far more frequently than they interact and communicate with members of the surrounding monolingual community'. They go on: 'In such a community, speakers generate their own bilingual norms of correctness . . .,' even though they 'may choose not to apply the norms'. Thus, 'interference is a continuum' and communicative competence becomes partly a matter of 'knowing how and when to use whatever varieties of each language they may command'; while 'the linguistic norms of any speech community must always be empirically (and quantitatively) discovered for that community'.

Elías-Olivares provides an excellent brief empirical study of bilingual norms in a Chicano speech community of East Austin, Texas, to close the section. The author describes how working-class and lower-class Chicanos switch selectively between any of four varieties of Spanish (Northern Mexican, formal; Popular, everyday; Mixed, 'Tex-Mex', 'Spanglish'; and Calo, 'Barrio language') and their characteristically limited English. The Spanish varieties 'are not used in a vacuum but through community rules of appropriateness . . . in this community we find that despite the opinions of laymen that Chicano speakers speak only one form of Spanish, called Tex-Mex and considered corrupt, there exists a language repertoire composed of a wide range of varieties or styles which might not conform to the rules of the formal variety but which serves to fulfil the communicative needs of the speakers'. According to Elías-Olivares Tex-Mex is still un-mistakeably Spanish, 'rich in the use of loan words' but with only 'a certain degree of grammatical interference from English'. In addition she shows that yet another code-switching style can be observed, namely the habit of switching quite rapidly between one or other of the Spanish varieties and English. It would seem, further, that in this neighbourhood 'to be a bilingual means precisely to be able to switch rapidly from one language to the other'. The main purpose of doing this is to 'express ethnic membership', respond to shifts in formality or respect, adjust to the appearance on the scene of other individuals, and so forth.

The final part of Elías-Olivares' paper (*Conclusion and pedagogical implications*) serves well to conclude this section of our book and to introduce the final section. She states here: 'An understanding of the language situation in these communities should help us to apply some of the findings to concrete educational problems, such as the imple-mentation of bilingual educational programs.' For instance, what variety or varieties are to be selected for teaching? What are the community's feelings on the matter? Might one encourage code-switching in the teaching of some subjects? Above all, perhaps, there is the question of teacher training. She writes: 'The general attitudes of teachers show very clearly that there is a need for the implementation of basic sociolinguistic principles in teacher training particularly those that deal with language varieties and their use in the communities.'

The papers in Section Four (*Designing the language curriculum*) come to grips with some practical problems of decision-making. First is Burstall's review of the evidence presented in the final report of the NFER (National Foundation for Educational Research) French Project (1964–74). The main aims of this study were: '(i) to investigate the long-term development of pupils' attitudes towards foreign-language learning; (ii) to discover whether pupils' levels of achievement in French were related to their attitudes towards foreign-language learning; (iii) to examine the effect of certain pupil variables (such as age, sex, socio-economic status, perception of parental encouragement, employment expectations, contact with France, etc.) on level of achievement in French and attitude towards foreign language learning; (iv) to investigate whether teachers' attitudes and expectations significantly affected the attitudes and achievement of their pupils; (v) to investigate whether the early introduction of French had a significant effect on achievements in other areas of the primary school curriculum.' In the discussion which follows the reader will be particularly struck by the implications—foreshadowed in our book by Rubin's estimate of certain characteristics of the good language learner—of the finding that pupils in small rural schools 'consistently maintained a higher level of achievement in French than did those in the larger urban schools'. One of the keys to the situation is here: 'The classroom situation in the small school tends to encourage cooperative behaviour and to lack the negative motivational characteristics of the competitive classroom in which success for a few can only be achieved at the expense of failure for many.'

Cohen and Swain take us to the North American context, discussing some of the pros and cons of the 'total immersion' model of language education. They explain: 'What the total immersion model does is reverse the usual order in many bilingual education programs from L1 first/L2 second to L2 first/L1 second as far as the medium of instruction and the introduction of reading are concerned'. While reading their paper, it may be useful to refer to the following table of options, and perhaps to read into it some further relevant sub-categorizations:

## Majority group

i)  Monolingual instruction in the dominant language;
ii)  Monolingual instruction in the subordinate language;
iii) Bilingual instruction.

## Minority group

iv) Monolingual instruction in the dominant language;
v)  Monolingual instruction in the subordinate language;
vi) Bilingual instruction.

Note that each of the distinctions dominant/subordinate, majority/minority, and monolingual/bilingual may not always be completely self-evident or clear-cut. Which of the two languages French and English is 'dominant', for example, in parts of Canada? Is Spanish in the American Southwest a subordinate language in the same sense as say Maori is in New Zealand—in view of the fact that Spanish is an international language? It should also be noted that no assumptions concerning 'first' languages should be read into these six categories: this applies particularly to minority group children, whose first language may well be that of the majority group, often in contrast with the first language of their parents.

Cohen and Swain's list of eight traditional characteristics of the school experience of minority groups not receiving any form of bilingual education (our category iv), best referred to (they suggest) as 'submersion' rather than 'immersion', contrasts strikingly with their list of seventeen characteristics of 'carefully planned immersion experiences' in programmes conducted in Canada and (to a lesser extent) the United States (generally restricted to our category ii). Note also their observation that 'for the minority group child who has already learned English—perhaps as an $L_1$—immersion education might be an appropriate model' (our category v).

Litteral's clearly argued proposal for a language curriculum for schools in Papua New Guinea rests firmly on his assessment of the general linguistic situation in the country and on past education policy on languages and some of the results of this policy. Litteral's reservations on the policy of education through English only harmonize well with those of Cohen and Swain on 'submersion' programmes generally, while his detailed proposal for a carefully phased curriculum appears to be well designed to achieve the goals of education as set out in these words: 'A minimal goal of education would be to extend the linguistic repertoire of every person so that he can read and write in his mother tongue and that as many people as possible become participants in a national communicative network. This implies universal literacy with most people able to use a national language (Pidgin or Hiri Motu). From the viewpoint of the nation, this goal involves spreading its communicative network as extensively as possible throughout the nation. The maximal goal for languages in education would be to extend the linguistic repertoire for the largest number of students possible to include the effective use of English. This would strengthen one national communicative network as well as strengthen the link with the international network.'

Craig's treatment of bidialectal education in the West Indies introduces us to the problem of what to do in that kind of situation where speakers are (to a greater or lesser degree) already capable of varying their performance along a linguistic continuum—which in the West Indies is a Creole/Standard continuum, but which elsewhere may be a more obviously monolingual non-Standard/Standard continuum (as in the case of Singaporean and Malaysian English, or Black/Standard English in the United States), or a more obviously bilingual native/non-native language continuum (as in parts of Europe, West Africa, or India). The influence of popular attitudes is always a considerable factor in such circumstances (compare also Haugen and Elías-Olivares in Section Three), and Craig gives priority to this in explaining why proposals that Creole be used as the language of primary education have not so far been implemented. It is entirely typical indeed that feelings of 'linguistic insecurity' exist not least in the minds of the speakers of the non-standard (here Creole) variety itself. These tend to be ambivalent feelings however: 'In effect it is an attitude that represents a type of socio-psychological dualism in which the low-status language is stubbornly preserved by its speakers as a part of their identity and cultural integrity, but at the same time these very speakers resist any measures which, by extending the societal role of their own low-status language, might impede their children's acquisition of the accepted high-status language.' Craig goes on to question the validity of the most obvious alternative to the educational use of Creole, namely a teaching strategy 'based on getting children to correct those characteristics of their own speech that differ from the language aimed at by schools', before putting forward a teaching programme which is informed by the basic principle that 'as far as the learner was concerned, the continuum between Creole and Standard consisted of four hierarchical strata of linguistic structures as follows: L, those common to both Standard and non-Standard speech and therefore within the production repertoire of the learner; B, those not usually produced in the informal, non-Standard speech of the learner, but known to him and produced under stress in prestige social situations; C, those which the learner would recognize and comprehend if used by other speakers (especially in a meaningful context), but which the learner himself would be unable to produce; and D, those totally unknown to the learner'.

Our final paper, by Wolfram and Fasold, ties in very closely with Craig's. As Craig writes: 'By the middle of the 1960's, the resemblance between the Creole language situations in the officially English-speaking West Indies and the non-Standard English problems in the United States of America had been perceived.' Like Craig, Wolfram and Fasold are concerned with the role of attitudes: 'As he is taught to read and write, as his classroom recitations are corrected, as he is assigned to speech therapists for special language work, as his standardized test scores are misinterpreted, the child gradually is taught that the dialect he has always known only as an efficient tool of communication is considered a distortion of proper English.' The main aim of their paper is however to review the advantages and disadvantages of various methods of teaching the spoken language, reading, and writing, against the background of four alternative goals for the pupil's control of the spoken language. Particular attention is given to four strategies for the teaching of reading to pupils whose everyday spoken language is markedly non-standard. Like Craig, Wolfram and Fasold question the assumption that attitudinal factors ('value conflict') are the whole story where language learning difficulties are concerned, and like him propose that 'linguistic conflict' as such plays an appreciable part. The linguistic make-up of a language continuum is entirely relevant both to the difficulties experienced by pupils and to decisions to be made by teachers and educational policy-makers.

The point is that not only are 'value conflict' and 'linguistic conflict' both relevant, but they are probably mutually determining anyway. This assumption merely reflects a basic perspective in sociolinguistics itself, namely that 'language' and 'context of situation' are closely related, perhaps even to the point of being indistinguishable. The present book rests on several basic concepts of just such a composite nature: communicative competence (Section One), speech community (Two), code diversity (Three), for example. If the book has a single overriding purpose, it is to open up some of the practical educational consequences of this very far-reaching theoretical perspective.

# Acknowledgements

Acknowledgements are made to the following publishers from whose texts earlier versions of the extracts and papers have been taken:

Georgetown University Press for 'A grammarian looks to sociolinguistics' and 'Sociolinguistic surveys at the national level' in Georgetown University Round Table on Languages and Linguistics 1972.
Teachers of English to Speakers of Other Languages for 'What the "good language learner" can teach us' in TESOL quarterly 9:1 (1975) and 'Bilingual education: the "immersion" model in the North American context' in TESOL quarterly 10:1 (1976).
National Society for the Study of Education for 'Children's Sociolinguistic Competence and Dialect Diversity' in *Early Childhood Education* (Seventy-first yearbook, Part II).
Arlington VA, Center for Applied Linguistics for 'Some Reflections on the Uses of Sociolinguistic Surveys' in *Language Surveys in Developing Nations: Papers and Reports on Sociolinguistic Surveys.*
Professor Einar Haugen for 'The Stigmata of Bilingualism' in *The Ecology of Language.*
Language Learning for 'Social factors, interlanguage and language learning' in Language Learning 22, 2, 1972.
Research Center for Language and Semiotic Studies, Indiana University, for 'The linguistic dimensions of a bilingual neighbourhood' in *Bilingualism in the Barrio* (Language Science Monographs 7, 1971, revised 1975).
Dr. Lucía Elías-Olivares for 'Language use in a Chicano community: a sociolinguistic approach' in Working Papers in Sociolinguistics No 30, Feb 1976, sponsored by S.S.R.C. Committee on Sociolinguistics.
Dr. Clare Burstall for 'Primary French in the Balance' in Educational Research, Volume 17, 3, 1975.
Robert Litteral for 'A proposal for the use of Pidgin in Papua New Guinea's Education system', in KIVUNG Special Publication No. 1 'Tok Pisin i go we?'
Dr. Dennis Craig for 'Bidialectal education: creole and standard in the West Indies' in International Journal of the Sociology of Language 8, 1976.
Prentice-Hall, Inc., for Chapter 8 of *The Study of Social Dialects in American English.*

# Communicative competence and language learning

# A grammarian looks to sociolinguistics

Charles J. Fillmore, University of California at Berkeley

1. Linguists of the 'generativist' tradition seek to discover, for each language, a system of formal principles capable of determining the grammatical sentences in that language and capable of associating with each of these sentences those structural properties on the basis of which it can be correctly interpreted.[1] Many of the methodological assumptions linked with this definition of the grammarian's task have been challenged from time to time in the last fifteen years; and many of these challenges, and the reactions they have produced, are relevant, I think, to the subject of this year's Georgetown Round Table.

In my first sentence I used the phrase *the grammatical sentences*. The objections to the generativists' initial view of their task can be organized around a discussion of each of the three words in that phrase. The first word is *the*. It has been assumed that there is, or ought to be, a determinate set of sentences for a grammar to characterize, and to support that assumption grammarians have needed either to take as an idealization a static and uniform speech community unrealizable in the real world, or to act as if the proper object of linguistic inquiry is a private-access body of data known technically as 'my dialect'. There are thoughtful scholars who have not wished to make either of these choices. The second word is *grammatical*. The decision to define the set of 'grammatical' sentences in a language as the data to be explained by a theory of grammar—as opposed, say, to a set of sentences found in a fixed body of texts—requires a reliance on certain sorts of intuitive judgments of native speakers. These judgments concern not only the grammaticality of sentences that belong to the language without question, but also, necessarily, the exclusion from sentencehood of certain candidates for grammaticality. Unhappily, the recurrent embarrassment of the generative grammarian is that his students and his critics are forever contriving situations in which the sentences he had needed to believe were ungrammatical turned out to be completely appropriate.[2] The third word in my phrase is *sentences*. It has been assumed, in a great many linguistic traditions, that the maximum unit of analysis, the unit within which all 'purely linguistic' generalizations have their scope, is the 'sentence'. But this is surely wrong.

2. The grammarian who has faced these problems sees no hope of constructing a grammar capable of assigning grammaticality indices to sentences unless the grammar can be taken as, or as a part of, a theory which takes into account linguistic contexts larger than sentences, as well as a great many facts about the process of communication, the functions of linguistic performances, and the social occasions and literary forms in which given sentences can have given functions.

I would like to go through a chain of arguments that leads one to this conclusion. Consider first a sentence like *You didn't take any apples.* Our grammarian must surely regard this as a grammatical sentence of English. He has failed in his work if his grammar does not contain the principles according to which this sentence can be generated. These principles must specify the form of negative sentences with simple verbs, the dependence of *any* on a set of contexts including negativity, and so on.

Next, look at a larger sentence: *You didn't take any apples, and Jimmy didn't, either.* Here we have a compound sentence, once again something clearly a grammatical sentence of English. Our grammarian must ensure that his grammar provides for sentence conjunction, allows for verb-phrase deletion in the second of two clauses that are related in the way these two are, assigns contrastive stress on an unlike subject in the second of two parallel clauses, as well as de-emphasis of *didn't*, and accepts *either* at the end of the second of two conjoined negative clauses, certain other conditions being satisfied.

But now consider a sequence of two sentences: *You didn't take any apples. Jimmy didn't, either.* The second sentence in the sequence is 'authorized' by the first sentence in the same way as what we saw for the second clause of the compound sentence, but here the generalizations have to be seen as applying across a sentence boundary.

A solution that is not too unnatural is that of regarding juxtaposition as a type of conjunction, and to say that although what we seek is basically a grammar of sentences, the notion 'sentence' needs to be generalized to include sentence sequences in coherent discourse.

But now consider a case where the two sentences are spoken by different people. A says *You didn't take any apples*, and B says *Jimmy didn't, either.* The same principles hold here, too, principles governing stress placement, ellipsis, and the rest; but the term 'sentence' cannot decently be stretched to include sentence sequences in discourse to which there is more than one contributor.

Grammatical theory, somehow, must take into its scope, as we have seen, conversation or two-party discourse as well as one-party discourse. Some of the new problems the theory must face can be understood by considering a two-line conversation in which A says *You didn't take any apples* and B says *You didn't either.* Here contrastive stress is assigned to the subject of the second sentence because it has a different referent, though not a different form, from the first sentence. The two sentences constitute a well-formed piece of discourse only if they are spoken by different people. Take now the opposite case, a conversation in which A says *You didn't take any apples* and B says *Because I knew they were rotten*. This time the pronoun in the second sentence is destressed because it has the same referent as the pronoun in the first sentence, though, of course, it has a different form. It is obvious, I think, that a theory of grammar must be informed by a theory of conversation, and certain understandings about deixis and pronominal reference that make up part of that theory.

Once the grammarian has made that decision, he becomes aware that in the way that some sentences are limited to occurrence as next-sentence in a discourse, some occur only as next-sentence in a discourse at a point where there has been a change of speakers. An illustration that does not only involve pronouns can be found in the sequence *Thank you—You're welcome*, a sequence which is appropriate only if its performance is divided between two speakers.

As a first approximation to the truth, we might be tempted to say that the only thing the grammarian needs to say about *You're welcome* is that it is an acceptable second-part next-sentence for *Thank you*. My next point, however, will be that a theory of conversation must necessarily take into account the functions of utterances.

Take a trivial example first, an exchange in which A says *You're welcome* and B says *Thank you*. We understand this as an exchange in which A is reminding B that B owes him an expression of gratitude and B, perhaps grudgingly, complies. We must, in short, identify the functions of the two utterances and the sequencing expectations that are determined by those functions, in order to explain both the bizarreness of the reversed order and the way we can interpret it.

But in fact we can imagine contexts in which the sequence *Thank you—You're welcome* is inappropriate. Consider a three-line conversation in which A says *You have lovely eyes*, B says *Thank you*, and A then says *You're welcome*. The sequence can be given an interpretation, of course, but we recognize it as bizarre by realizing that the function of *You're welcome* is partly that of acknowledging that one has done somebody a favor. A compliment cannot stand as a compliment if its speaker acknowledges that in saying it he has done his subject a favor.

There are still larger sequences in which the judgments get reversed again. Consider this time the following conversation: A says *You're a linguist, you ought to be able to help me. I'm writing this paper and I need to come up with an example of an indicative sentence in English having a second-person subject, and I can't for the life of me think of any. Can you help?* B says *You have lovely eyes*. A says *Thank you* and B then, appropriately, says *You're welcome*.

Matters are different there, of course, because one of the sentences is, as they say, 'mentioned' rather than 'used'. But is is precisely our understanding of the sentences and our knowledge of the workings of a conversation which enables us to know which of the sentences we just overheard was capable of being a quoted sentence and which were not. And that is what we needed to know in order to find the conversation acceptable.

Take an even more ridiculous case. A says *Good morning*. B says *What did you say?* A says *What did you say?* and then B too, again says *What did you say?* Here there are three occurrences of the same sentence, but the range of interpretations possible for each of the three is different. A says *Good morning*. B says, *What did you say?* to indicate that he did not hear what A said. A says *What did you say?* either to indicate that he did not hear what B said or to give an untruthful answer to B's question. B then says *What did you say?* either to indicate that he didn't hear what A said this time either, or to give a truthful answer to A's question.

The point of all this is that conversations, or discourse samples in general, are not well-formed or ill-formed as such, but only on particular interpretations. These interpretations have to be based on assumptions about what is going on in the conversation, who says which lines, what has been said before, whether one is lying or telling the truth, and so on. There is no way, in short, of talking about grammaticality or well-formedness without getting in many ways involved in the details of social interaction by means of language.[3] Inquiry into the ways in which settings authorize linguistic choices can be made respectable and fruitful when motivated by something nobler than the desire to show that some grammarian is mistaken with his asterisks.

3. The issues in sociolinguistics that will concern me most directly are those of what has been called 'microsociolinguistics',[4] the study of language behavior in encounters between people on particular social occasions. We can refer to knowledge of appropriate situated language use as 'communicative competence'[5] and express it as the ability to bring into association 1. instances of language behavior, 2. communication act functions, and 3. the classes of social occasions in which the particular instances of language behavior can have the given functions.[6]

A sociolinguistic model of communication must specify the various possible components of a communication event and must provide a typology of the settings in which communicating takes place in a community, the participant roles which these settings create, and the functions which individual communications can have in these settings. Something along the line of the Bühler-Jakobson model, as this has been exemplified and made familiar to this audience by Hymes,[7] can serve us as a useful starting point, especially, I think, if we are not particularly concerned to work out the pairing that Jakobson sees between the 'factors' and the 'functions' of speech.[8]

The basic factors of a communication event are these: the identity of the sender of a message, the identity of the intended receiver or addressee of the message, an awareness in the sender of an interceptor or witness to the communication event, the code shared by the interlocutors, the topic and the specific content of the message, the encoded form of the message, the properties of the channel through which the message is transmitted, the setting or social occasion within which the message plays a role, and the function which it serves in that setting.

In talking about the various functions and aspects of situated language use, we can take any of various points of view: the sender's point of view can be usually expressed as the sender's intentions, the receiver's point of view can be taken as the receiver's reactions, and the analyst's is the interpretation of what is going on between sender and receiver.[9]

I will now attempt to summarize the various communication act functions, keeping in mind these separate points of view where necessary, and giving some indication of the linguistic concomitants of messages having these functions.

Take first the job of notifying the addressee that there is going to be some communicating. The receiver's work is to know whether he is being addressed. If he is a physician named Abercrombie and feels somebody poke him on the shoulder and hears somebody say *Dr Abercrombie*, his job is easy. If she is a young lady in a crowded street and hears somebody say *Oh, Miss!*, she does not know for sure.

The sender's job is more complicated. He must decide whether or not he wishes to be polite, because on the basis of that decision he will choose between, say, *Oh, sir!* and *Hey, mister!* He must decide whether he knows the person's name, title, age, sex, status, race, kinship affiliation, etc., in order to know whether to say *Oh, Mommy, Mr. Smith, Doctor, Jimmy, Hey, gringo* or what you have.

The sender can act to identify himself by giving his name, or—to take the receiver's point of view—he can identify himself unintentionally by means of his voice quality, his handwriting, or his style, for example. The job the sender has in identifying himself to his addressee involves deciding whether or not the addressee recognizes his voice, knows his name, has visual contact with him, has a specific kinship relationship to him, and so on. On such matters depends the choice among such locutions as *It's me, This is Harvey Schwartz, I'm Harvey Schwartz, I'm Mr. Schwartz, My name is Harvey Schwartz*, and *It's Daddy*.

The so-called 'contact' or 'phatic' function of communicating, which can be thought of as absorbing the matters of speaker identification and addressee notification, is that of keeping the channel open, of guaranteeing that the receiver is attentive. I am inclined to separate this into two functions, the 'contact' function by which the sender is assured or attempts to guarantee that the message is being processed in real time (consider the *uh huh, uh huh* of speech) and the 'phatic' function by which people 'keep in touch' for the sake of maintaining a social relationship between them conducible to communicating even though they may have very little to say.[10]

The 'emotive' function of language is seen in language behavior which expresses (to take the sender's point of view) or exposes (to take the receiver's point of view) the sender's real or pretended inner life, his attitudes and feelings. Certain lexical items, like *gosh, ouch* and *alas* are limited to locutions serving this function. Certain grammatical processes seem also to be so limited, for example the use of *so/how* with adjectives, as in *He's so tall!* and *How tall he is!*, or the type of adverb inversion exemplified by *Little did I suspect that I was being betrayed* and *Never had I seen such a sight*, to speak only of English. And, of course, there are a great many paralinguistic cues to one's inner life, some typically under conscious control, others not.

The 'reactive' or 'conative' function of communication has to do with the effect of a message on the feelings, actions or understanding of the receiver. Again, situations can be described from the point of view of the sender's intentions or the receiver's reactions. 'Teasing' can be thought of from the point of view of the sender's malice; 'persuading' can be defined in terms of the beliefs or actions induced in the receiver; 'insulting' can be taken as ambiguous in this respect, as we can see by noting that both of these usages are acceptable: first, *He didn't even know that I'd been insulting him* and *I didn't mean to, but apparently I insulted him.*

A taxonomy of the things that people do to each other when they communicate can be one basis of a semantic analysis of communication-act verbs in a language, and that classification in turn would be a good start toward an analysis of the specific communication-act functions that are associated with particular choices of linguistic material. I am inclined to think that in fairly precise ways the appropriateness of choices of lexical items, paralinguistic features, some grammatical and phonological processes, will be determined by the nature of the communication act, whether it be insulting, blessing, flattering, accusing, asking, commanding, promising, or what have you.

The so-called 'referential' function of language has to do with the communication of the 'propositional content' of the message. Again there is the difference between what the speaker intends to communicate and what the receiver is able to figure out. In the most typical case of communication, the receiver is not able to figure out what the sender intends. In certain subtle cases, the receiver is able to figure out more than what the sender intends: some receivers are reputed to be skilled in this way to a particularly high degree, and these are: psychiatrists, private detectives, and Kremlinologists.

In the analysis of the communication of content, the analyst's point of view takes one into an awareness of the greatly detailed mass of background information which is shared by the interlocutors and which accounts for many of the deletions, pronominalizations, instances of definite reference not explained in the context, and the use of presuppositions unjustified in the context.

The aesthetic or 'poetic' function of language can be spoken of from the receiver's point of view in terms of his appreciation of the way in which the message form was constructed; from the sender's point of view it consists in making choices so that future receivers will appreciate the resulting form. The analyst, taking his aloof point of view, asks such questions as whether the conventions which determine values in this area are universal or community-specific, whether the receiver's appreciation takes the form of the belief that the effect he perceives was intentional on the part of the sender, and so on.

The 'situational' function of communicating has to do with the ways in which the interlocutors' perception of the setting or social occasion is related to linguistic choices they make. From the sender's point of view the relation can be either a determined or a determining one. In some cases, that is, the speaker's perception of the nature of the setting guides his choice of linguistic form, while in some cases choices which the speaker makes in speaking are what determine the nature of the occasion, or the style level.

It is not likely that there is a fixed and finite number of discrete types of social occasions provided by a given culture for communicative interaction; but it is clear that many fairly well-defined types of them can be enumerated—as, for example, the insult ritual between close friends, psychotherapy sessions of the nondirective type, classroom discussions on topics where the teacher has mastery of the subject and the students do not, haggling between customer and merchant on the price of an item, and so on. These occasions can be ranged according to the degree to which the associated language behavior is highly routine or fairly unconstrained. And they can be divided into occasions in which the interaction is, to use a distinction due to Gumperz, 'transactional' or 'personal'.[11] If it is transactional, the exchange has a fixed purpose and there is a fixed way of achieving that purpose and acknowledging that it has been achieved.

Social occasions can also differ from each other by the specific ways in which the usual expectations of normal, friendly conversation are suspended: this typically shows up, as pointed out in recent unpublished work by Michael Moerman, as a difference between types of interaction periods which do or do not have fixed beginnings and ends. When the committee meeting is called to order, several changes occur: interaction becomes transactional, only certain topics will be welcomed, the right to speak is narrowly limited, and the time at which the participants can return to normal sorts of conversation needs to be clearly marked. Before a class session formally begins, it can be expected that people will ask questions under the normal conditions: once the class is started it then becomes appropriate for one member of the group to ask questions that he thinks he already knows the answers to, or in fact to answer his own questions if nobody else does. Before the session with one's psychiatrist begins, one expects a question like *When are we gonna meet next time?* to receive as a response something like *What about next Tuesday at four o'clock?* Once the session has begun, the same question would elicit instead the response *Why did you ask that?* It is obviously of great importance for discourse analysis to have secure knowledge, on a given text, of the nature of the interaction or the purpose of the communication, since expectations about sequencing and topic and right to speak may be very different from one setting to another.

4. The linguistic properties by which differently situated instances of appropriate language behavior can differ from each other are extremely extensive.

They include the choice of a code, as in the switch from classical Arabic to colloquial Arabic along with a change from lecture to class discussion,[12] using standard Japanese rather than the local dialect when politeness is called for,[13] using Spanish for courting, but switching to Guaraní once the purpose of the courtship has been achieved,[14] and so on.

Certain sorts of activities bring into play certain linguistic routines, activities such as marrying, congratulating, greeting, offering condolences, making an arrest, introducing people to each other, and so on. Somewhat similar is the choice of particular locutions or grammatical properties in connection with specific types of activities. Examples are telling people about their inner wishes as a way of giving instructions (*You wanna make a left at the next corner.*), using the phrase *talk about* when estimating a sum of money (*We're talkin' about $60,000.*), using demonstratives while scolding (*Get that beaver out of this house this instant!*) or asking stereotyped scolding questions like *How many times have I told you not to bring your beaver into the living room?*

The choice of personal pronouns and address forms can vary, in widely different ways in different communities, as studied in classical papers by Brown and Gilman,[15] Paul Friedrich,[16] and Brown and Ford.[17] And there is much more to be done.

The appropriate choice of lexical items can be determined by such things as the age, sex, race, class membership, occupation or education of the sender, addressee, or perceived audience. Javanese, for example, as we have learned, has a wide range of synonyms differing in level of politeness.[18] *Medication* is a middle-class substitute for the upper-class and lower-class word *medicine. Honey*, as a term of address, is used to and by waitresses in restaurants of the Holiday Inn variety and downward, in my observation. For all I know, it may be used elsewhere, too, but almost never, I would guess, by a male to a male.

It may be that inflectional categories, as in Koasati, or conversational sentence particles, as in Thai, are chosen on the basis of the sex of sender and/or addressee.[19] Different patterns of stress and intonation usage for the two sexes have been noted frequently. That paralinguistic features are selectively used in the same sorts of sociolinguistic settings that we have been considering has recently been amply documented in a survey article by Crystal.[20]

5. The connection between appropriate language choices and the social settings in which their use can be authorized may be thought of in the style of the 'ethnomethodologists' in terms of the 'work' which the participants in a conversation must perform. This work consists in general in detecting certain controlling features of the social situation, in knowing what it is that one wants to accomplish in this situation, in remembering or being able to reconstruct the relevant expectations regarding language behavior for such settings.

The nature of this 'work' can be illustrated by returning to the matter of speaker-identification. If Mr. James Smith is checking in at a hotel where he has made advance reservations, he says *My name is James Smith*, because he knows that that is the name the inn-keeper must look up. If he is introducing himself to a small child in a context in which it is necessary to provide the child with an address form for him, he says *I'm Mr. Smith*. If he's introducing himself to a new neighbor and wishes to give the neighbor the right to determine the level of friendship they should expect of each other, he says *I'm Jim Smith*, thus allowing the other the option of calling him either *Jim* or *Mr. Smith*. If he is introducing himself in one of those modern settings that call for intimacy but not familiarity, as in a sensitivity training group, he says *I'm Jim*.

Or take a situation discussed in slightly different terms by Robin Lakoff,[21] where a hostess is offering a guest a piece of cake. If the guest is a small child, our hostess knows that no child is embarrassed to have it known that he is hankering after a piece of cake, so she can simply say, *You can have a piece of cake, Jimmy*. In offering cake to an adult, the hostess can ask if the guest would like some cake (*Would you like to try a piece of this cake?*) or can say something which presupposes that the guest does not want any (*You must have a piece of this cake. I insist.*); but the offer *You can have a piece of this cake* will not do.[22]

6. The question a grammarian must ask when he considers the various matters I've been talking about is: Where does autonomous linguistics—if there is such a thing—fit in this picture? I despair of answering this question, because although I would like there to be a special job that only linguists can do, I am not at all sure what that would be or whether it would be interesting. I do have a proposal, which I will present at the end of my talk, on how to find out what autonomous linguistics is; but I can warn you now that it is not a very practical proposal.

I no longer believe that it makes sense to talk about a grammar generating a set of grammatical sentences in a language, unless the term 'grammatical' means nothing more than 'capable of being parsed.' I think of the grammarian's job as that of discovering and describing the elements, the structures, the processes and the constraints which are somehow made available to the language user as instruments for communicating, but I find myself more and more tending toward the study of how and for what purposes and in what settings people 'use' their grammars.

Many of the side issues of linguistic theory require an accounting in the larger theory—as, for example, grammaticality judgments, the processes of language change, and the treatment of linguistic 'mistakes'.

There are clear cases of grammatical sentences (*I love you.*) and there are clear cases of ungrammatical strings of words (*the a of of*); but it seems to me, as I have already indicated, that decisions about the unclear cases will have to be based on understandings of situations of use and not on such a formal basis as that of finding the simplest grammar which generates all the clearly grammatical sentences and fails to generate all the clearly ungrammatical sentences and letting the grammar make the decision for the unclear cases.

Theories of language change must take into account the fact that settings are not only determining of but determined by language behavior. That is, I can select a certain class of lexical items, or transformations, or an articulatory set, or a voice quality or hesitation pattern, either because I perceive that I have a particular position in the conversation group, a position of affinity or authority, for example, or I can choose linguistic material for the sake of symbolizing and therein creating that affinity or that authority. I can center my vowels to let you know that I am one of you, if that is what it takes; or I can pronounce all my underlying /r/s to let you know that I am being formal or pompous or what have you. As Weinreich and others have pointed out, neither of these influences on the final form of my speech can be explained on the basis of such a minimal sociological variable as 'density of communication'.[23]

Speech modification that comes about as a result of consciously or unconsciously imitating the speech of the people one wishes to become affiliated with creates an interestingly asymmetric situation, because certain kinds of complexities in a linguistic system unperceived by the imitator make the imitation process obvious to members of the imitated group (all of which suggests to me that being a spy must be extremely risky work). To one person, the difference between *who* and *whom* is a difference determined by certain syntactic facts; to another person, the principle is that educated people say *whom* in lots of places where the rest of us say *who*. (The practical part of this principle is: When in doubt, say *whom*. Recently a secretary at Berkeley, on being asked if Professor Berlin was in, said *Professor whom?*). To one person the difference between /nyuwz/ and /nuwn/ is a difference in the phonological representation of two lexical items, the two items being different at both ends; to another, the principle is that your better type of person says /nyuw/ where ordinary people say /nuw/, and such a person ends up as the Columbus, Ohio, radio announcer who introduces the /nyuwn nyuwz/.

Data about linguistic 'mistakes' thus permit some sort of accounting in sociolinguistic terms. In the extent to which speakers of a language are motivated to seek mastery of more than one code or style or must acquire control of many different sets of expectations governed by different sorts of social occasions, the speaker must frequently monitor his own productions to evaluate them according to his imperfect perception of the setting and his imperfect mastery of the expected sorts of language behavior. The relationship between the kinds of mistakes, stammerings, false starts, missed agreements, etc., and the contexts in which one feels insecure or carefully attended to must be partly explainable in terms of the complex task that a sender has.

7. It has sometimes been proposed that sociolinguistic principles can be incorporated into a theory of grammar. Some years ago, from this platform, DeCamp proposed that transformational grammar was particularly hospitable to the facts of sociolinguistics, especially as this concerned dialect or style, because of the use of binary features and the redundancy rules by which the choice of one property of a word or segment commits a speaker to the choice of other properties.[24] If a structure could be marked as [+Pompous], say, then the presence of that feature could trigger certain transformations, could require the selection of certain lexical items and the rejection of others, could trigger or constrain certain phonological rules, and so on.

The list of features one might think of for this purpose could include terms like Pompous, Deferential, Insulting, Female-Speaker, Male-Speaker, Child-Speaker, Emotive, Excogitative, Hysterical, and innumerably many more; but it is difficult for me to see what these features could possibly be features of. If they are to be features of lexical items, then the theory will require an extremely elaborate system for assigning style or dialect judgments to the selection restriction apparatus in some way. If they are to be features of the sentence as a whole, then it is probably not true that transformational grammar is especially suited for sociolinguistics, because I know of no satisfactory proposals for dealing with 'features' of elements larger than lexical units. But much more seriously than that, the one fact that I find least suited to the incorporation of sociolinguistic features into the grammar of a language is that exactly the same sorts of conditions that in one community determine the choice of pronouns or inflectional endings, determine in another community the choice of one language rather than another.

I have no doubt that the theory of transformational grammar is flexible enough to get around that embarrassment—by accepting the performative analysis, by taking a strong version of the theory of a universal semantic base, by assuming a universal theory of sociolinguistic variables and by assigning sociolinguistic features to the highest performative verb—but when an analysis requires that much use of brute force, the facts that led to the analysis are much more interesting than the theory which got reshaped to incorporate them.

8. The central theoretical problem as I see it, is that of determining how to capture the ability of a person to know his language. I find it helpful to conceive of the total theory of linguistic abilities as a very specialized branch of Incarnation Theory. Suppose we assume that some minor god wishes to cross the line, wishes to pass as a member of the human community. It has the standard Divine Sensorium by which it is able to perceive in an instant all of space and time, it is able to assume any form or to occupy and control any existing creature, but it needs to be told how to talk and what constraints it needs to impose on its unlimited potential in order not to give away its divine origin. It will need to acquire the local grammar, or maybe more than one local grammar, and a large portion of the lexicon of that language or those languages. It will need to identify itself as a member of the community with respect to age, sex, family position, social status, educational background, occupation, geographical origins, etc.; and it will need to equip itself with a fairly coherent set of opinions about the world and a set of affective preferences, together with a strategy for changing these, though this last is not necessary for an adult. It will need to be able to perceive among its interlocutors whether they are people it is supposed to know, how its biography is shared with theirs, if and how they are related to it, and so on. It will need to notice what sorts of social occasions it finds itself in or what sorts of social settings its own action has put it in. It will need to know what linguistic conventions and routines govern

conversation on these occasions, what it and its interlocutors are expected to accomplish with each contribution to the conversation, when it can appropriately talk at all and when it should remain silent. And it will apparently need to know how to vary its speech from time to time and how past decisions to vary its speech in one respect might require it to vary its speech in some other respect more often or less often so that certain proportions come out right.

This is an enormous undertaking, as you see—and even at that I have said nothing about what it will need to know about how people perceive the world in order for it to acquire the semantics of the system—but it all seems to be part of the job.

My proposal for determining the boundary between linguistics and other disciplines connected with a speaker's control of language use, is to start a project for writing an instruction manual for an Immigrant of the sort I have in mind, to have on this project a large and capable research team with workers from a great many academic disciplines, and to determine empirically which tasks the linguists can carry out without any help from the others.

## Notes

First published in *Report of the 23rd Annual Round Table Meeting on Linguistics and Language Studies*, edited by R. W. Shuy, Georgetown University Press, 1973.

1. For a discussion of some of the practical and conceptual difficulties with this definition, see my paper 'On generativity' in P. Stanley Peters, ed., *The goals of linguistic theory*, Prentice-Hall.
2. I do not wish, on this last point, to be understood as putting down armchair linguistics. Far from it. I am pointing out only that the intuitive judgments which the grammarian needs to consult cannot be those of grammaticality alone.
3. I think that one way to become particularly conscious of the working of context on appropriateness judgments for discourse is to practice constructing sample texts for which no supporting context is conceivable, and to practice devising contexts for contrived or bizarre texts. Schegloff has mentioned certain locutions that are appropriate over the telephone but not in face-to-face conversation [Emanuel Schegloff (1968), 'Sequencing in conversational openings', *American Anthropologist*, 70. 1075–1095], and I have been interested in situations of the opposite sort. One might be inclined to think that a text like the following, containing something of each type, has to be bad. *Hello, this is Chuck Fillmore. Could you send over a box about yea big?* Speaker identification by means of the formula *This is X* is not

appropriate in face-to-face encounters, yet the size-indicator *yea* requires that the interlocutors be in visual contact. A setting which could authorize the text, however, is one of communication by videophone. Texts which cannot be contextualized at all are fairly easy to construct, as for example, a letter that begins *To whom it may concern* and ends *As ever, Mary Lou.*

4. The term, I believe, was first used by Joshua Fishman.

5. The term is from Dell Hymes (1969), 'Models of the interaction of language and social settings,' in John McNamara (1967) *Problems of bilingualism: Journal of social issues* 23.8–28.

6. My name for the first term of this triad is left deliberately vague, so as to include such things as the choice between speech and silence, the choice between one language and another, the choice between first name or title plus last name, the choice between performing or not performing a contraction, the choice of a paralinguistic feature, etc.

7. Dell Hymes (1962) 'The ethnography of speaking', in T. Gladwin and William C. Sturtevant, eds. (1962) *Anthropology and human behavior.* Anthropological Society of Washington, D.C., pp. 13–53, reprinted in Joshua Fishman (1968) *Readings in the sociology of language*, Mouton, pp. 99–138.

8. Roman Jakobson (1960) 'Linguistics and poetics', in Thomas A. Sebeok (1960), ed., *Style in language*, M.I.T., pp. 350–373.

9. We can take as the simplest case one in which all three of these points of view are identical: the receiver reacts in precisely the way that the sender intended, and both sender and receiver perceive the situation in the same way that the analyst does. (The secretary, for example, in the usual way and for the usual purpose, says *Good morning* to her boss.) Cases where the sender's and receiver's points of view differ include cases of deceit, where the sender knows better what is going on than the receiver, cases of 'humoring' someone, where the receiver has the upper hand, or cases of two-way mis-communication, as in conversations between linguists and sociologists. A case where the sender's and receiver's points of view are identical but differ from that of the interpreter is the case where the interlocutors share a background of expectations, values and beliefs which the analyst must discover for himself or must impute to the situation in order for it to make sense to him.

10. The cultures that are the most comfortable to live in are those which offer their members a well-defined repertory of types capable of providing the content of messages whose function is merely phatic.

11. John J. Gumperz (1964) 'Linguistic and social interaction in two communities', in Gumperz and Hymes (1964) *The ethnography of communication, American Anthropologist* 66. 6 II, 137–153.

12.Charles A. Ferguson (1959) 'Diglossia', *Word* 15. 325–340.
13.Samuel E. Martin (1964) 'Speech levels in Japan and Korea', in Dell Hymes (1964), ed., *Language in culture and society*, pp. 407–412.
14.Joan Rubin (1963) 'National bilingualism in Paraguay', Yale dissertation (1968) 'Bilingual usage in Paraguay', in Fishman (1968), op. cit.
15.Roger Brown and Albert Gilman (1960) 'The pronouns of power and solidarity', in Sebeok (1960) op. cit., pp.253–276.
16.Paul Friedrich (1972) 'Social context and semantic feature: the Russian pronominal usage', in John Gumperz and Dell Hymes, eds., (1972) *Directions in sociolonguistics*, Holt-Rinehart-Winston, pp. 270–300.
17.Roger Brown and Marguerite Ford (1961) 'Address in American English', *Journal of abnormal and social psychology* 62. 375–385, also in Hymes (1964) op. cit., pp. 234–244.
18.Clifford Geertz, 'Linguistic etiquette', chapter from his *The religion of Java*, The Free Press (1960); reprinted in Fishman (1968) op. cit. 283–295.
19.Mary R. Haas (1944) 'Men's and women's speech in Koasati', *Language* 20. 142–149, reprinted in Hymes (1964) op. cit., 228–233.
20.David Crystal (1971) 'Prosodic and paralinguistic correlates of social categories', in *Social anthropology and language*, A.S.A. Monograph 10, pp. 185–206.
21.Robin T. Lakoff (1971) 'Language in context', ms.
22.The guest, in her turn, may confess to the most debilitating lust. Something like *Oh, all right, why not?* is inappropriate, whereas a sordid confession like *The very sight of it makes my mouth water* is quite in place.
23.See William Labov (1963) 'The social motivation of a sound change', *Word* 19. 273–309, Labov (1968). 'The reflection of social processes in linguistic structures', in Fishman (1968) op. cit., pp. 240–251. Uriel Weinreich (1957), 'Research frontiers in bilingualism studies', *Proceedings of the Eighth International Congress of Linguistics*, p. 191; Uriel Weinreich, William Labov and Marvin Herzog (1969) 'Empirical foundations for a theory of language change', in W. P. Lehmann and Yakov Malkiel (1969), ed., *Directions for historical linguistics*. John J. Gumperz (1958) 'Dialect differences and social stratification in a North India village', *American anthropologist* 60. 668–681.
24.David DeCamp (1970) 'Is a sociolinguistic theory possible?' Georgetown University Monograph Series on Languages and Linguistics. 22. 157–173. Washington, D.C., Georgetown University Press.

# What the 'Good Language Learner' can teach us
Joan Rubin

The differential success of second/foreign language learners suggests a need to examine in detail what strategies successful language learners employ. An indication is given of what these strategies might consist of and a list of several widely recognized good learner strategies is given. In addition to the need for research on this topic, it is suggested that teachers can already begin to help their less successful students improve their performance by paying more attention to learner strategies already seen as productive.

It is common knowledge that everyone learns his first language with a fair degree of success, the reason being that everyone is born with the ability to learn a language and then grows up in a community in which he needs to function to some degree through language, the rules of which are imparted to him in the normal course of the day. Yet, it is equally common knowledge that some people are more successful (however this is defined) than others at learning a second language.[1] This differential success is often explained by saying that 'X has more language learning ability than Y.' Yet there is something curious here: if all peoples can learn their first language easily and well (although some have more verbal skills than others), why does this innate ability seem to decline for some when second language learning is the task? Although one of the more essential skills which many people try to acquire through formal education is competence in a second or foreign language, the success record for attempts to help students acquire this skill has been notoriously poor.[2]

More positively, we can observe that this ability does not decline for all students studying a second language. We all know of students who learn a second language in spite of the teacher, the textbook, or the classroom situation. How do these individuals achieve their success? I would like to suggest that if we knew more about what the 'successful learners' did, we might be able to teach these strategies to poorer learners to enhance their success record.

Good language learning is said to depend on at least three variables:

aptitude, motivation and opportunity. Of the three, the first—aptitude
—is assumed to be the least subject to manipulation; how subject to
change it is, is a question frequently discussed in the literature. Some
authors feel that language aptitude is 'a relatively invariant characteristic
of the individual, not subject to easy modification by learning' (Carroll
1960: 38). Others (Politzer and Weiss 1969; Yeni-Komshian 1967; and
Hatfield 1965) have demonstrated that language aptitude can be improved somewhat through training; still others have pointed to the
intricate interrelationship between aptitude and motivation.

There are two major tests of language aptitude currently in wide use:
one by Carroll and Sapon and one by Pimsleur. That by Carroll-Sapon
(Carroll 1965: 96) uses mainly linguistic parameters as criteria to predict
language learning success: 1. phonetic coding, 2. grammatical sensitivity
—the ability to handle grammar, 3. rote memorization ability, and 4.
inductive language learning ability—the ability to infer linguistic forms,
rules and patterns from new linguistic contexts with a minimum of supervision and guidance. The test by Pimsleur (1966) adds a motivational
dimension and identifies three components: 1. verbal intelligence—
familiarity with words and the ability to reason analytically about verbal
materials, 2. motivation to learn the language, and 3. auditory ability.
These tests are to be used with those who have not had prior experience
with a foreign language.

While these tests are helpful in predicting success, they give the
language teacher and learner little direction as to what can be done about
a person's ability. Commonly, the poorer student may notice that the
better student always has the right answer but he never discovers why,
never finds out what little 'tricks' lead the better student to the right
answer. For the student who wants to improve his learning, aptitude
tests don't give enough detailed information about the kinds of habits a
learner will need to develop. Rather than letting him just admire the
good student and feel inferior, we need to isolate what the good learner
does—what his strategies are—and impart his knowledge to less successful learners.

By strategies, I mean the techniques or devices which a learner may
use to acquire knowledge. Some of the strategies which seem to be
important are the following: 1. The good language learner may be a good
guesser, that is, he gathers and stores information in an efficient manner
so it can be easily retrieved. He may listen to a phrase, pick out the
words he understands and infer the rest. He may actively look for clues
to meaning—in the topic, setting, or attitudes of the speakers. His guessing strategy may be stratified from the more general to the specific so
that he gets the most information from each question or sentence. 2. He
is often willing to appear foolish in order to communicate and get his
message across. 3. He will try out his knowledge by making up new
sentences, thus bringing his newly acquired competence into use. I will

give more details on good language learner strategies later in this paper, but it is important to recognize here that tests of aptitude are meant to find the minimal number of dimensions to predict success without detailing all of the many strategies involved. If the focus is to help students improve their abilities, then these strategies should be looked at in much greater detail.

A second variable mentioned frequently in regard to good language learning is that of motivation. Several articles discuss those aspects of motivation which are essential for good language learning. Gardner and Lambert (1959) have isolated two kinds of motivation, by now well-known: instrumental and integrative. They find that the latter correlates more with successful language learning. While it is generally agreed that the best language learning occurs in the country/region where the language is spoken or when the language is the most common one at home, some would go so far as to say that the classroom is no place to learn a language. Macnamara (1971) points out that the essential difference between a classroom and the street as a place to learn a language is motivation. According to Macnamara, the student seldom has anything so urgent to say to the teacher that they will improvise with whatever communicative skills they possess to get their meaning across. However, the good language learner seems to have a high motivation to communicate, no matter where he is. The problem is how to provide the necessary motivation for others within the school framework—if that is possible. Cooper (1973: 313) also emphasizes the need factor in promoting language learning: 'If we want to enable the student to use English, then we must put him in situations which demand the use of English.' With proper motivation, the learner may become an active investigator of the nature of the language to be learned. Francis (1971) feels that students will learn to do what they themselves exert themselves to do.

A third variable mentioned above was opportunity. This includes all those activities both within and outside the classroom which expose the learner to the language and which afford him an opportunity to practice what he has learned. We have all noted that the good language learner takes and creates opportunities to practice what he has learned while the poorer learner passively does what is assigned him. The good language learner uses the language when he is not required to do so and seeks opportunities to hear the language (attends foreign language movies, joins foreign language clubs, listens to T.V. or the radio, uses the foreign language with other students outside class). What is important here is to discover what advantage students take of the opportunities they either have or create. I agree with Ervin-Tripp (1970) who suggests that there has been too much attention on the input to the learner and too little on what is going on in the learner himself. She suggests that the focus on opportunity alone without considering the use that the learner is making of such an opportunity will not allow an adequate model of language learning. 'Any learning model which predicts language learning on the basis of input without regard to the selective processing by the learner will not work, except for trivial problems.'

If language learning is really the acquisition of communicative competence as well as of linguistic competence, then we need also to examine how the good language learner defines opportunity as exposure to many different social situations so as to get a proper feel for the circumstances in which a language code is to be employed.

It is clearly difficult to separate these three variables (aptitude, motivation, opportunity) since they do impinge on one another. An individual with lots of natural ability and motivation but with little opportunity may have difficulty in acquiring a language. If opportunity is present, but there is little motivation or poor learning skills, then we may expect that the language learning will proceed slowly. Equally, a person with lots of natural ability and opportunity may fail to learn because of poor motivation.

What is clear is that the good learner has or creates all of these and the poorer learner does not. If we are to improve the success of the classroom teaching, we will need to know a great deal more about the learning process.

## The good language learner

While there is little systematic work relating language learning strategies to success, there are a number of observations which can be made about individuals who are good language learners. I have been able to isolate some of these by observing students in classrooms in California and Hawaii, by observing myself and by talking to other good language learners, and by eliciting observations from some second language teachers. As I have begun to observe classes, what fascinates me is how often the teacher plows ahead with the lesson seemingly with little awareness of what is going on in each student, and often without directing the attention of the poorer students to how the successful student arrives at his answer. This is, many foreign language teachers are so concerned with finding the best method or with getting the correct answer that they fail to attend to the learning process. If they attended to it more, they might be able to tailor their input to their students' needs and might be able to provide the student with techniques that would enable him to learn on his own. Indeed, no course could ever teach all we need to know about a language and the teacher must find the means to help the student help himself, when the teacher is not around.

The task of observing these strategies is a complicated one because they necessarily involve cognitive processes which neither the learner nor the teacher may be able to specify. However, when our attention is focused on observing these strategies, I think we may find it easier to isolate some of them. Just recently, I discovered that by using video-tape more of these strategies would be observable than by just using a tape recorder.[3] With the video-tapes we hope to help learners and teachers see what is going on in the classroom. We hope to be able, as well, to abstract the learner strategies by interviewing the learner about his behavior during a particular classroom while showing him a tape of his behavior.

In spite of the fact that we are only beginning to isolate these strategies, I think that it is useful to list some of the ones found thus far. They remain general but give an idea of the kind of strategies I think we ought to be looking for.

## Strategies

1. The good language learner is a willing and accurate guesser. It seems that the good language learner is both comfortable with uncertainty (indeed he may enjoy it) and willing to try out his guesses. A good guesser is one who gathers and stores information in an efficient manner. The good guesser uses all the clues which the setting offers him and thus is able to narrow down what the meaning and intent of the communication might be. In this sense, he is carrying over into his second language behavior something that all of us do in our first language interactions. We never comprehend all that the speaker intended and we are always using whatever clues the environment, and the discourse may give us.[4] Guessing is based on what we know about the social relationship between the speakers, the setting, the event, the mood, the channel and all of the other parameters that Hymes has isolated for us in the ethnography of communication (Hymes, 1972). It is based on what we know about the rules of speaking (Cf. Paulston, 1974, for some examples of the importance of knowing these). It is based on factual probability (Twaddell, 1973). It is also but not exclusively based on what we know about grammar and lexicon.

The good guesser uses his feel for grammatical structures, clues from the lexical items he recognizes, clues from redundancy in the message. He uses non-verbal clues, word-association clues, outside knowledge (his general knowledge of society, of similarities to his native language). He makes inferences as to the purpose, intent, point of view of a message or communication.

The ability to guess seems to relate to one's first language as much as to one's second. Mueller (1971: 153) calls our attention to the fact that people may vary in their ability to comprehend what they hear or read in their native language. The fast reader and the good listener can understand while paying attention to a minimum of cues. He can overlook unknown words, or can read even though focusing only on content words. Such a person guesses, or makes inferences about, the meaning of words or sentence structure. A wrong guess does not disturb him, but is quickly corrected from the subsequent context. Carton, who directed an important initial study on the role of inferencing in language learning, concurs: 'Individual learners vary according to their propensity of making inferences, tolerance of risk and ability to make valid, rational and reasonable inferences.' (1966, 18). Carton also suggests that there are three steps to guessing: 1. scanning, confirmation, and testing for adequacy, 2. assessment of probability that the inference is correct, and 3. re-adjustment to later information.

The ability to guess changes as one gets older; adults seem to stratify their guessing from the more general to the specific, gathering the most information from each question. In two separate articles, Jerome Bruner and N. H. Mackworth (1970) and F. A. Mosher and K. R. Hornsby (1966) have shown that adults use different strategies in guessing than do children and that they are more efficient guessers.

The importance of guessing and inferring has been recognized for a long time in second language learning (see for example, Twaddell 1967 and 1973) yet the details of how this is to be taught are not at all clearly worked out. Twaddell does make some fine suggestions about guessing in his more recent 1973 article. Some texts assume that guessing will take place, yet none train students directly to do so.[5]

2. The good language learner has a strong drive to communicate, or to learn from a communication. He is willing to do many things to get his message across. He may use a circumlocution, saying 'the object on top of your head' when he doesn't know the word for hat. He may paraphrase in order to explain the different meaning of a phrase (for example, one student explained that the term 'snack bar' had a different meaning in Japan than it does in the United States). He will use gestures to get his message across or spell a word when his pronunciation is not clear. He will use a cognate, from any language he knows, to try to express his meaning. He may not limit himself to a particular sentence construction but will use those constructions he does have to the fullest. For example, he may use 'going to go' if he doesn't know the future in English, the important point being to get the message across (Richards, 1971, discusses similar strategies). He may try to form new words by nominalizing a verb or verbalizing a noun and then checking the response. Having this strong motivation to communicate, the good learner will use whatever knowledge he has to get his message across. This strategy has an important by-product in that if he is successful in communicating, his motivation to participate and acquire the necessary tools to do so will be enhanced.

3. The good language learner is often not inhibited. He is willing to appear foolish if reasonable communication results. He is willing to make mistakes in order to learn and to communicate. He is willing to live with a certain amount of vagueness.

4. In addition to focusing on communication, the good language learner is prepared to attend to form. The good language learner is constantly looking for patterns in the language.[6] He attends to the form in a particular way, constantly analyzing, categorizing, synthesizing. He is constantly trying to find schemes for classifying information. He is trying to distinguish relevant from irrelevant clues. He is looking for the interaction or relation of elements (using as a basis for this analysis information from his own language or others that he has learned). Naturally, the more experience a learner has with doing this sort of exercise the more successful he will be. It has often been observed that a person learns his second or third foreign language more easily than his first just because he has had practice in attending to the important formal features of a language.

5. The good language learner practices. He may practice pronouncing words or making up sentences. He will seek out opportunities to use the language by looking for native speakers, going to the movies or to cultural events. He initiates conversations with the teacher or his fellow students in the target language. He is willing to repeat. He will usually take advantage of every opportunity to speak in class; indeed, in any one class certain students seem to stand out and are called on more frequently.

6. The good language learner monitors his own and the speech of others. That is, he is constantly attending to how well his speech is being received and whether his performance meets the standards he has learned. Part of his monitoring is a function of his active participation in the learning process. He is always processing information whether or not he is called on to perform. He can learn from his own mistakes.

7. The good language learner attends to meaning. He knows that in order to understand the message, it is not sufficient to pay attention to the grammar of the language or to the surface form of speech. He attends to the context of the speech act, he attends to the relationship of the participants, he attends to the rules of speaking, he attends to the mood of the speech act. In learning one's first language, some scholars have suggested that meaning comprehension is prior to structure acquisition. Macnamara (1972) argues than an infant doesn't start to learn his first language until he can understand what is said without hearing the utterance. In the case of the second language learner, the learner already has a known structure and a lexicon which can be

used to sort out some of the message. Thus, context is less prominent, although still very important for the second language learner.

He sees language as serving many functions, and he looks for ways to convey these functions. He knows that in any social interaction, there is room for the interpretation of the speaker's intention. He knows that many cues to the message are to be found in observing the nature of the interaction. There are a whole host of social dimensions which the good language learner uses to help in his understanding of the message and to enable him to frame an appropriate response.

The good language learner may try to isolate those features which give him maximum intelligibility. He may develop a feeling for those phonological cues which best enhance intelligibility. In English, this might mean that he emphasizes accurate production of intonation patterns over that of individual sounds because of the intimate relationship of these patterns with syntax. In English, some mispronunciation of individual sounds will be tolerated if intonation patterns are accurate.

There are lots of other things which the good language learner does which need exploring. Some other hints are in the literature for memorization techniques. Carroll (1966: 104) suggests that 'The more meaningful the material to be learned, the greater the facility in learning and retention.' It might be expected that the good language learner finds ways to make the things he must memorize more meaningful. Carroll (1966: 104) also suggests that: 'The more numerous kinds of association that are made to an item, the better are learning and retention.' Again we need to observe what the good language learner does to enhance associations.

## Further research

The above list offers some good insights into the cognitive processes that seem to be going on in good language learners. A recent article by Stern (1974) lists some additional learner strategies which enhance our insights into the process. However, this is just a start and more systematic and deeper observation will need to be carried out. To do so a number of factors need to be taken into account first since it is clear that considerable variation between learners may be expected.

The learner strategies (of even successful learners) will vary with: 1. The task—some material may require rote memorization while other material may require oral drill. 2. The learning stage—language learners may in fact use different strategies at different points in time in the learning process. 3. The age of the learner—it is probably true that adults do better guessing (having at their disposal multiple hierarchies of redundant cues) while the child has not yet developed such hierarchies. Children on the other hand may be freer in adapting to new situations and to acting out a communication. 4. The context—if second language learning takes place in the classroom with little or no opportunity for practice, the type of strategies used may well be more limited and distinct from those used where the learner has an opportunity to and perhaps has an obligation to use his language for real communication purposes. 5. Individual styles—some people are not comfortable unless they have something written in front of them or unless they have the grammatical points under consideration in front of them. Some people learn better by visual means while others learn better by auditory means.[7] We should expect that there would be many different kinds of 'good language learners.' 6. Cultural differences in cognitive learning styles—in some societies, listening until the entire code is absorbed and one can speak perfectly is a reported form of learning; in others successive approximation to native speech is used as a learning strategy; while in still others rote learning is the most common learning strategy. Good learners may have considerable insight to contribute to their learning difficulties and to their preferences for instructional methods.

By looking at what is going on inside the good language learner, by considering how he is successful, what strategies, what cognitive processes he uses to learn a language, we may be led to well-developed theories of the processing of linguistic information which can be taught to others. Perhaps we can then establish procedures to train others to use these or similar procedures to acquire a second language.

In the meantime, teachers can begin to look at what the good student does to acquire his skill. They can stop, if so doing, inhibiting the use of communicative strategies in the classroom, that is, use of all sorts of clues to guess at meaning. Rather they should encourage students to transfer what they know about the world and about communication to second language learning. I agree completely with Twaddell (1973) who says that 'The learner must be allowed, must be encouraged, to accept temporary vagueness in the early stages of familiarity with a given word.' Indeed, I would say that the early learner should be encouraged to accept temporary vagueness in many other areas of language learning. In this sense, he will be replicating the more natural communication process where the participants in communication do not always hear, understand or properly interpret what is being said to them; still they do not panic but continue the conversation and see if the item becomes clarified in the course of the dialogue.

The teacher should help students understand how topic, context, mood, human relationships help him narrow down the possible meaning of a sentence, or a word. He should help the student guess what the linguistic function of a particular item might be. In this sense, the teacher would be helping the student learn how to learn a language.

When we have researched this problem more thoroughly we will be able to incorporate learning strategies into our methodology, we will be able to help the learner select the appropriate method for his own learning style and we will be able to adapt the strategy to the particular cultural learning style. The inclusion of knowledge about the good language learner in our classroom instructional strategies will lessen the difference between the good learner and the poorer one.

## Notes

First published in *TESOL Quarterly*, 9, 1, 1975.

1. This difference may not occur with very young children learning a second language in a natural setting with the kinds of communicative demands made in the use of a first language.
2. This evaluation of the success record seems to be generally agreed upon by teachers as well as students, no matter whether the success criterion is passing the course, acquiring certain skills (reading, writing, speaking and understanding) or actually putting to use what has been learned. Indeed, students in many American universities have been so dissatisfied with the profits from second language courses, they have petitioned with success to have the language requirement removed.
3. I am indebted to Roger Prince, a graduate student in the English as a Second Language Program at the University of Hawaii, for his willingness to explore the use of video-tape in this research.
4. What is fascinating to me is that most language classrooms discourage this normal communication strategy by telling students not to guess or by not asking the good guesser how he got there.
5. The direct method assumes that the student will guess the appropriate cognates found in the target language yet never allows the teacher to refer to the mother tongue so that the guessing is expected of the student but is never a part of the teaching strategy.
6. This is what Carroll, Sapon and Pimsleur have called 'grammatical sensitivity and inductive language learning ability.'
7. Individual learning styles are reported to be affected by several variables as well: (a) general cognitive style (b) personality traits (perfectionism, self-confidence, extroversion) (c) past school experiences (d) educational achievement (e) experience in learning other foreign languages.

# Children's sociolinguistic competence and dialect diversity
Susan Ervin-Tripp

## Assumptions

The more we study speech in natural settings, the more we find systematic variation within every speaker, reflecting who he is addressing, where he is, what the social event may be, the topic of discussion, and the social relations he communicates by speaking.[1] The regularities in these features of speech make them as amenable to analysis as the abstracted rules called grammars. Competence in speaking includes the ability to use appropriate speech for the circumstance and when deviating from what is normal to convey what is intended. It would be an incompetent speaker who used baby talk to everyone or randomly interspersed sentences in baby talk or in a second language regardless of circumstance. It would be equally incompetent to use formal style in all situations and to all addressees in a society allowing for a broader range of variation.

With respect specifically to social dialects we assume that all varieties of English are alike in many underlying features. The child in a community with social dialects of English is in a very different situation from an immigrant. Even though he may not understand all details of Standard English, those he fails to understand or use may be relatively superficial from a linguistic if not a social standpoint. In casual discourse, intelligibility of Standard English to a nonstandard speaker is not likely to be the major problem, as it can be for a speaker of another language. Since gross unintelligibility is not present, motives for learning may be different.

As a result of mass media and education, as well as pressures towards 'proper' speech in many homes, we assume that children who use many nonstandard features may often understand more of the surface features of Standard English than they reveal in their speech. In this sense a kind of bilingualism may exist at the comprehension level, as it does with those Spanish or Navaho speakers who can understand more than they produce.

Finally, we assume that social groups vary in the uses to which they most often put speech and in the value they attach to different uses, so that the range of uses of speech by a child is to be ascertained. On the other hand, certain values can be found universally in every social group. We ought to discover which speech events, for example, are evaluated aesthetically. We assume that aesthetic values are present in every society; whether they are focused on speech and, if so, on which kinds of speech is to be learned.

## Previous research

*Systematic correlates of variations in dialect features.* In speakers with a wide repertoire of language or dialect variation, the internal linguistic structure of that variation and its co-occurrence with semantic and social features can be examined. Sam Henrie found that deletion of verb affixes by five-year-old black children was related to semantic features of the utterance and was not a random feature. It has been known for some time that the form *be* as in 'He be outa school' is semantically contrasted with *is* and carries meaning that Standard English cannot easily translate. Henrie found that by the age of five, children selected *be* most often for habitual actions ('they be sleeping') or distributed nontemporal states ('they be blue'), least often for momentary acts.

We have learned that the frequency of standard features may increase when (a) the child is role-playing doctor or teacher, (b) the child is in the schoolroom or being interviewed by an authority figure, (c) the child is interviewed alone rather than in a group, (d) the interviewer uses only Standard English rather than variable speech. Labov noted, for example, that in formal style black teen-agers used the plural suffix more, though the redundant third person verb marker remained infrequent. Since none of these studies except Labov's has focused on fine detail, we might be willing to pool them all as indicating a kind of formal-informal dimension. Fischer, for example, noted that New England three- to ten-year-old children increased their use of '-in' suffixes (fishin) over '-ing' suffixes (fishing) in the course of an interview, presumably relaxing into more casual style. Fischer noted, as others have, that girls in his group used the more formal variant more; Kernan's examples of formal features in role-playing usually involved girls.

This kind of variation corresponds to what Blom and Gumperz call situational switching and Houston calls 'register,' where the primary determinants appear to be setting, situation, addressee, and topic. Overlaid on these features, which in bilinguals often generate sharp switching of languages, are variations in linguistic features like '-in' and '-ing' which may or may not form coherent styles. Gumperz calls these 'metaphorical switching.' These may be viewed as reflections of changes of function or intent within the particular interaction, that is, the variations between dialect features can be considered linguistic devices for realizing intent or social meaning. In a given conversation, different speech acts or structural units within the conversation and different foci or speech episodes often may be demarcated by changes in the frequency of socially significant speech variables. Blom and Gumperz describe these phenomena with respect to dialect variation between a village dialect in Norway and Standard Norwegian. The phenomena are analogous to American dialect feature variation.[2]

An example of a simple analysis of classroom interaction (under John Gumperz's guidance) with these concepts may illustrate what I have in mind. Mary Rainey studied a teacher in a black Head Start class. She selected the alternation between '-ing' and '-in' suffixes for observation, since they are related both to formality and to dialect. The teacher regularly used '-ing' in formal teaching and story reading but in these situations she used '-in' when she was trying to get attention or closeness. Rainey calls '-ing' the *unmarked* or usual form for formal teaching. On the other hand, the unmarked form for informal or casual interaction was '-in' and in these situations '-ing' was used for marked emphasis. ('Where are *you* going, Ezekiel Cato Jones?') A contrast in *register* is the comparison of casual interaction with formal teaching; *marking* is the change in meaning indicated by a shift from the normal features of that register.

The notion that formality lies on a simple dimension seems well founded empirically in Labov's studies. With addressee and setting constant, he was able to accomplish style changes in '-ing' and in phonological alternatives by topical changes (e.g., to a more emotional topic) or by task changes (to reciting a childhood rhyme, to reading) which affected the consciousness or 'monitoring' of speech. Labov found in his Lower East Side New York study that a full range of style variation in interviews was not adult-like until around fourteen or fifteen, but there is other evidence certainly that some variation exists before that time. Typically, children use the more informal forms more often than adults as one would expect from their exposure to informal home situations.

In contrast to Labov's unidimensional view of monitoring, Claudia Kernan has used this term in speaking of 'monitoring black' and 'monitoring white.' These terms refer to speech which veers away from the normal expected, or unmarked vernacular. This monitoring is analogous to Blom and Gumperz's metaphorical switching. What are the social factors that go along with monitoring black? Some examples were parodying the speech of quoted persons to indicate their social characteristics.[3] On other occasions, speakers might be alluding to shared ethnic identity.

Many black public figures like Dick Gregory and Bobby Seale are skilled at these allusions to ethnic identity through 'monitoring black'.[4] On the other hand, such allusions are common in everyday discourse, according to Kernan, and Gumperz has located instances in recordings made by a black-community worker of interaction between his wife and teen-age boys, for instance:

> You can tell me how your mother worked twenty hours a day and I can sit here and cry. I mean I can cry and I can feel for you. But as long as I don't get up and make certain that I and my children don't go through the same, *I ain't did nothin' for you*, brother. That's what I'm talking about.

In speakers of Hawaiian pidgin, systematic register variation occurs between features of pidgin phonology, syntax, lexicon, and intonation and those features of Standard English known to the speaker, with social inputs such as age of addressee, relative status, familiarity, sex difference, and whether the addressee is an islander or mainlander. But within this registral variation, reference to shared, personal island experience even in a formal mainland setting can bring about style shift towards pidgin.

In a tape of Chicano bilingual interaction analyzed by Gumperz and Hernandez, loan words, exclamations, and sentence connectors were used as allusions to ethnic identity. These superficial items might even appear in relatively monitored speeches, such as political interaction. But in informal interaction where the speakers have no values deriding language switching, the bulk of the switching consists of changes in whole sentences or clauses underlying them. These code shifts have a social meaning similar to marking or style shifting in dialect variation. They can, for example, allude to ethnic identity, and depending on context carry special meanings of confidentiality or personal involvement. In these cases the switching is often quite unconscious and affects a deeper level in the sentence production process. In dialect style shifting, the parallel between these superficial and deep shifts would be the contrast between the isolated use of single features like *be* or exclamations and lexical items compared to more pervasive changes in paralinguistic and phonological features affecting longer units of discourse.

Labov has commented that if a speaker masters a fully consistent standard register, he may be unable to switch to the vernacular except through the use of markers whose frequency is not like that in an unmarked vernacular. He loses his fine sense of context-defined inherent variation. In some of the black monitoring observed by Kernan, forms were used that were caricatures and do not occur in any vernacular style.

The notion of marking or foregrounding information has been

formally developed by Geoghegan. He has found, in working on alternations in address forms, that one can identify a regular, expected, reportable, unmarked form which is predictable from social features such as setting, age, rank, sex, and so on. This would correspond to register or situational or unmarked style as used above. Register does not carry meaning because it is predictable from known social features. Deviations from the unmarked alternatives carry social information such as positive and negative affect, deference, and anger. Thus 'marking' is the same as Gumperz's metaphorical switches. Kernan's 'monitoring' carries information to the listener because it deviates from the speaker's usual style in that situation. In her examples the information concerned attitudes towards addressees or persons referred to or quoted. Since these changes in speech are often unconscious, they can only be studied from taped natural conversations, not from informant reports.

*Sociolinguistic development.* I hope it is clear from this discussion of registers, styles, marking, and monitoring that these concepts are still being developed and changed and that attention to them will be fundamental in any research on children's understanding of the social aspects of language. Since work has been largely on adults, we do not know at how young an age and under what social conditions it is possible for speakers to show register or style variability in their speech.

My guess is that the first social features that will appear are major setting and addressee contrasts, since we find very early that bilingual children change language according to locations and persons. Martin Edelman, for example, examined the relation between reports of the expected language for given settings and language dominance as judged by fluency in emitting isolated words in a particular language associated with a given setting. The children were Puerto Rican bilinguals in New York, six to twelve. The pattern did not change with age, merely the amount of English dominance. Children knew significantly more English words for education and religion, but not for family and home.[5] Church, school, and home are unambiguous settings, for which dominant language was reportable by the children.

In addition, when nursery school children role-play they often adopt consistent speech patterns in accordance with the social categories involved—mothers and babies, doctors, cowboys, teachers, puppets. These situational patterns are relatively stereotyped but do reveal quite early use of language with consistent feature changes. What we do not know is what features change and what social cues can be generalized beyond particular persons.

The instances we have observed of speech variation for intent may not be socially conventionalized in young children. One can only surmise how the metaphor they seem to express has been learned. For example, children will use infantilized style as a marker for dependency needs, but it is not clear whether this style is in fact drawn from the child's own earlier repertoire or is some stereotype of infant's speech. I have heard children of four years use telegraphic sentences to a foreigner just learning English and thought it an imitation but Eurwen Price reports that four-year-old English monolinguals in a Welsh nursery school who assumed the Welsh teachers knew no English spontaneously spoke telegraphically, e.g., 'Me cars now', yet they clearly had not heard such speech from the fully bilingual teachers. The most striking feature of these style shifts is that they are transitory and that within a given conversation they may merely mark the onset before reversion to unmarked style.

We know that consistent code changes in second languages can be learned early very rapidly. Edward Hernandez, in Berkeley, has been studying a Chicano monolingual of three who became relatively bilingual within six months from nursery school exposure, though his English at that time was considerably simpler than his Spanish. We do not know how early or under what social conditions completely consistent control over the situational selection of two social dialects can be mastered. Part of the problem is that we know relatively little about the linguistic features of such competence. Greenlee, who observed bilingual five-year-olds, commented that they already had learned not to speak Spanish before outsiders, but that in her small sample of their own interaction there were code shifts for marking emphasis, indicating addressee, and quoting.

*Stylistic consistency.* In the more formal types of situations, bilinguals can learn relatively separated codes. Even metaphorical switching tends to be at fairly high syntactic nodes if both lexical alternatives are available to the speaker (i.e., he doesn't have to use vocabulary from one variety since he lacks words). Some bilinguals even have a range of formal to informal styles in both codes.

One of the major differences between the variation found in most bilinguals and in speakers with forms from various social dialects has been argued by Kernan. She points out that there is a lack of co-occurrence restrictions, or stylistic consistency, in the samples of black speech. One changes register, or monitors, by increasing or decreasing the frequency of certain variables, sometimes categorically. But if one examines the variables which show stylistic variation, one finds the variants side by side. For example, 'She has a morning class and a afternoon class, and she have their name taped down on a piece of cardboard.' She found the same variation in preschoolers: 'They seen the bird, saw the ducks.' For these reasons, she does not think that standard variants are dialect borrowings, but rather that they are integral to the dialect.

Labov, who has examined both individual and group styles in teen-age and adult Harlem speakers, has been impressed by the inconsistency of their formal style features, especially in the formal test situations typical of schools. 'Whenever a subordinate dialect is in contact with a superordinate dialect, answers given in any formal test situation will shift from the subordinate towards the superordinate in an irregular and unsystematic manner.' Claudia Kernan also found, in classroom correction tests, that students had no stable notions of what the standard alternative was among the alternatives in their repertoire. Labov, McKay, Henrie, Kernan, and indeed everyone who has collected considerable samples of speech of dialect speakers have found that the full range of most standard forms will appear *some time* in their speech. That is, the problem of standard speech is in most cases not that the form is outside the repertoire but that the speaker *cannot maintain a consistent choice* of standard alternatives and not make slips. There is inadequate co-occurence restriction between the standard forms whether they are dialect borrowings or not.

This is what we would expect if in fact the features that standard speakers use to identify standard and nonstandard speech are often used for metaphorical signalling by nonstandard speakers. They may hear a higher density of standard features as carrying a particular connotation in a given situation. But some features are *not* varied for this kind of meaning, and since various combinations of features co-occur there is no strong sense that any consistent style is required. In addition, there is considerable 'inherent variation' according to Labov's work, which may not carry any connotations at all. In Standard English this inherent variation is not heard as marking the speaker as incompetent in Standard English, but since in any nonstandard English the variation includes features which are criterial to listeners' judgments of standardness, it appears to be socially inconsistent to outsiders.

In advising parents who rear bilingual children it is usual to point out that they should maintain consistency of speaker, occasion, and setting so that the child can be aided in predicting which form to use. But in the case of any nonstandard English the great bulk of the informal styles heard in the community by children contain a high degree of variability between standard and nonstandard features, since the variability is inherent in the dialect. A child who is to maintain a consistent choice of the standard alternative must mark it categorically in his storage, or at least have some linkages between forms which will make sequential occurrence of standard forms seem normal for him. If the child heard pure standard or nonstandard forms, this learning would not be a problem.

He would learn the standard style as a second language with as brief and trivial interference as we normally find in immigrant children.[6] But this is not what he hears. He hears highly variable speech lacking in co-occurrence restrictions or predictability from segment to segment, at least at the grammatical level. Small wonder that many speakers are very uncertain as to which is standard and cannot do classroom correction tests comfortably.[7]

This line of thinking leads me to an outlandish proposal. If the problem is to identify 'pure styles' and to store them with sufficient separateness to permit stylistic consistency, might it not be appropriate to help identify them by using 'monitoring styles' of a sort, by having children role-play, parody, or use narrative styles in which a relatively extreme nonstandard without inherent variation on key features might seem appropriate and the other children could call them on failures? The converse would of course be role-playing a journalist, doctor, legislator, and so on, in Standard English grammar. The social appropriateness of such a move in a school might very well be questioned by parents who believe the school is the place for Standard English, but such games might enhance maximum adeptness in style switching. There is of course some precedent for permitting and encouraging a range of styles in dramatic play, even in school. In addition, there may be community tradition for such uses, as in the black speech act called 'marking' which parodies speech.

In courses helping adolescents to master register changes, Waterhouse has found that even students who did not speak Standard English consistently were as a group critical of press releases in a role-played press conference if they contained non-standard features like copula deletion. The group itself, without pressure from the teacher, exerted constraints on role-players to keep a consistent register. The method saves the actor from being teased about speaking Standard English and potentially may be transferred to situations where the teacher is not present.

The practice of giving students drills in Standard English, which has developed in some schools, is based on the assumption that the variants do not exist in their repertoire. It also assumes that there may be massive problems of failure of communication. But studies of social dialects in fact show the frequency of non-standard forms to be small but socially important because of prejudice against nonstandard speakers. Where the standard variants exist in the child's repertoire already, and where some already are markers of social meaning, the teacher has a special objective quite different from that of basic second-language learning. The teacher needs to find the most effective way to give a child training in situational switching which will allow him to use the forms consistently in writing and in speech situations where he may be affected by fatigue, fear, and by concentration on the content of what he is saying. That seems to be what parents want to happen.

If a child is forced to speak only Standard English, he is robbed of an essential rhetorical tool. An example from Gumperz and Hernandez illustrates deliberate use of style shifting:

> Student (reading from an autobiographical essay): This lady didn't have no sense.
> Teacher: What would be another way of saying that sentence?
> Student: She didn't have any sense. But not this lady; she *didn't have no sense.*

The child who is bilingual or speaks a nonstandard variant has style variation available which signals social meaning which may be unexpressible in Standard English. Where these meanings have analogues in style shifts within Standard English the teacher who is able to understand the child's intent can view it as part of his task to enlarge his own and the child's repertoire to include several ways of signalling these meanings, depending on the audience.

*Comprehension of features.* Interpretation of studies of the possibilities of variation in produced speech requires better evidence on what features children can hear. Because of the evidence that many variants occur freely if unpredictably in children's output, it is sometimes assumed that all children understand all features of Standard English. Jane Torrey's work using comprehension tests such as choice of pictures is a model for studying these problems. She found that sibilant suffixes had markedly different probabilities of being understood or produced, depending on their grammatical functions. Almost all the black children in her Harlem sample understood a plural suffix and produced it regularly, almost none understood or produced a verb suffix marking number, as in 'the cat scratches,' vs. 'the cats scratch', and about half understood and produced the copula, the possessive, and the verb suffix denoting tense, as in 'the boy shut the door' vs. 'the boy shuts the door.' Torrey has not reported the performances of children who usually hear Standard English to see if some developmental factors are present. This study, of course, isolates the features from contextual redundancy by selecting sentences in which only the suffix must be the cue, as one must to discover whether a particular linguistic cue can be interpreted alone.

The kind of evidence that Labov, Kernan, Baratz, and others have obtained, showing that in imitation tasks children *translate* into their own dialect, may be insufficient indication of comprehension of particular features, since the sentences contain redundancy. For example, Baratz found that white children translated 'It's some toys out there' into 'There are some toys out there,' and black children often did the reverse. But this does not indicate that either group 'understood' the first words, rather that the rest of the utterance made obligatory this form in their output. Error analysis of imitation materials with less redundancy would discover what syntactic and morphological features are employed. Torrey's findings are not inconsistent with the important fact that in everyday situations most Standard English may be intel- ligible grammatically to all black lower-class children, since in many situations language is redundant.[8]

A recent study by Weener attempted to separate phonology from whatever semantic and syntactic sequential probabilities are tested by memory for 'orders of approximation' to English by six- and seven-year- olds. From the standpoint of syntactic differences, this method gives rather gross results and is unlikely to be sensitive to whatever syntactic differences occur in the formal output of lower-class black and middle- class white informants. The interesting finding in this study was that when asked to remember these strings of words, the lower-class black children and middle-class whites did equally well with the materials read by a middle-class speaker, but the whites had trouble remembering the same materials read by a black speaker. That is, just as we might expect on social grounds, black children have more exposure to middle- class white phonology and can interpret it more easily than the sub- urban Detroit white children could interpret southern black speech.[9]

The Weener results remind us that the critical factors in adjusting to phonological differences, as in adjusting to 'foreign accents,' are likely to be experience and attitude toward the speaker. Studies of the mutual intelligibility of speakers in varieties of social settings allowing for both differences in contacts and in types of speech exposure and for differ- ences in social attitudes towards the other group would inform us about factors causing changes in intelligibility in our pluralistic society. These studies need to focus on comprehension as such, not output measures like the cloze procedure, and it would be helpful if they would dis- tinguish fine-grained feature interpretation (as of the plural marker in Torrey's work) from grosser referential intelligibility and the under- standing of allusion and metaphor.

One of the most significant findings in Kernan's work and in recent studies of John Gumperz is that there is considerable informational or connotative content in choice among referential equivalents in the speaker's repertoire. A full competence in comprehending the speech of others includes these social interpretations. So far, most research on information-transmission has been focused on shapes, colors, and lo- cations rather than on the equally systematic communication of hostility, affection, and deference. It is possible that the latter matters are of greater practical significance—for example, in the classroom where teacher and pupil need to communicate respect for each other. If teachers cannot understand when a pupil makes a conciliatory move, for instance, disaster could follow.

*Subjective reaction tests.* Along with studies of comprehension, we need more information about children's attitudes towards speech varieties and their sense of norms of register and style. There have been numerous studies in which people rate voices out of context (except of topic) by Labov, Tucker and Lambert, and Williams, for example. Such ratings necessarily tend to be of people or categories of people, since this is all the information the listeners can discover. It turns out to be the case, when specific features used in ratings are examined, that listeners tend to give 'categorical' judgements, as Labov first pointed out. They will judge intelligence, ambition, and honesty just from 'accent.' They do not react to frequencies reliably but, as June McKay has suggested, tend to pick out the 'lowest' ranked social feature, even if it is rare, as an indicator of the speaker's social ranking—provided, of course, it is not contextually accounted for as 'marking,' such as parody, irony humor. Williams has found that teachers tend to judge race from a few features. The work of Triandis, Loh and Levin, and Lambert implies that teachers will then treat the children by their group stereotype. From a practical standpoint, knowing which features are perceptually critical might help those who aim at giving the children the option of choosing when to be ethnically identifiable from phonology.

One of the fundamental ideas in sociolinguistics, as emphasized earlier, is that speech in fact and in its norms is context sensitive. We accept baby talk to infants but not to adolescents. As a measure of children's development of style norms, judgments of the sort just discussed need to be made where the social context is made clear in some way. It remains to be seen how children react to anomalies—by laughter, criticism, imitation perhaps. Children as young as five will criticize others who are doing role-playing for using the wrong terminology for the role, e.g., 'You can't say "honey"; you're the baby.' Such studies are the judgmental analogue of the role-playing method of studying actually produced style and register changes, and the two kinds of studies should be paired to permit study of the extent to which judgments are finer than ability to produce the forms critical to the judgments. Labov has found that by mid-teens speakers who did not themselves produce the most formal alternatives in New York phonology shared the opinion of the rest of the population on what variants were socially higher.

Claudia Kernan has commented that certain genres of folk literature, such as songs, poetry, and narratives would be ludicrous in Standard English, and Labov found that childhood ryhmes often forced use of the most casual vernacular. It would be of great value to know how sensitive are children to these social co-occurrence constraints, especially on genres brought into use from outside the school to enlarge the children's fluency in the classroom. If they react to some kinds of performances as sounding wrong in Standard English, or vice versa—if some require Standard English—then efforts by the teacher to mismatch these types of discourse with the wrong style may make the children uncomfortable and silent. For these reasons studies of judgments may help guide teachers toward culturally appropriate varieties of language.

*Functions of language.* One of the major issues that has come to the fore in sociolinguistics and in applied work in education has been the question of varieties of language function. Bernstein (2) has pointed out that in England, middle-class parents train children in a considerable amount of explicitness about referents, as though they were talking to a stranger or blind person and no shared assumptions obtained. The result of this training (possibly through the use of known-answer question drills) is that children perform verbal tasks very well in test situations with minimal verbal stimulation. The difference in stress on overelaboration of detail vs. terseness of description, based on shared assumptions, shows up in a variety of studies. Hawkins found that lower-class English children described pictures with many 'exophoric' pronouns, which required that the listener see the picture, as indeed he did. Middle-class pupils elaborated nouns and adjectives which specified information the examined must already have known from seeing the picture. Williams and Naremore found that when children were asked to be specific, class differences disappeared. But when terse questions were asked, the middle-class children assumed they should give complicated elaborate answers and, the lower class, that only minimal necessary responses were needed. Labov has cited examples illustrating the bewilderment of a child taken into a room by a tester and told to 'say what is in front of you' when both the tester and the child could see quite well what it was.

The implication, of course, is that children may have learned that the function of such communication is to convey information. If they have not been brought up on 'known-answer' questions and taught to display their vocabulary and disregard whether the hearer knows the information, they may not understand the intent of such questions.

Claudia Kernan described such an incident during her study of the speech of Oakland black youngsters. She asked one child, 'Where do you live?' and got a vague answer, 'Over there,' with a vaguely waved thumb. Shortly after, her husband asked the same question. The answer he got was, 'You go down the stairs, turn left, walk three blocks . . .'

What was the difference? Her husband had never been to the child's house—but she had picked the child up there.

Social-class differences in transmission of referential information may be a function of 'set.' If so, they can be easily changed by instruction or brief training. Studies by Cowan, Coulthard and Robinson, and Robinson suggest that they are to some degree the effects of socially different ways of viewing the function of the act asked of them, or the 'rules of the game.' It is possible of course that skill in the particular domain of vocabulary or previous experience with materials might aid in such performances too.

Of considerable value to sociolinguistic work are studies of skills in language developed by children. For example, children often spontaneously play with sounds in the preschool years, and invent games transforming songs by simplified transformations like pig Latin. Where these skills become socially organized, they may develop into identifiable speech categories: nursery rhymes, songs, sounding, toasting, rifting, or rapping. These, in some cases, include oral traditions, knowledge of which is part of the developing competence of children. These may include not only general stylistic features but sequential rules. Children's skill is repeatedly evaluated by peers and highly appreciated. Houston has even argued that in the rural poor that she studied, lack of toys resulted in more storytelling, language games, and placing more value on linguistic creativity, spontaneous narrative, and improvisation. She has shown that black lower-class children excel in story enrichment during retelling. Having recently seen a group of forty highly educated adults and their children around a campfire without even one person being skilled enough to carry on storytelling, I can believe education can produce cultural impoverishment!

Analysis of the structure of communication within communities could make us better able to draw events from children's repertoire into the schools, better able to use them in testing competence to identify biologically based retardation, and better able to understand how children interpret tasks they are given to do. Within these speech categories, stylistic variations involving the standard-nonstandard dimensions are important carriers of emotional significance. The ability to convey meaning depends on this range of variation. We can expect that as children have contact with members of varied social groups they will learn skill in a wider range of speech categories, learn each other's oral traditions, and learn devices for conveying information about social intent from each other's dialects. We are already seeing these changes in Berkeley children in integrated schools. Labov has pointed out that the black children he studied valued language highly for cleverness in besting others; this attitude, if fully understood by teachers, could, he proposed, be a basis for enlarging language competence.

## Notes

First published in *Language Acquisition and Communicative Choice*, edited by Anwar S. Dil, Stanford University Press, 1973.
All the references are to be found in the bibliography.

1. For further discussion of these points see Hymes, and Ervin-Tripp. The furthest development of the importance of repertoire in social meaning has been in the work of John Gumperz.
2. A striking finding of this study was that speakers valued the local vernacular highly and *could not believe* that they employed Standard Norwegian words and features for certain kinds of speech. The relation between the vernacular and a standard has been an educational issue in many parts of the world; studies in other places might often be relevant to developmental issues in the United States.
3. A vivid example of completely unconscious marking which was not a direct imitation appeared in Labov's study of Lower East Side New York speech. A Negro without ethnically distinctive speech told a story about a dangerous experience. In the dialogue he included, he represented his own speech in his typical unmarked casual style, but he also represented the speech of the person he feared, since that person was supposed to have threatened someone with a gun. This voice was rasping and rapid, with 'country' southern Negro features. He later reported that the other person was—a Hungarian!
4. An example from Bobby Seale, an expert at such monitoring, in a speech at a 'Free Huey' rally: 'If the United States government and the courts . . . did this they would have to choose black people from the black community to sit on their juries. They would have to choose some of them mothers who been working twenty years in Miss Ann's kitchen scrubbing floors like my mother done. They have to choose some of the hard-working fathers. They have to choose some of them brothers standing on the block out there wondering where they gonna git a gig!' In the discussion of press reports of the Black Panther Party, he says 'the paper's going to call us thugs and hoodlums . . . but the brothers on the block . . . gonna say, them some out-of-sight thugs and hoodlums up there, and the brother on the block is going to say, who is these thugs and hoodlums. In fact, them dudes look just like me. In fact, I know John, George, Paul. In fact, I know Bobby Hutton. Hey, man, I know that dude, over there. Hey man, what you cats doin with them rods?' Voice quality and intonation change demarcates the quotation as well as the style shift apparent in a transcript. This monitoring style was found in a rally with a largely black audience but not in a radio interview on the same subject matter.
5. The discrepancy between the children's report about neighborhood

language, which they rated as predominantly Spanish, and their word-fluency scores, which were significantly higher in English for the task of naming objects in the neighborhood, illustrates the problems of using tests rather than recordings of natural conversation. It is possible that most 'doorstep conversations' common in the Puerto Rican neighborhoods were in Spanish but that vocabulary for nameable shops and objects was primarily English, and likewise that considerable English was in fact used in conversations which speakers believed were in Spanish. John Gumperz has particularly emphasized the difference between questionnaire answers and actual behavior.

6. Here we distinguish immigrant children from children in those bilingual communities where the same conditions of admixture of English and other forms may obtain in some cases. Many instances have been observed in which bilinguals cannot identify the language of the provenance of a form because it is used in both their codes.

7. Kernan developed a method for identifying when speakers knew the 'proper' standard form. She asked teenagers to correct nonstandard sentences. She found that such forms as deleted copula, negative inversion (can't nobody jump), 'ain't' and 'done' plus participle, and hypercorrect verb suffix (they runs) were consistently identified, but the students were uncertain about many other forms. Labov has had the same results, showing that some forms are stigmatized and are identified as nonstandard, but others are not.

   Six-year-old: She done ate up all of my potato chips.

   Mother: Done ate! She has . . . have ate up all my potato chips.

8. This statement may sound overoptimistic. There are many registers outside of the everyday experience of most people. In the more open enrollment in universities, there may be many students encountering for the first time, with discouraging results, not only new vocabulary and subject matter but also lecturers who use complex nominalizations and unusual types of sentence embeddings. The assumption that syntactic learning ends in childhood is not socially realistic, but there has been little systematic study of complex registers.

9. In studies which disconnect syntax from phonology, there is a serious confounding because of the likelihood of some co-occurrence rules or rules of style consistency between the two levels. Nonstandard syntax with 'standard' or media-announcer phonology is bizarre and quite different in meaning from nonstandard syntax and congruent phonology. In the same way, the standard syntax and stereotyped stage nonstandard phonology employed by Stern and Kieslar was so bizarre a combination that black children could not understand it very well. In the Weener study the syntax had no clear identity and the black speaker's phonology was a natural formal reading style.

# SECTION TWO

# Language, education and social change

# Sociolinguistic surveys at the national level

W. H. Whiteley, University of London

I should like to introduce my paper with two quotations from recent articles (1966) by Charles Ferguson. The first is as follows:

> The fact remains that the availability of accurate, reliable, information on the language situation of a country can be influential in making policy decisions and is of tremendous value in planning and carrying out the implementation of the policies.

and the second:

> It is assumed here that a full-scale description of the language situation in a given country constitutes a useful and important body of data for social scientists of various interests.

These constitute two kinds of justification for carrying out a sociolinguistic survey at the national level; they may, of course, be regarded as—and perhaps ideally are—complementary, but they need not be, and since they may require different kinds of research workers for their implementation, more usually probably are not. It is evident that the first quotation embodies a view of sociolinguistics which underlies much recent work (Shuy and Fasold 1971) and which is probably also influenced by political considerations. My own experience of such surveys is limited to the recently completed Survey of Language Use and Language Teaching in Eastern Africa, which carried out surveys at this level in Uganda, Kenya, Ethiopia, Tanzania, and Zambia, and involved the deployment in each country of two full-time research workers, a team leader, and various part-time research workers, for periods of up to one year. As a result of my participation in the Survey in Kenya I should like, first, to consider very briefly to what extent the first of the above objectives can be realized in the present socio-political climate, and secondly, and at greater length, to raise some of the problems that are involved in making statements about the language situation of a country at the national level, assuming that a 'full-scale' description of this kind subsumes a comprehensive study of language behaviour.

It must be recognized at the outset that there was little relevant experience on which the Survey could draw in the field of language-planning as far as Africa was concerned, though the experience of planners in Norway, India, and Turkey might have given us cause for scepticism. The newly independent states of Africa might lean heavily on expatriate economists to create, modify, and recreate their National Development plans: but they had not hitherto invoked the expertise of linguists, and, as was suggested on more than one occasion at Survey Council meetings, the view that '. . . the finding of suitable answers to language questions . . . is of crucial importance in their economic, political, and social development' (Ferguson 1966: 1) was one which was largely formulated—however imaginatively—in expatriate terms.

So the objective embodied in the first quotation was written into the proposal for the Survey and remained, for many associated with the project, an important goal. Yet, allowing for the facts that language choices may not 'set quickly and decisively' and that they are not determined 'simply on the lines of rational analysis' it has still to be remarked that even by the time the Survey was being planned all the nations involved had been operating a set of language choices for some years, whether accompanied by planning or not, and it was noticeable that co-operation between the Survey teams and Governments was most fruitful in precisely those cases where choices had been most explicitly made, and where the Survey teams were able to provide the service of documenting and evaluating the implementation already achieved. Einar Haugen once commented (1966) that in the history of the world all the successful examples of language planning had had the participation of linguists, and some years earlier the Leverhulme Conference on Universities and the Language Problems of Tropical Africa (1963) had recommended that linguists should participate in fields where information was needed on which practical decisions concerning language could be taken. So much can be accepted, but when the decisions were made, the opinions of linguists were not invoked. Of course, history may subsequently appear to substantiate Haugen's claim, but it will be a difficult case to prove. Linguists may identify problems within particular communities yet fail to persuade the members of their relevance from *their* point of view.

The decisions were taken on political grounds and in conformity with particular political ideologies, but coloured inevitably by particular configurations of historical forces. Tanzania's choice of Swahili as a national language was in part a gesture of independence, in part a reflection of her socialism and her concern that all levels of the population should be involved and able to understand the objective of Party policy, given that the great majority of Tanzanians could hope for no more than primary schooling. In Kenya, where socialism is differently conceived, the de facto adoption of English as an official language in many sectors is in conformity with an essentially élitist ideology, where the country is administered by a professional Civil Service not very different from that inherited from the Colonial Government and clearly separated from the Party. The whole question of the place given to making decision on language choices within the total scheme of political decision-making demands attention. As Colinn Leys has recently pointed out '. . . speaking generally, political leaders do not want one particular goal beyond all others. Like the ordinary people whose affairs they try to manage, they have a multiplicity of goals they want to achieve and most of the time they are pursuing them all more or less simultaneously'. (Leys 1971: 110) There have to be priorities, of course, and in different cases it is evident that the political returns on deciding to use a particular language in a particular sector may not be commensurate with the risks involved. Thus a decision to use English at one level may need to be offset by a decision to encourage, for example, the teaching of the vernacular at the University. Even where the main lines of a policy are clear, there are still opportunities for decisions to be made on political grounds to trim the approach, e.g. the establishment of a National Swahili Council in Tanzania in 1967–68 in opposition to the University based Institute of Swahili Research. At this level the presence of a political scientist in a survey team would be welcome, always assuming that the socio-political climate were not positively hostile to this.

The Survey proposal listed three important spheres in which decisions relating to language questions must be taken: national unity and identity, access to modern technology, and international communication. To these one might add a fourth, internal communication. The second and third of these pose no great problem at the moment; all the East African states having opted, formally or informally, to continue using English. The first, however, is another matter, not least because the term 'national' is variously understood and realized. For lack of suitable alternatives Uganda's Ministers and former President, Milton Obote, used English on national occasions; in Kenya some Ministers use English and some, like the President, use Swahili, which he has referred to on at least one recent occasion as the national language; in Tanzania Swahili is used on all national occasions. So far as internal communication is concerned, while it may be possible for a bureaucracy using Swahili to function efficiently in Tanzania, in Kenya it is English that is used as the medium for official communication from the centre through the Province, down to the District level. At the intra-district level between officials and between central government officials and people the local vernacular is used. In Uganda a similar situation obtains though Swahili is a less efficient articulator between the lines of communication coming down from the centre and the situation at the periphery. (Criper and Ladefoged 1971) In all these spheres the major decisions had been taken.

To sum up, I do not believe that in the present socio-political climate it is realistic to imagine that sociolinguistic surveys are likely to be influential in making policy decisions. Indeed I think it could be argued that it would be presumptuous to entertain such an expectation, bearing in mind that the kind of problems posed by these multilingual nations, require that special training be given to potential language planners of a kind not hitherto available. On the other hand there are no such objections to describing the language situation, and I should now like to turn to a consideration of the extent to which this is a realistic objective at the national level.

Here again, it must be recognized that there were rather few precedents for such an enterprise, and little basic data available, e.g. in Kenya very little language data is provided by the Population Censuses of 1962, 1969. As the first Survey team went into Uganda, Joshua Fishman was finishing off his two-year study of a Puerto Rican neighbourhood in New York and the experience and insights therefrom benefited us all; but Fishman was at pains not to minimize the difficulties of handling even so small a universe as a neighbourhood of 400-odd persons, and left no doubt that these would be magnified as one's universe expanded. Whether it would be possible, as he envisaged, ' . . . to generalize from individuals to entire neighbourhoods or countries . . .' (Fishman 1968: I, 9) in half the time, had to be discovered.

As an introduction to the discussion I present a sociolinguistic profile of Kenya (Table 1), obtained by applying the criteria set out by Stewart (1968). This is not intended as a criticism of Stewart's approach but rather as a device to throw into relief some of the problems that the surveys of a multilingual country like Kenya entails. The profile of necessity simplifies to a considerable extent, thus:

1. Language-type. The problem of a 'standard' form for Swahili. While a standardized form of Swahili was used as a model in education and elsewhere during Colonial times, both in Kenya and Tanzania, there has been a tendency during the past twenty years to assert and develop a local standard in each country. In Tanzania this has mainly been the result of language planning in the period since independence. In Kenya it has largely arisen as a reaction to other models which co-existed, of which the most important were the following:

*Sociolinguistic profile of Kenya (After Stewart 1968)*

| Class II (+50% users) | Swahili | Sop(d; L=V, H=English) |
|---|---|---|
| Class III (+25% users) | English | $S_X$(British norm)op(d: L=V, L=Swahili) |
| Class IV (+10% users) | Kikuyu | Vwcgo |
| | Luhya | Vwgo/Sre$_p$ |
| | Kamba | Vwego |
| | Luo | Vwgo |

*Sociolinguistic profile of Kenya—cont.*

| Class V (+ 5% users) | Nandi/Kipsigis | Vwgo |
|---|---|---|
| | Gusii | Vwgo |
| | Meru | Vwgo |
| | Mijikenda | Vwgo |
| Class VI (− 5% users) | Somali | Vgo |
| | Turkana | Vg |
| | Swahili | Vgl |
| | Swahili | $P_1$ (English pattern) |
| | | $P_2$ (Asian pattern) |
| | 22 others | Vg |
| | Arabic | Cr |
| | Sanskrit | Cr |
| | Prakrit | Cr |
| | Latin | Cr |
| | Hindi | Swg |
| | Gujarati | Swg |
| | Bengali | Sg |
| | Konkani | Vr(g) |
| | 4 others | Vg |

The population of Kenya was c. 11,000,000 in 1969.

Classes represent percentage of users within the polity. Upper case letters refer to language types, thus S=Standard; V=Vernacular; C=Classical; P=Pidgin. Lower case letters refer to language function, thus: o=official; p=provincial; c=capital; g=group; r=religion; w=wider communication; l=literary.

For a fuller discussion of the symbols see W. A. Stewart 'A linguistic typology for describing national multilingualism'. In: *Readings in the sociology of language*, ed. by J. A. Fishman, The Hague, Mouton, 1968.

(a) The coastal varieties of the language with their literary and historical traditions (Vgl), influenced by Arabic phonology and lexicon and by dialectal features (e.g. the dental/alveolar, aspirate/unaspirated oppositions in stops) characteristic of other Swahili dialects—even in Tanzania—but not generally elsewhere in Kenya.

(b) The very low-status varieties used between Asians/Africans; Europeans/Africans ($P_1$ and $P_2$) to mention the two most important varieties. The low status of the language as a whole in some areas is in part related to the recollections of the settings in which such varieties occurred and to present awareness that they still persist.

(c) The 'very difficult' variety of Swahili heard over Radio Tanzania. Recognizing that in rural Kenya childrens' exposure to Swahili in the pre-school period will vary very widely, not only quantitatively but qualitatively and also that their subsequent use of the language is also likely to be very variable, the Kenya Institute of Education has been engaged over the past few years in producing Primary School Courses which aim at a somewhat simplified version of the former standard, which keeps Arabic influence to a minimum at both phonological and lexical levels and which seems to aim at a relatively modest level of competence. It is rather early yet to assess the impact of this new standard on usage.

Where children have access to a radio, this is likely to be their most persistent source of exposure to the language, except on the coast; but here too the models are very varied; from the announcers from the coast whose first language is Swahili to their colleagues from up-country whose Swahili sometimes appears to have been translated from English and bears an unmistakeable intonational imprint thereof.

Thus in Stewart's terms the standardization of Swahili may be said to be both polycentric (i.e. different sets of norms exist) and exonormative (i.e. based on foreign models of usage), but the situation is probably not susceptible to formulaic generalization at the national level. The important point is that the term Swahili covers a number of linguistic varieties which differ in social status and function. Whether the concept of a 'continuum' as developed by the Creolists is useful here is not certain, though the situation described by DeCamp (1961: 61–84) for Jamaica, where individuals of different status in different parts of the country control different spans of the continuum, shows many similarities with the Swahili situation in Kenya, though the possibility of measuring the discreteness of the many varieties by some of the currently available techniques (Bailey 1971: 341–48) remains to be carried out.

2. Language functions. The use of 'o' and 'p'. It is not possible to assign 'o' to any language as 'a legally appropriate language for all politically and culturally representative purposes on a nationwide basis' unless one clarifies or refines the rubric somewhat. In broadcasting, for example, many of the major vernaculars are used to reach speakers across the whole nation, and this is inevitably so where social mobility has resulted in perhaps 25 per cent of Kikuyu and some 12 per cent of Luo being resident outside their home areas. Smaller numbers of other groups are similarly placed. Again, most of the major vernaculars are used at district and sub-district levels for some official purpose or other depending upon the local situation, the nature of the occasion and the heterogeneity of the speakers. They are also used in the courts.

It must also be noted that the language situation in education is not revealed by such a profile. English, in more than half of the country's schools, is the medium of instruction throughout the system. In the remaining schools it is the medium of instruction after the first year or two. Swahili is taught as a subject right through the system, including the University, except during the first year or two in rural schools. Some basic skills are still acquired in the vernacular in those schools which are not following the English-medium approach; but apart from this the vernaculars are not encountered again during the educational process until the University, where courses are planned in the major vernaculars along with the study of Linguistics.

3. Degree of use. The difficulty of using a national Class rating can be illustrated with reference to English and Swahili. To say, for example, that English is used by 30 per cent of the population obscures the fact that this may represent a figure of say 80 per cent of those living in towns, but only 25 per cent of those living in rural areas. Nor is the very wide gap between the generations and the sexes revealed; thus in a sample of Kipsigis, 77 per cent of the men under 30 claimed competence in their first language, Swahili and English, while only 4 per cent of those over 30 made such a claim. On the other hand the incentives to acquire and to demonstrate competence in English are very great, since it is from this source that economic and social status are believed to flow. Many young Kenyans who are being encouraged to use Swahili by the Party are quick to point out that those who currently enjoy both wealth and power did not acquire it through the use of Swahili.

Again, the figure for Swahili conceals the fact that Kenya comprises an economically little-developed coastline with almost 100 per cent Swahili speakers, including most of those who use it as a vernacular; an economically highly developed central area where perhaps 50 per cent may be Swahili speakers; and large areas in the west and north-west of the country where fewer than 15 per cent of the population may be Swahili speakers. Some consideration ought also to be given here to level of competence: a good deal may be inferred from an account of the settings in which particular languages are used, since for each setting there is probably a minimal 'threshold' below which effective communication cannot take place. On the other hand there are a number of settings in which it is not competence so much as social appropriateness which determines the choice of language. Gumperz has given many illuminating examples in his writings, and our experience in Kenya has provided ample confirmation of this, particularly in encounters between members of the public and government officials. Thus, a man wishing to see a government officer about renewing a licence, may state his request to the girl typist in Swahili as a suitably neutral language if he does not know her. To start off in English would be unfortunate if she did not know it, and on her goodwill depends his gaining access to authority reasonably quickly. She may reply in Swahili, if she knows it as well as he does and wishes to be co-operative; or in English if she is busy and not anxious to be disturbed; or in the local language if she recognizes him and wishes to reduce the level of formality. If he in return knows little English, he may be put off at her use of it and decide to come back later; or, if he knows it well, he may demonstrate his importance by insisting on an early interview and gain his objective at the expense of the typist's good will. The interview with the officer may well follow a similar pattern, being shaped on the one hand by the total repertoire available to each other, and on the other by their respective positions in relation to the issue involved (Whiteley 1972, Ch. 12; Parkin 1972, Ch. 8). Yet it emerged from our sample surveys that there were in any case a substantial number of people whose competence in both English and Swahili was below the threshold for the settings being considered and probably restricted to isolated words and phrases. Even the settings themselves may prove an unreliable guide to usage: typically, at District centre level and above, retail trade was in the hands of Asians, and trading was carried on between them and the local population in Swahili; below the District level, it might be noted, numbers of Asian traders learned enough of the vernacular as was necessary to carry on their trade. As the policy of Kenyanization takes effect and Kenyans (especially Kikuyu) move into this sector, and, moreover, as the educational system turns out an increasing number of school-leavers with increasing competence in English, there is some evidence that English is being favoured by the younger and Swahili by the older generation.

Finally, the diglossia situation and the absence of it raises a number of interesting points which cannot be generalized in terms of a single national pattern:

(a) In some rural areas there appears to be a situation of stable diglossia with bilingualism, restricted usually to men, in which a vernacular is L and English H. Where women are not monolingual, they may use Swahili rather than English.

(b) In other areas, especially nearer the coast, the pattern for both men and women is to use the vernacular as L and Swahili as H.

(c) Within the framework of Government service there is an interesting complementarity of work-language where status differences are involved. Here, while English is retained as H, Swahili is used as L.

(d) An increasingly common phenomenon among the younger generation, now that both English and Swahili are taught from the Primary School upwards, is what might be termed triglossia, with Swahili occupying an intermediate position between English and the vernacular.[1] Thus English is used with agents of Government, especially those senior to oneself, e.g. in hospitals, Police, Post-office, Administration, etc.; Swahili in trade, bars, and with agents of Government of equal or junior status to oneself; the Vernacular in and around the homestead and at church.

The incidence of monolingualism varies widely: from the higher than 35 per cent reported in our survey from such diverse groups as Luo, Kipsigis, and Meru, to nil, reported for some Kikuyu and Luyia groups. However, we lacked material from the pastoral peoples of the north and north-east parts of the country where the incidence of monolingualism is reported to be high.

Two quite general comments remain to be made. 1. Within the context of a single national profile it is not possible to see the contrast between the urban and rural areas. While probably no more than 8 per cent of the total population lives in towns, they include Nairobi, the capital, a city of more than half a million people, the seat of government and centre of prestige. It is linguistically heterogenous, where the rural areas are homogeneous; while the vernaculars dominate the rural areas, it is Swahili which is the common man's public language of the city. As Parkin has pointed out from his study of urban housing estates in Nairobi what emerges clearly is the persistence of Swahili as an important, growing medium of communication at all status and educational levels, apparently regardless of whether it has been taught at school or not. (Whiteley 1972: Introduction; Parkin 1972: Chapters 5–8).

2. Regional differences are such that it does not seem to be meaningful to describe the language situation except in terms which allow full weight to be given to them. The sort of factors I have in mind are the following:

(a) Demographic. Ethnic homogeneity varies widely, in the rural areas, from virtually 100 per cent among the larger groups to below 50 per cent in some of the smaller; and it seems to be the case that—all other things being equal—competence in Swahili increases with heterogeneity. Area of occupation may also be significant. For example, the Somali and related groups who comprise only 3 per cent of the total population, occupy almost half of the total land area of the country in the strategically important northern frontier region, with an average density of between 2–10 to the square mile. Monolingual to a high degree, intensely loyal to their language and very sensitive to events in the neighbouring Somali Republic, their importance far outweighs their numbers, and the provision of programmes in Somali together with broadsheets is an important aspect of Kenya's language policy. Finally, pressure of population may be important. This is undoubtedly one factor among many that has contributed to the steady emigration of Kikuyu into other parts of the country, so that substantial minorities are now being created in areas which had previously been very largely homogeneous, thus they numbered barely 1000 in Baringo in 1962, but over 12,000 by 1969.

(b) Socio-economic. Over the period of Colonial administration the different regions followed different lines of development. This was dictated by such factors as the siting of Missions, the alienation of land for European settlement or enterprise, the possibility of developing cash crops, and so on. Some areas became richer than others, acquired better communications and social services, including education. This resulted in differential opportunities for farming, employment, and so on, which in turn provided a range of incentives to add to verbal repertoires. Kipsigis who gained a reputation for service in the Army and the Police acquired skills in Swahili which were of little value to them after their return home; Luo who worked on the railway or in the port at Mombasa also acquired skills in Swahili which were quite uncharacteristic of the rural areas to which they subsequently returned where we noted one of the highest figures for ($L_1$ — English) competence and one of the lowest claiming some competence in Swahili (c. 33 per cent).

The above discussion has focused on the kinds of problems that remain obscured by a simple nation-based approach to the formulation of sociolinguistic profiles, and it is evident that any subsequent profiles will need to be multi-faceted if they are to take account of the range of variables encountered. Alternative approaches have, however, been adopted. Fishman and others have utilized the concept of 'speech community', which he has recently defined (1971) as one '. . . all of whose members share at least a single speech variety and the norms for its appropriate use'. Such a community may be as small as a 'single closed interaction network' or as large as a county. The largest speech community in Kenya by such criteria would be co-terminous with the ethnic group, and smaller communities could be set up in accordance with the purposes of the research under consideration. Fishman goes on to suggest that some speech varieties are referentially, rather than experientially acquired and reinforced and that 'nations' are likely to be speech communities of this kind. He goes on '. . . the standard variety of a language is most likely to be that variety that stands for the nation as a whole and for its most exalted institutions of government education, and high culture in general. It is this variety which comes to be associated with the mission, glory, history, and uniqueness of an entire "people". . .' As will be appreciated from points already raised, it is questionable whether this can be said of either of the two standards in Kenya, English or Swahili, at the present time. What could be said is that for many Kenyans each is associated with a syndrome of values in terms of which the other is delineated, thus those who hold that English is a mark of economic and social status, conferring a desirable form of modernity, and a sense of political unity, may also hold that Swahili is a symbol of lower achievement and status, which offers no sense of modernity and is less effective as a unifying force. In contrast, those who hold that Swahili

is an important symbol of authenticity which confers a sense of unity
both within the nation and within the wider East African Community,
may also hold that English as a Colonial heritage, has only a limited role
at the national level. A third stance is also maintained, whereby both
English and Swahili are held to confer national unity, and both are
invested with some elements of modernity and authenticity. The difficulties of using this 'speech-variety'-based definition of community
arise when dealing with second and third language competence, and can
be illustrated by taking the set of those who speak a variety of English in
Nairobi—leaving aside here the question of deciding what constitutes
a given variety. It would need to take account of the fact that a large
number of the set also share a variety of Swahili, and a smaller, though
still very substantial number a variety of Kikuyu. Similarly, account
must also be taken of the numbers of Kamba, Luo, Luhya speakers, etc.
Of the Kamba speakers a larger number speak Kikuyu than Kikuyu do
Kamba, and a similar asymmetry characterizes the Luo/Luhya pattern
of bilingualism. If one now suggests that this community might be enlarged to include the set of, say, rural Luo, who also share this variety of
English, thus creating a larger community, one runs up against the
difficulty that the two sets are underpinned by different qualitative
factors and are thus not comparable in terms of both requirements.

Fishman himself stresses, later on in the same chapter, the fact that
a basic definitional property of speech communities is 'density of
communication' and thus approaches Gumperz's early definition as
'any human aggregate characterized by regular and frequent interaction
over a significant time and set off from other such aggregates by differences in the frequency of interaction' (Gumperz 1964: 137). To base the
definition of speech community squarely on sociological criteria leaves
one free to examine verbal repertoires, both as properties of the community and of their constituent members. Thus, one might select for
examination the repertories for types of contrasting communities, e.g.
urban/rural; pastoral/agricultural; rural work-groups/urban work-
groups; manual workers/'white collar' workers, in different parts of the
country and gradually build up a pattern for the nation on the basis of
these parameters. At a lower level still, one might examine role-
differentiation within the communities. These studies, however, are
essentially directed at the relatively small communities, with a high level
of internal interaction, from which Gumperz's own illuminating material
is drawn. More, recently, however, Gumperz has amended his definition
of speech community thus, '. . . any human aggregate characterized by
regular and frequent interaction by means of a shared body of verbal
signs and set off from similar aggregates by significant differences in
language usage' (Gumperz 1968: 219). This raises some problems.

First, all 600,000 Gusii could be said to share a body of verbal signs; but they are not, as a body, characterized by frequent or regular inter-action: the Fishman definition fits better here. Second, if the body of verbal-signs is the defining characteristic of the community, it is difficult to accept the view that '. . . the totality of dialectal and superposed variants regularly employed within a community make up the *verbal repertoire* of that community' (Gumperz 1968: 230). If a group of employees constitute a speceh community, X, by virtue of their inter-action through code Y, any other codes employed by the members will be the markers of their membership in other communities, i.e. domestic, religious, etc. and thus individual not community repertoires. Clearly one may start either from a sociologically defined community, i.e. in terms of intensity of social interaction, or from a linguistically defined one, i.e. in terms of shared linguistic code. In the former case one might aim at a characterization of verbal-repertoires across a country for communities of comparably varying degrees of intensity of interaction. In the latter one might work towards establishing the members' verbal-repertoires in terms of various social variables, e.g. age, sex, education, etc. In either case, it seems to me, such studies will need to proceed in close collaboration with detailed ethnographic studies. The survey has made a good start here with a number of intensive studies of Nairobi: from David Parkin's work in African housing estates (1972: Chapters 5–8); to Janet Bujra's study of the strongly islamized community of Pumwani (1972: Chapter 9) and Barbara Neale's study of a Jain com-munity (1972: Chapter 10). The sample surveys that were carried out in the rural areas were at the somewhat superficial level associated with rather short questionnaires and interviews: but they have revealed interesting patterns of linguistic competence and frequency in the rural areas, and have highlighted a number of interesting problems for future work: i.e. the extent to which the dominance of the vernacular in rural homesteads is being eroded by the younger generation's competence in English, the position of Swahili in the domain of trade, whether com-munities in the rural settlement schemes break up into constituent ethnic groups each with its own vernacular or adopt Swahili as inter and intra-group language, whether there are recurrent patterns of language behaviour within Government service which transcend regional differ-ences, and so on.

After a year in the field, and several months of writing up, one acknowledges a better understanding of the range and complexity of the problems entailed in making a sociolinguistic survey of a country such as Kenya. What has been achieved is certainly not a full-scale descrip-tion of the linguistic situation; nor even a characterization of it in national terms; yet a good deal of reliable and accurate data will have been assembled and made available; some areas of darkness will have been illuminated, which are perhaps of more than local interest, and a base will have been set up from which future workers can explore.

One final point: if what has been achieved so far is not to remain of purely academic interest to a scholarly universe remote from that from which it derives, it must be integrated into local institutions and used as a basis for further locally-based research. Only in this way will local scholars, operating from within the ideology of their particular governments, be able to influence the decision-making process in the way that Charles Ferguson envisaged in the first of the quotations with which I began this paper.

## Notes

First published in *Report of the 23rd Annual Round Table Meeting on Linguistics and Language Studies*, edited by R. W. Shuy, Georgetown University Press, 1973.

I should like to express my thanks to Dr. Peter Hill of the Institute of Education, University of London; Dr. David Parkin of the University of Sussex; and Professor John Gumperz of the University of California, Berkeley, for reading and commenting on an earlier draft of this paper.

1. The situation seems to be not dissimilar to that described by Fishman ('Bilingualism with and without diglossia; diglossia with and without bilingualism', *Journal of Social Issues*, XXIII/2, 1967, 31) for East European Jewish males who use Hebrew, Yiddish and, more recently, English in intra-group contact. In the East African context the importance of changes in the status of both English and Swahili for the overall sociolinguistic picture is such that the recognition of 'triglossia' seems useful.

# Some reflections on the educational use of sociolinguistic surveys
Sirarpi Ohannessian and Gilbert Ansre

## Education

Education in most modern societies is increasingly becoming one of the most important agents for social change. This is more so in newly independent nations where often the aim, content, and method of education are quite new, and the whole process is geared towards bringing about drastic physical, social, and often psychological change. Also, substantial funds are directed to education as the major means by which nationals can prepare themselves to take complete responsibility for their political, economic, and social as well as educational affairs. Language in education, therefore, is of crucial importance. An analysis of educational needs from a language point of view is invaluable for educational planning in such countries.

Language in education is also of importance in the more technologically 'developed' countries. In the United States, for instance, attention has been turning to the problems of minority groups who speak other languages than English or other than standard varieties of English. Here there is a great need for sociolinguistic information on such matters as what the linguistic factors are in considering an American 'educated', what the effects of other forms of a language are on status in a society, whether or not development of minority dialects or languages is conducive to educational growth and not just change, what the role of language is in group solidarity, and so on. There is also a need for information on dialect variation and use, the distribution of various languages and dialects in school systems, the degrees of bilingualism in various groups, language shift, attitudes among both minority groups and the majority group towards the language or languages of others, styles of learning prevalent in minority groups as compared with what the majority-oriented educational system demands, and so on. To give one example, the choice of an appropriate and acceptable variety of Spanish for use in bilingual education programs in the southwestern United States could benefit greatly from information on attitudes among both Spanish-speaking and non-Spanish-speaking parents, teachers, and linguists in the community towards such a choice.

It is beyond the scope of this paper to attempt even a brief discussion of the variety of levels and aspects of education whose planning and execution would benefit from reliable sociolinguistic information in various parts of the world. It might, however, be useful to focus on the situation in one area (sub-Saharan Africa), to look at only one or two aspects of education in it, and to consider in what ways sociolinguistic surveys could provide helpful information.

Typically, countries in sub-Saharan Africa have won independence relatively recently, and as politico-geographical entities their boundaries often are the result of recent colonial history rather than of a closely-knit socio-cultural unity among their citizens. These, in greatly differing numbers, speak a wide variety of languages and dialects which are often mutually unintelligible but on most of which relatively little linguistic work has as yet been done. In some cases not even a reliable list of languages and dialects spoken in the country exists. A great number of these languages have not been reduced to writing, and in many only a few tracts from the Bible exist as literature. These languages have often been closely associated with ethnic identity in the past, and as a consequence are regarded, by at least some, as divisive rather than unifying elements in the work of nation-building.[1] In general, population mobility is encouraged to 'mix' ethnic and therefore linguistic groups, and modern industrialization has helped bring about, at least in some of the urban areas, linguistically very heterogeneous communities.

In discussing language in education, we should not be limited to the medium of instruction in the classroom alone. We ought to consider the teaching of specific languages as subjects in the curriculum and the effect they have on the cultural awareness and psychological sense of value of the student. Educational authorities stand to gain a lot from sociolinguistic surveys which give information on how the teaching of and about an indigenous language gives the students and the population at large a clearer sense of the worth of the language in the society as well as a better sense of national identity, even in the face of occasional linguistic diversity.

Also typically, these countries rely in varying degrees on the former colonial language (which usually only a minority commands efficiently) for administrative, economic, social, and educational purposes and sometimes as a unifying factor in nation-building. Patterns of multiple language use or language 'complementation' are developing in some of the countries, and these may become stable. For instance, in Tanzania, the numerous languages and dialects that are spoken by ethnic groups are used for personal and social purposes and fulfill the role of the intimate home language. An African *lingua franca*, Swahili, fulfills the function of the national language and serves a great many official purposes. A world-language, English, serves the role of an official international language which is also used for a number of internal official purposes. In Senegal, Wolof and French serve somewhat parallel purposes, but countries like Ghana, Nigeria, and Zambia lack a national *lingua franca*, though some of their major languages are widely understood and used in the regions where they are mainly used only in the spoken form and have not been vigorously promoted in education.

One of the most important decisions in the educational systems of these countries is what language or languages should be used as media of instruction at various levels in the process of education. The question is very closely related to language choice on a national level, often reflects the pattern of language complementation in the country, and is, in the main, a political decision based on the socio-economic needs of the community, especially manpower needs. In all these cases (e.g. Tanzania, Senegal, Ghana, Nigeria), a detailed knowledge of the sociolinguistic situation would help in decision-making, for though the choice is a political one, it should be an educated one based on the sociolinguistic data of the country. It is, however, sometimes assumed that once decisions are made and plans drawn up, 'specialists' can find easy ways to carry them out. On the contrary, further decisions are necessary for the most effective implementation of a language policy at the very many levels in education, and a great deal of information and insight into the actual linguistic situation is crucial.

The choice of a language as a medium of instruction for the early primary grades is one very important part of the decision. At this level, education is more widely available than any other, but, because the dropout rate is usually very high after the first few years, these early years of schooling are likely to be all the formal education that a large proportion of the population will have. Whatever the pattern of language complementation in a country, or in its educational system, in essence three major alternatives for choice of a medium of instruction exist, although many variations regarding time of introduction of a language, duration of use as medium, and simultaneous use in varying content areas are possible. The alternatives are: (a) the child's mother tongue; (b) an African national or regional *lingua franca* (often not the child's mother tongue); and (c) a world-language, in this case English serving as an example.

The language in which a child is initially taught to read is one major aspect of the choice of a medium of instruction in early primary education. The choice for each child is limited to only one language, generally one of the three alternatives given above. (In some cases it may be a religious language, e.g. Arabic or classical Ethiopian.) A wise choice will need a great deal of psycholinguistic, sociolinguistic, and pedagogical information. Some of this information will be necessary in considering all three alternatives for initial literacy, and some will be peculiar to each. The following paragraphs will briefly discuss some of these considerations.

If the *first* alternative (i.e. the child's mother tongue) is being considered, the types of information needed for decision-making will include such factors as the number of 'languages' in which it will be necessary to have reading materials and the type and quality of existing materials as well as of available literature in, and on, these languages. These are basic types of information, but more specific detail will be necessary before action can be taken. For instance, if materials are to be prepared in a particular language, it will be necessary to decide on exactly which variety of the language is to be used for the purpose. Such a decision will need to take into account not only linguistic factors but the attitudes of the community. The feelings of the people as to what constitutes separate 'languages' and which dialects or varieties of these languages they consider as suitable and acceptable for use in education will be very important factors in deciding on the choice of a variety for teaching reading since, presumably, these languages would also serve as media of instruction in the early years. Also, specific information on the distribution of the speakers of various languages and dialects in classes to be found in industrialized urban areas, in provincial towns, and in rural areas will greatly affect decisions.[2]

Perhaps it would be useful here to illustrate some of these points with the example of a project which is in some ways unique in modern Africa in that it has been able to take advantage of a language survey, to rely on linguistic and sociolinguistic information gathered through years of research in the area, and to have trained linguists and the government of a state cooperate in the scheme. The project is currently (1972) being carried out in the Rivers State in Southern Nigeria and represents perhaps the most serious attempt made so far to prepare materials for initial literacy in the majority of the languages of a complex multilingual area in Africa. The following is taken from a brief account of the project given in a paper entitled *The Rivers Readers Project*,[3] by Kay Williamson of the University of Ibadan, a linguist whose area of special interest is Ijo, one of the major languages of the area. Dr. Williamson is a member of the committee of three which coordinates the project.

According to the classification of the Greenberg survey of the languages of West Africa (*Languages of Africa*, *1963*), the languages spoken in the Rivers State belong to some five different linguistic groups, two of which are Benue-Congo and three Kwa. Within each group, there are several different languages, some with subdivisions in themselves, each comprising several dialects. In her account, Dr. Williamson identifies the relative size of school populations in each of the languages that she lists under the five divisions.

Before the creation of the Rivers State in 1967, the area had been part of the Eastern Region in Nigeria and the policy had been (as in many other anglophone African countries) to start primary education in 'the vernacular' and switch to English as a medium of instruction in the higher primary grades. But the lack of suitable materials in many of the minor languages had often (as elsewhere) meant starting reading in English, or, for a large number of children, in another African language that was not their mother tongue. The creation of the Rivers State saw a great revival of interest among groups in their own language and heritage. Neither the choice of a single language for the entire area nor that of only a few languages appear to have gained acceptance for initial literacy. The Rivers State Government, therefore, agreed to sponsor the Rivers Readers Project, whose aim was to publish materials for the primary schools in some twenty languages and major dialects of the State, the intention being that 'so far as is reasonably possible, each child should be introduced to reading in his own language before he is expected to begin in English.'

It may be of interest to look at some of the important decisions the project had to make and to consider how sociolinguistic information on the situation helped in their making. One of the first things to decide was what constituted a language for purposes of the project.[4] Those involved in the task found that, in addition to the linguistic information available, the single most important factor in determining this was 'the expressed feeling of a group of people that it constitutes a distinct and internally cohesive linguistic community,' although this coherence differed from one area to another. For example, North-Eastern Ijo is considered a single language in the Ijo group of the Kwa languages. It has three dialects, but it was decided to produce separate readers in each of the dialects because the three communities felt themselves to be clearly distinct, had separate country councils, and had an earlier tradition of publications. On the other hand, a single reader was produced for Ikwerre, which had two major dialect groups that could be recognized as separate languages. In this case, however, their speakers were willing to attempt to overlook great dialectal diversity in their desire to create a single common standard language, so a single reader was produced for both (with the possibility that another dialect may be used when the book is revised).

Another important factor that affected decisions was the size of the community. When a linguistic community was very small, such factors as the desirability of its integration into a larger group as well as economic factors had to be taken into account. The general policy, however, was 'to study the situation further and decide each case on its own merits'. A further factor that was taken into account was the existence of a previous tradition of writing in the language, since this made the acceptance of another language for reading difficult. Where no such tradition existed, materials were prepared, but it was sometimes necessary, when consensus was difficult, to make arbitrary decisions in the choice of a linguistically 'more central' variety.

The organization of the project may seem somewhat irrelevant here, but it is perhaps one of the most important elements in the effective use of sociolinguistic information. The project, as Dr. Williamson points out, is a cooperative effort involving moral and financial support from the Rivers State Government (and some support from UNESCO and The Ford Foundation); cooperation from linguists at the University of Ibadan, members of the Institute for African Studies, the Department of Education, the Institute of Linguistics at Zaria; language committees that check expression and wording in texts; and a number of individuals—materials writers, teachers, and so on. The Ministry of Education organizes conferences to familiarize teachers with the some 30 books and other materials that have so far been published. The important point in all this is that linguistic and sociolinguistic information in and of itself may not be enough, but that the concerted efforts of those in a position to make policy decisions; those capable of providing linguistic and sociolinguistic information; and the actual administrators, materials writers, and teachers can, together, produce substantial results provided there is also interest and enthusiasm for the task. The Rivers State Project appears to rely to a great extent on such interest and willing cooperation on the part of the people involved in it.

Although linguistically complex, a community or a school in a rural area such as the Rivers State generally draws the great majority of its children from the same area. Classes, therefore, are on the whole linguistically homogeneous. Many communities in Africa, however, especially the large urban centers, draw school children from a large variety of geographic areas and have linguistically very mixed populations, so that the teaching of reading in the child's own language presents more serious problems here than in rural areas. (It is interesting to note that Port Harcourt, the only city in the Rivers State, uses English from the beginning.) Information on language distribution in such multilingual areas, therefore, is of great importance for decisions on the language of initial literacy.

In an industrial area such as Zambia's Copperbelt, for example, it is not uncommon to find ten or more different mother tongues claimed in a class of about 40 children. Linguistically mixed communities in which such classes are found are generally neither uniform nor stable in composition, so that fairly precise information (preferably periodically updated) can serve as a very important basis for satisfactory decisions. Of equal importance is information on the language competencies of teachers in the African languages they may be expected to teach, since they, too, may not form a stable population. It seems evident that information on all these factors would help in deciding whether the economic and administrative problems involved would make it feasible, or indeed possible, to provide the right materials in the right languages to be taught by the right teachers to the right children in such linguistically mixed communities.

It would be necessary in such a situation to find out whether there are fairly homogeneous groups or patterns of bilingualism and multi-ligualism among the children, and what, in actual fact, their 'first' languages are. If these are trends in language shift from a number of minor languages to the major regional language, it may be more feasible to abandon the idea of providing instruction in all or most of the languages and decide on a few 'major' ones. This, in effect, is the second alternative listed above and will be discussed later.

It has already been mentioned that the existence of a written tradition is an important factor in the choice of a language for initial literacy. In considering a program for teaching reading in most of the indigenous languages, it will be essential to know whether the languages in question have been reduced to writing, whether their orthographies are adequate, and whether there is any need for reform and standardization. Many African languages were first reduced to writing by missionaries, some of whom had little or no training in linguistics. Traditions have grown round these orthographies, and people have become very attached to them. However, there are also occasional inconsistencies in spelling, sometimes found in the same text. Since consistency in spelling is generally regarded as desirable for educational purposes, some consideration is likely to be given to the problems of orthography in most programs concerned with teaching reading in primary schools.

Any contemplated change in an orthography, however, appears to rouse intense emotions. Such emotions are found not only among speakers of languages that have had many centuries of written history (and might, therefore, be in need of reform because of centuries of sound change in the spoken language) such as West Armenian, but also in languages that have a relatively short written history such as Lozi in the Western Province of Zambia. Experience has shown that it would be rash to launch on any orthographic change without information on the attitudes of each linguistic community to its graphology. The history of the earlier attempts at improving and unifying the orthography of Twi and Fante, two branches of the Akan language of the Gold Coast, is a good example of the problems that beset precipitate action which doesn't take into account the attitudinal and practical aspects of the situation.[5] A careful survey of the situation would provide such information and suggest not only a feasible and hopefully acceptable system of orthography but strategies that would take into account attitudes and perhaps involve members of the community in order that standardization or reform (if indeed necessary or desirable) might be achieved with the least amount of friction.

Other important factors that would affect decisions are the economic value and other advantages of each mother tongue for purposes of literacy. For instance, are there any disadvantages in acquiring initial literacy through a minor language in order to attain employability in such fields as agriculture, trade, the crafts, technological occupations, and for further education? What is the proper type of manpower needed for a self-sustaining economy? Is the use of the indigenous language advantageous for basic (permanent) education? Will it help in early conceptualization and generalization ability? Is it truly necessary for the majority of people to learn the 'official' metropolitan language to be able to function well in the nation? In assessing these and other factors, it would also be necessary to consider the less quantifiable but perhaps more important aspects of having status accorded to one's mother tongue at school, the sense of pride and identification which learning through it might provide to the child. It would also be necessary to consider the more tangible benefits of receiving instruction through a language that is familiar to the learner, especially when only a limited time is likely to be spent at school. A survey might, for instance, be able to demonstrate which ones, among early school dropouts who learned to read in their mother tongue or in an initially unfamiliar language, could best function in various occupations, follow written instructions, and assume responsibility for supervision, provided, of course, that teachers and materials are available to teach through the medium of these languages.

So far only the first alternative in the choice of a language in teaching beginning reading has been discussed. If the *second* alternative, i.e. teaching through an African *lingua franca*, is being considered, there are two different but basic sets of questions to be asked. First, if there is an indigenous national *lingua franca*, what is the proportion of areas in which it is a 'first' and an effective 'second' language? For what proportion of the school population would it be necessary to prepare materials with a 'second language' approach to the teaching of reading, i.e. materials that do not assume that the child understands what he is being taught to read? For instance, if materials were to be prepared in Swahili for speakers of other Tanzanian languages who did not know the language, they might first make provision to teach orally the Swahili words and sentences that the children would be taught to read later. On the other hand, such provision would not be necessary for Swahili-speaking children, and the choice of such words and sentences would not necessarily have to take into account their suitability for oral classroom teaching. Other questions to be asked would include: Are there speakers of some languages for whom Swahili is more comprehensible than to others? What is the degree of exposure that children have to Swahili prior to coming to school? How available is it in all parts of the country in radio and television broadcasts?

If, on the other hand, regional *lingua francas* within a country are being considered for this second alternative, the answers to a number of other questions will influence decisions. In most of these countries, for a variety of reasons (including wider comprehensibility, number of speakers, previous missionary activity in the language, and so on), certain languages have been established as 'regional' languages and some have become *lingua francas*, mainly in the areas where they are widely spoken. In considering them for initial literacy, some of the information needed for decisions would include: What are the degrees of intelligibility between this regional language and those of the children in class in each region? What proportion of the present children speak it as a first language? How does this differ in various types of communities such as rural and urban areas? What are the attitudes of ethnic groups to having their children taught to read in a 'near' or 'related' language? Are the regional languages acceptable to all groups? What varieties of these major languages should reading materials be in? For instance, are 'town' varieties more useful or acceptable than 'rural' or more 'pure' varieties? If the latter, then which particular one? What are the attitudes of communities (mother-tongue speakers and others) towards such a choice? Are there abundant written models of these languages on which to base materials? Are standard forms developing in some regional languages? Questions regarding orthographies would again have to be asked, as well as questions about grammatical descriptions, about teachers and their proficiency in the languages, about materials, and so on.

The *third* alternative for initial literacy will probably be related to the choice of a major European language (e.g. English or French) as a medium of instruction from grade 1; otherwise reading will probably be introduced in an indigenous language. Such a choice would have to be based on a consideration of many of the answers to the questions asked above and an assessment of the advantages of each alternative, since problems in beginning reading in a language often totally unknown to the child when he comes to school would include psychological, pedagogical, and cultural factors.

Information on the extent to which English is used by various groups in the community would affect decisions for its use for initial literacy. What proportion of the population does actually use English and for what purpose? For what groups or occupations is English vital? Will it be put to use by early dropouts, by unskilled laborers, and so on? What is the extent of the use of English in urban versus rural areas?

Should initial literacy in English be accessible to all children? What are the manpower resources of the country for teaching English? Are there sufficient numbers of competent teachers and inspectors for all classes to start in English from grade 1? If not, should resources be husbanded so that the teaching of English is more effective for fewer numbers? If so, two principal choices may be open. One would be to postpone all teaching of English to the upper grades; the other to teach it to selected groups. Here decisions will be necessary on the criteria for the selection of groups. Should language aptitude be a criterion? If so, how should it be measured? What are other criteria for the selection of groups? How acceptable and reliable are they? What are administrative and professional problems in carrying such selection out? What are the attitudes and aspirations of parents for their children in this regard? Would teaching initial reading in English to selected groups be regarded as discriminatory? Would it be the beginning of an unfair class system in the country? These are not new problems but have been debated for a long time.[6]

An important aspect of this third alternative is that if literacy starts in English, further problems regarding the time and manner of introducing literacy in indigenous languages have to be solved. Although the world-language may be important from economic and manpower-oriented points of view, the teaching of local languages is regarded as of very great importance in these countries as a means of providing a sense of identity and pride and as a major way of preserving the cultural heritage of their peoples. Questions similar to those asked for the first and second alternatives will again have to be taken into consideration for beginning reading in an indigenous language, as well as such questions as the transfer of skills (negative as well as positive) to reading in the mother tongue (or the *lingua franca*), from English orthography; the question of types of reading material if the languages are not being used as media of instruction; and the cultural content of such reading materials if only a few languages are to be taught to all ethnic groups in the community. Apart from these, the question of the possibility of increasing national productivity in industry when education is given mostly in the indigenous language rather than in the metropolitan language is pertinent.

Another, but very important, dimension to the question of initial literacy is that of existing educational conditions in the country. What are the prevalent practices in teaching reading? Through what methods and in what languages are children being taught to read? Are practices uniform throughout the country? If not, where and how do they differ? Are there any schools where literacy has started in English? If so, what difference has this made to reading ability or educational performance? In what types of schools and under what conditions has such teaching been carried out? Are there any factors in text materials, in teacher competence, or physical facilities that might affect apparent differences in results in different language medium schools? Are there motivational factors that affect the learning of reading in one language or another? Are there better prereading materials for English than the other language (or languages)? Systematic and objective information on past and current experience can be very important factors in formulating courses of action.

The problem of teachers has come up in every single one of the alternatives under consideration, and some aspects have already been mentioned. Surveys may study the pattern and process of the selection and training of teachers. They may look at practices in posting, teachers' attitudes, and the effectiveness of their work, as well as point to possible avenues for improvement. Important questions in some of these countries are: What does the actual process of training for teaching language and literacy consist of? What is the linguistic content of it for indigenous languages? Is there any provision for teaching these languages to children who do not already speak them? Who trains teachers? What is their experience and preparation? Is training related to any research or experimentation in language teaching? How aware are those in charge of teacher preparation of modern developments in language teaching theory and practice? Is there any experimentation in teaching methods in progress?

In many developing countries there is evidence of high interest in the teaching of local languages both on the part of authorities and of the community. This interest is sometimes reflected in the press. The provision of money, time, and trained personnel for the teaching of these languages, however, has often given way to other, more pressing priorities which the nation needs. Status for the languages and advancement opportunities for those who teach them are sometimes lacking. A sociolinguistic survey could study the situation; verify the existence of such inadequacies and lacks (or their absence); determine the attitudes of administrators, teachers, parents, children, and the community in general towards indigenous languages; and suggest alternative courses of action. For instance, do teachers want to teach these languages? If some do not, what are the reasons for it? What effect does this have on their teaching? Are there opportunities in the country for advancement through the use of these languages? Do opportunities exist for the teaching of (or through) these languages? What are teachers' attitudes towards teaching local languages versus teaching English? Is doing the latter more prestigious? Does this draw the better teachers to teaching English? Is it desirable to change this attitude? If so, by what means and what methods? Clear answers to these and other such questions could help in decisions both on the allocation of resources to the teaching of these languages and on the preparation of teachers for them.

These have been only a few and rather random examples of the hosts of questions that would need reliable answers for decisions on just one aspect of educational planning—language choice for initial literacy for young children—in one specific area of the world. It is perhaps unnecessary to take up other aspects of education for similar treatment here, but it seems reasonable to argue that, all things being equal, decisions would have a more sound basis with the type of information such surveys could provide if the funds, manpower, and time were available.

At this point it might be useful to give one or two negative examples. One is from the educational scene in the United States. In recent years, substantial amounts of federal funds have been directed towards bilingual education programs in various parts of the country (over 86.3 million for the fiscal years 1969–72 under Title VII of the Elementary & Secondary Education Act). The awarding of these funds to various projects, however, has not been based on 'hard', systematic facts about the current sociolinguistic situation, and clear criteria for the allocation of funds has been generally lacking. As a result there has been a considerable amount of duplication of effort, especially in such areas as materials production. Funds have, in some cases, been allocated to programs in areas with a far lower percentage of non-English speaking elements than others, and in other cases assumptions on such aspects of the situation as the language proficiencies (e.g. ability to command English) of children coming to school for the first time have proved to be unreliable. Even if a very small proportion of the funds available for bilingual education had been spent on an overall assessment of the relevant sociolinguistic situation in a few major areas such as New Mexico, Texas, New York City, and California, the utilization of funds might have been far more effective.

An example from Ghana in the 1950's is the Accelerated Development Plan in Education, advocated for the use of English as a medium of instruction from the first year in school. This, of course, failed because of the unrealistic nature of the proposals. If time and resources had been spent on a carefully planned survey of the linguistic competence of both the pupils and the teachers and the attitudes of parents to this recommendation, the educational system of that country would have been spared some of the resulting deficiencies in the pupils' command of both English and the Ghanaian languages.

It can be argued that a great deal of the types of information discussed above is already known to Ministries of Education or that it can be easily obtained through the normal channels of the educational system. It is possible that some of the information is indeed to be found in Ministry of Education files or in the experience of inspectors, headmasters, and teachers, but it is doubtful that systematically collected information of all the types discussed above is readily available to those who need it. It should perhaps be stressed that some of this information can only be obtained through sustained, controlled, objective observation in carefully selected areas and classrooms. Some of it will need to be collected and analyzed by people with many years of highly technical training in linguistics and related fields and competent in sophisticated research techniques and statistical analysis. Almost all of it, however, needs the special skill of the sociolinguist to interpret for the specific situation under study. If scholars with such training are nationals of the area and are available, it seems obvious that they are the best to carry the responsibility for surveys, not only because of their deeper knowledge of the area but from the point of view of continuity in the implementation of decisions based on a survey. Even if such scholars are not available, however, a survey is likely to be far more useful if as many nationals of the area as possible are involved in it, and all available local resources are tapped for the collecting of information.

Apart from serving a useful purpose as a basis for decisions on language policy in education, sociolinguistic surveys can be invaluable sources of teaching material in teacher training colleges, in secondary schools, and in universities. They can be the basis for 'know your country' or 'district' or 'region' courses or units in secondary schools and university programs. They can provide a much clearer picture of the language situation, not only to the potential language teacher but to all teachers (who, in effect, are often language teachers as well as teachers of their own subjects) and to all administrators and inspectors as well as the educated layman. The findings of surveys on the structure and relationships of languages can form first steps in the preparation of reference grammars, pedagogical grammars, and text materials, and the linguistic, sociolinguistic, and psycholinguistic research carried out by surveys can form the foundation for further investigation in these areas. The educational value of such knowledge is very great. Many people—especially in developing countries—who are highly educated in other fields are very limited in their knowledge of such demographic data on their own country. The more sophisticated they are in this area, the more relevant their education will be to their environment.

## Notes

First published in *Language Surveys in Developing Nations*, edited by Sirarpi Ohannessian, Charles A. Ferguson and Edgar C. Palomé, Center for Applied Linguistics, 1975.

1. For tribal identity and modern ethnicity see Fredrick Barth, ed., *Ethnic Groups and Boundaries: The Social Organization of Culture Difference* (The Little, Brown Series in Anthropology), 1969.

2. In a paper entitled 'St. Stephen of Perm and Applied Linguistics', Charles A. Ferguson discusses, in quite a different setting, the types of consideration to be taken into account in language choice, choice of an appropriate variety as standard, and in devising a writing system for a non-literate society. He uses as his major example the work of a fourteenth century Russian Orthodox bishop. In Joshua Fishman, Charles A. Ferguson and Jyotirindra Das Gupta, eds., *Language Problems in Developing Nations*, New York, John Wiley and Sons, 1968, pp. 253–265.

3. Williamson, Kay, 'The Nigerian Rivers Readers Project', *The Linguistic Reporter* 14:6 (December 1972), p. 1–2.

4. For a discussion of what may be defined as 'language', 'dialect', and 'variety', see the introduction to Charles A. Ferguson and John J Gumperz, 'Linguistic Diversity in South Asia', *International Journal of American Linguistics* (Publication 13 of the Indiana Research Center in Anthropology, Folklore, and Linguistics, Part 3) 26:3 (July 1960), p. vii.

5. See K. O. Dickens, 'Unification: The Akan Dialects of the Gold Coast', *The Use of Vernacular Languages in Education* (Monographs on Fundamental Education), Paris, UNESCO, 1953, pp. 115–123.

6. See, for example, *Report of the Commonwealth Conference on the Teaching of English as a Second Language* held at Makarere College, Uganda from January 1–13, 1961. Printed on behalf of the Commonwealth Education Liaison Committee by the Government Printer, Entebbe, Uganda, vi, 56 pp.

# SECTION THREE

# Standard and non-standard: what target should the teacher aim at?

# The stigmata of bilingualism
Einar Haugen

## I. The Ambiguities of Bilingualism

There is a strange kind of lopsidedness in the literature on bilingualism. Perhaps I can put my finger on the problem by saying that I have been a bilingual as far back as I can remember, but it was not until I began reading the literature on the subject that I realized what this meant. Without knowing it, I had been exposed to untold dangers of retardation, intellectual impoverishment, schizophrenia, anomie, and alienation, most of which I had apparently escaped, if only by a hair's breadth. If my parents knew about these dangers, they firmly dismissed them and made me bilingual willy-nilly. They took the position that I would learn all the English I needed from my playmates and my teachers, and that only by learning and using Norwegian in the home could I maintain a fruitful contact with them and their friends and their culture. In the literature I found little mention of this aspect. What I found was a long parade of intelligence tests proving bilinguals to be intellectually and scholastically handicapped. When I came to read about the trilingual Luxembourgers, I learned that they were considered untrustworthy, presumably by the French and German whose languages they spoke without becoming either loyal Frenchmen or loyal Germans. My own happy experience with bilingualism, which enabled me to play roles in two worlds rather than one, was apparently not duplicated by most of those whom the researchers had studied.

The reason for this discrepancy has only become clear to me after I realized that in speaking of bilingualism, many people are quite simply not talking about the same thing as I. Linguists like Uriel Weinreich, Werner Leopold, William Mackey, and myself, who have been concerned with bilingualism over the years, have offered definitions that were based on the literal meaning of the word and its relation to the learning of two languages. Having defined our universe in terms of second language learning, we found bilingualism in every country and on every level of society, from the aborigines of New Guinea to Joseph Conrad and Albert Schweitzer. But those children in our Southwest or in the ghettoes of

New York who have enjoyed the tender concern of educational, psychological, and political authorities have one feature in common that is not
mentioned in any academic definition of bilingualism. This is the fact
that for many people 'bilingual' is a euphemism for 'linguistically handicapped'. It is a nice way of referring to children whose parents have
handicapped them in the race for success by teaching them their mother
tongue, which happens not to be the dominant language in the country
they now inhabit. The term has enjoyed a semantic development not unlike that of 'minority group', a term one would not normally apply to the
English aristocracy or to American millionaires. Even the Bilingual
Education Program, financed by our Congress since 1965, suggests by
its wording that it grew out of concern with the children's inadequate
English and not out of tenderness toward their native language. Its first
goal is 'to develop greater competence in English', and the limitation of
its benefits to 'families with incomes below 3,000 dollars' shows clearly
enough that it is mostly a kind of poor relief and thereby confirms the
association of 'bilingualism' in the popular mind with poverty and
alienation.

This view is of course not limited to the United States. Bilingualism
is a term that evokes mixed reactions nearly everywhere. On the one
hand, some people (especially academics) will say: 'How wonderful to
be bilingual!' On the other they warn parents, 'Don't make your child
bilingual!' In a recent article Mackey points out the necessities that
impel speakers in small countries to learn second languages and says,
'In many countries to be educated means to be bilingual.' (Mackey
1967: 18). Unfortunately, the converse is also true: in many countries
to be bilingual means to be uneducated. If we look around at the countries
where bilingualism has risen to the status of a national problem—say
Belgium, Canada, Finland, Ireland, Wales, Yugoslavia—it has usually
been due to the refusal of a dominated social group to submit to the
imposition of the language of a dominant group. The power relationships
of victor over vanquished, of native over immigrant, of upper class over
lower class: these have bred bilingualism as it is commonly understood.
The fact that it is unilaterally imposed by a dominant group is a major
source of the pejorative connotations where these exist. It is part of what
keeps underprivileged groups underprivileged, and it is taken up for
general discussion only when it forms part of a syndrome of segregation.
Our neighbor Canada offers a charming example of the ambiguities of
the situation. The English-speaking Canadians are heartily in favor of
bilingualism, so long as it means that the French will learn English; the
French, however, think of it as requiring that all the English learn
French. But in the meanwhile the French are doing what they can to
ensure that Quebec at least will remain all French—and no more
bilingual than is absolutely necessary.

## II. Necessity is the Mother of Bilingualism

Fortunately, there are other kinds of bilingualism without this stigma. In many countries it is part of the privilege of the upper classes to be bilingual. In the Middle Ages all men of learning were bilingual; the great reformer Martin Luther spoke in a mixture of Latin and German which has been fascinatingly preserved for us in the records of his table talk (Stolt 1969). The aristocracy and royalty of Europe were normally bilingual: in Russia and Romania they spoke French, in Hungary Latin, etc. There are bilingualisms of a humbler sort which have not raised any serious problems. Wherever neighbors have lived peacefully together, a rough and ready bilingualism has arisen as part of daily intercourse. And, of course, second languages have been taught for ritual purposes, fulfilling a special function in the lives of even very simple tribes.

If we try to find a common feature in all of these and many other 'bilingual' situations, we can turn to the definition offered by Uriel Weinreich in his well-known *Languages in Contact*: Bilingualism is 'the practice of alternately using two languages' (or more, as he points out in a footnote) (Weinreich 1953: 1). There is no need, however, for a bilingual to use both his languages: it is enough that he know them. I would therefore change the definition to 'knowledge of two languages'. This brings it within the field of linguistics, since (as we have been learning recently) it is the task of linguistics to explicate the speakers' knowledge of their language. We may even take a step further and say that a bilingual has *dual linguistic competence*, the potential of performing in two distinct languages. The crucial point is not the number two, since one or both of the competences may and usually will fall short of full native competence. The bilingual may have only one and a half competence; it is still more than one, and we shall have to admit him to the company of bilinguals. The ideal bilingual is of course two native speakers rolled inside one skin; but he is about as likely to occur in real life as Chomsky's 'ideal speaker-listener in a completely homogeneous speech-community' (Chomsky 1965: 3).

It is only because bilinguals fall short of being ideal bilinguals that they offer anything of interest for either sociolinguistic or linguistic research. The proper study of bilingualism is the *interrelationship* between the two languages of the bilingual, both on the level of competence and performance, if these can be distinguished. Before I analyze this relationship, however, I shall offer a few sociolinguistic thoughts on the best ways of distinguishing various kinds of bilingualisms. The clear difference between learning a first and a second language is that the first is a universal human acquisition, while the second may meet resistance from the first and is not in the same way universal. The only reason for learning a second language is that the first does not suffice for the speaker's communicative needs.

Most of the learning situations fall into one of three typical kinds: *supplementary*, *complementary*, and *replacive*.

(a) *Supplementary:* the second language is learned as a supplement to the first language, for certain occasional needs, as what the Germans would call a *Hilfssprache*. Say one travels briefly to a foreign country; or one is anxious to read a foreign writer. Such needs are individual and sporadic, even when they are built into the school system.

(b) *Complementary:* the second language fulfills a complementary function with the first in the life of the speaker. This could include a dialect speaker who learns to read and write the standard, or a Yiddish speaker who learns Hebrew for his religious activities, or a Belgian who speaks Flemish at home and French at his place of business. Such situations tend to remain stable over a long period.

(c) *Replacive:* the second language gradually comes to fulfill all the communicative needs of the speaker so that he fails to use the first language at all and does not pass it on to his descendants. This is the situation of many immigrant and subject populations; in a fully bilingual group one of the languages is superfluous.

Any given social situation can have elements of all three; and a community may have individuals who are in various situations. The three situations may even follow one another chronologically by the gradual change of the generations. The monolingual speaker of A may pass through the *supplementary* use of B (Ab), the *complementary* (AB), and the *replacive* (aB), coming out at the end as a monolingual B.

Before we leave the sociolinguistic aspects, let me point out that most speakers in most societies are more concerned with communicating than with the medium in which they communicate. Such concepts as language loyalty and language purity are instilled by teaching and are not inevitable accompaniments of language use. They are factors to be reckoned with when they do exist, but most untutored speakers are untouched by them. This is one reason for the many language shifts and for the impact that bilingualism has had on the history and structure of languages. Power demands compliance, and often gets it even if it means rejection of the mother tongue; but this says nothing about how long it can take or what cultural losses it may entail. As so often in human life: to those that have shall be given. To most real bilinguals the learning of a second language is a necessity, and the problem for the educator and social planner is to make the process preserve human dignity rather than destroy it.

## III. Linguists Squint at Bilingualism

In my years of following the growth of linguistics in America since it was a gleam in Bloomfield's eye, I have been impressed by the cleavage between what I would like to call the Procrusteans and the Heracleans.

The Procrusteans take delight in devising models and theories. If a bit of data sticks out here and there, they are not averse to lopping it off in the name of elegance. Men like Saussure in France and Hjelmslev in Denmark were eminent Procrusteans, whose rigid dichotomies made for neat classifications. Bloomfield's behaviorism was such an approach, which compelled him and his followers to exclude data to fit their theories. The corrective furnished by Chomsky's generative approach is in danger of becoming another bed of Procrustes. What used to be called patterns is now called rules, and anything that cannot readily be formalized as a rule is trivial and uninteresting. Who are the Heracleans? They are the followers of Heracles, who had no theory other than that monsters should be liquidated when they appear and that Augean stables should be cleaned when the stench becomes unbearable. They can even gather the manure and make it yield a fertile crop, by putting the data into piles until some kind of pattern emerges. Otto Jespersen in Denmark and Edward Sapir were such thinkers, whose insights were brilliant and who were willing to do the hard work necessary to justify them. Uriel Weinreich was this kind of thinker in American linguistics.

Bilingualism has not fared well in the textbooks of linguistics in this country over the past thirty years. There is not one single general textbook of linguistics since Bloomfield that has taken adequate account of the topic. Even he had no special rubric on it, but treated it under several headings, especially 'borrowing', which is only one of the interesting aspects of bilingualism. Gleason's *Introduction to Descriptive Linguistics* just brushes the topic in one of his twenty-eight chapters. However, with his usual acumen he suggests that it might be a valid objective to make 'an empirical description of the range and significance of variation . . . as a characteristic feature of language'. This might even become 'the basis for a second type of linguistic science', for which we lack a name. Actually, in 1953 Weinreich offered the term *differential description* and in 1954 I proposed *bilingual description* (parallel to a *bilingual dictionary*), or alternatively *dialinguistics* (1954). Even without a generally accepted name, the field has flourished, as I learned to my somewhat bemused regret after I recently undertook to survey the output of the last decade and a half for the tenth volume of *Current Trends in Linguistics*.

One reason for the neglect of bilingualism and allied fields is that historical linguistics has fallen into disfavor generally. But it is an error to confine the topic to the diachronic axis, for bilinguals have two simultaneous competences and are functioning in a synchronic context. The reason is probably deeper: it is that most theoretical linguists have felt unequal to coping with linguistic diversity and variability. The structural phonemicists were anxious to reduce the multiplicity of phonetic variation to the smallest possible number of units, the phonemes. This was easy enough for positional variants, which came to be called 'allophones'; but other kinds of variants were simply lumped as 'free variation' and left out of account. Now William Labov has picked up the challenge and proved conclusively that some kinds of linguistic variation can be statistically linked to variations of social class and situation: for New Yorkers the more formal the situation, the more post-vocalic *r*'s they use and the lower they make their *o*'s. To most of us this makes excellent sense, since the notion of an absolute either-or was never very congenial. However, this is not an approach that can easily be fitted into either a structural or a generative approach to language, though efforts are being made. It certainly is not a part of the now orthodox theory, which is built on the concept of a homogeneous society.

All this is preliminary to my suggestion that the emphasis on linguistic uniformity may have passed the point of fruitfulness. It was axiomatic to the structuralists as it seems to be to the generativists that any given language formed a system. Meillet's famous dictum has been the model for all such thinking: 'Une langue est un système où tout se tient.' No one would deny the value of this epigram, if only as a memorable and challenging formulation which cries out for falsification. It is clear enough that the necessities of communication require a basic network of distinctive structures in a language. But their realization is only a shade less arbitrary than the words for 'horse' or 'apple' or 'tree'. What relationship can one find, for example, between the fact that English has the interdental fricatives $/\theta/$ and $/\delta/$; a set of suffixed morphemes in $/$-s, -z, -iz$/$; that these can signal either plural of nouns or third person singular present of verbs; that English has a past tense; that English replaces finite verbs in questions and deletions with the pro-verb *do*; that English has no word for French *langue*, but does have one for *home*, etc. We know from the history of English that it was more or less accidental that just these forms became fixed as a co-occurrent set of entities in standard English. We know from dialectology that other forms of English and Germanic exist in which some or all of these features may be absent. But the full confirmation of the arbitrariness of this system can be found in the variable and intermediate systems of bilinguals.

## IV. The Competence of Bilinguals

The key to the bilingual's competence lies in the necessity for *alternating his codes*, a process usually referred to as *switching*. Switching occurs in response to some kind of *triggering*, a term introduced by Michael Clyne (1967). The most obvious kind of trigger is the entry into the conversation of a new *addressee*, who does not understand language A or to whom it would not be appropriate to speak it. Often, also, a new *topic* may trigger a switch, if the speaker or his listener is more comfortable in speaking about this topic in language B. Certain *domains* of life (Fishman's term) demand one language rather than another, either because they are more appropriate or better known. Finally, internal needs of the speaker himself may trigger the switch: we shall call this *expressive* switching. For a variety of reasons which we cannot always identify, the speaker shifts back and forth from language to language. In some cases it is stylistic, if one language has a special tone of humor or appeal that the other lacks. With some speakers the switches seem to be almost completely random, when they are speaking to other bilinguals.

Now experience with bilinguals shows that they differ greatly in the precision with which they can switch from code to code. Some speakers take pride in staying within one language at a time and making a clean switch, while others tend to overlap the languages and produce what has been called 'ragged' switching (Hasselmo 1961). We need not describe further the character of such switching, only point out that clean switching requires a clear code marking of each rule and each lexeme that is stored in the speaker's memory. Such code marking may be called *tagging*. If I may comprise lexemes and rules under the term *items*, one can say that an effective bilingual must have a tag on every item and that he must see to it that the tags do not fall off! For within his brain the tags are all that keep his two codes apart. When he reaches into his store of items for the formulation of a new sentence, the tags block him from coming out with the wrong items.

In other words, there is no such thing as two separate storage tanks for the languages: in switching the bilingual activates a feature which keeps the items of language B inactive while he is speaking language A. It has been suggested, e.g. by DeCamp, that such a switching feature is part of the base rules 'whose presence triggers all the necessary changes which the subsequent components of the grammar must make in any derivation marked with that feature'. (1968: 4) However, it seems to me that the essential characteristic of the feature marking is that it is negative. Each Item learned is marked by the situation of learning: but for the monolingual this feature is redundant. The speaker does not mark the items as $[+A]$ until he begins to learn B, which must then be marked as $[-A]$. At first we can say that there develop two polar oppositions in which $[+A, -B]$ contrasts with $[-A, +B]$. Tagging is established at the time of learning and is reinforced by use.

There are many problems in tagging, however. All human languages have some overlap, which is greater the closer they are. In terms of tagging, this means that there are items which are $[+A, +B]$. These interlingual identities form what has been called *sandwich words* (Clyne), or in the terminology of the Japanese *haiku* poets, we may call them *pillow words*. Having lost the blocking effect, they tend to disorient the speaker and make him lose his linguistic bearings. They will rise into the speaker's consciousness even when they ought to be blocked, and having used them, he will be strengthened in his error by the reinforcement of having used them in a new situation. The negative feature will gradually be weakened and the area of overlap between the codes will be enlarged. Every act of performance will alter his competence by ever so little.

Let me give you an example from my own experience of such loss of marking. There are two common Norwegian words *plugg* and *svamp*, which are ultimately cognate with English *plug* and *swamp*. I choose these among thousands of examples because they have a highly characteristic phonological form. They feel thoroughly native in each language, and their meanings are well known even if they are of relatively low or medium frequency. I have more than once been blocked by the word *plugg* because of the overlap in meaning in English *plug*. In both languages the reference is to 'an object used to stop a hole or a gap', but I would be hard put to it to find an object which both languages would agree in so designating. The most common application in English today, an electric plug, is known in Norwegian as *kontakt*, which offers further problems of recall since it also means the same as English *contact*. Most of the objects known as *plugg* in Norwegian would be called *peg* in English, and so it goes. As for the word *svamp*, a bilingual rather intimately known to me once said: 'I find it hard to remember that Norwegian *svamp* does not mean a *swamp*.' In this case there is no actual overlap at all, since there is no object that could be identified by this word in both languages. However, the meanings have in common a purely abstract sense of 'a moist, porous object': in English a 'marsh', in Norwegian a 'sponge'.

It belongs to the story that while the two bilinguals referred to were struggling to keep them apart, the community of speakers in the rural sections of the Middle West did not even bother to try. The swamps they had to drain on their farms were called *svamp*, not *myr*, and the plugs they put in their houses were called *plugg*, and not *kontakt*. But more than that: while the American Norwegian speaks of spark-plugs as *sparkplugg*, in Norway the spark-plug is known as a *tennplugg*, in which the first element is Norwegian, the second a clear case of borrowing from English.

These examples show with sufficient clarity what some of the bilingual's problems are. If the parts of a language were really a rigid, inflexible system, in which every item somehow presupposed every other, such freedom of transfer would be impossible. There is nothing in the structure of Norwegian or any other language to stop speakers from introducing new meanings of familiar words in imitation of similar words in other languages. Nor is there anything to stop a speaker from replacing familiar words like *myr*, of feminine gender, with *svamp*, of masculine gender, or to make new words like *sparkplugg* or *tennplugg*.

In these cases there is a clear diaphonic equivalence of $_E/w > v/_N$ or $_N/u > ə/_E$ and a diamorphic equivalence of *swamp/svamp* and *plugg/plug* such that the words lose their tags and become a part of both structures. The $[-N]$ and $[-E]$ have been turned into $[+N, +E]$ and the storage problem of the bilingual has been correspondingly reduced.

## V. Intermediate Structures and Variable Competence

The examples I have given so far have been lexical, and some may object that the lexicon is not part of the language. This point of view I do not share, since my experience with language has been that without lexicon I have nothing to communicate. There is a kind of *looking-glass linguistics*, which quotes Alice in Wonderland to prove that grammar is more important than lexicon. It is extremely popular in introductions to linguistics to quote *Jabberwocky* to show that a sentence can be grammatical without conveying any meaning. As Humpty Dumpty explained to Alice, whatever meaning Lewis Carroll's nonsense conveys is due to the similarity of the content words to well-known English terms: *slithy* means 'lithe' and 'slimy'. A sentence consisting of all content words will usually convey some meaning, while one consisting of all form words will convey none. The only purpose of the form words is to establish more precise relationships between the content words. The form words, too, have to be tagged, and they can be transferred into the zone of overlap, until it becomes impossible for the bilingual to distinguish them with confidence.

In the world of the bilingual anything is possible, from virtually complete separation of the two codes to their virtual coalescence. The reasons for this are clearly rooted in the possibilities for *variable competence* in the human brain.

The deeper reasons for this are seen in the process we ordinarily refer to as language learning. The many recent studies of first language learning have demonstrated how a child builds up its knowledge by a combination of memorization and creativity, in which he generalizes from inadequate evidence and is corrected by his environment until he learns the limits of his rules, i.e. the constraints of his language. In learning a second language he is at every point both guided and misguided by his first. To the extent that the two processes go on side by side, they show mutual influence: each code may be different because of the existence of the other.

There is an enormous variety of second language learners. I shall concentrate on three typical ones with which you are all familiar: the *child*, the *pupil*, and the *adult*.

1. The child learner may acquire language B simultaneously with A, as did Ronjat's son and Leopold's daughter in the classic studies by their

fathers (Ronjat 1913; Leopold 1939–49). These studies show that at first the children try to fuse the two into one, and only after a time does it dawn upon them that daddy and mummy speak differently and that their systems must be kept apart. The struggles of the learners to accomplish this end and their eventual success in doing so offers us many striking instances of intermediate language structures. Similar developments occur when children are transported into a new linguistic milieu at a later age: while they are building up language B, their language A may suffer considerable weakening and dilution. A body of data was furnished me by a Norwegian mother [Åse Gruda Skard] whose children (aged 4 and 7) lived in Washington, D.C. for a time. While they shifted easily back and forth between the languages, there were numerous examples of overlapping. These often involved a considerable adjustment to the system of the host language. There were loanwords in their English like *screeve* 'write' (for N *skrive*) and *stain* 'stone' (for N *stein*) and there were loanshifts like *wash up* for 'washing dishes', *I'm angry on you* instead of *at you*, *pack up* instead of *unpack*, etc. The sentence 'We buried and buried' was meant to be 'we kept carrying', but telescoped Norwegian *bære* with English *carry*. Their Norwegian showed a much more serious shift, being supported only by home conversation. 'I can beat you' came out as *Jeg kan bite deg*, which literally would mean 'I can bite you'. A verb like *lage* 'make' got its meaning extended by being inserted into a word-for-word Norwegian translation, e.g. *Tass laget meg skrike* 'Tass made me cry', for the standard *Tass fikk meg til å skrike*. There appeared to be few if any limitations on the extent of mutual interpenetration. In time such children would either forget one of the two languages or develop both to maturity, or else leave one in its childhood form with inadequate vocabulary while the other developed to maturity.

2. The school learner is under the severe handicap of having no speech community behind him. As has been said by someone, neither he nor his teacher has anything to say to each other. The pupil will learn exactly as much as the school is willing to force upon him and not all of that. While he is pre-adolescent, he can still learn a great deal if the school sees to it that language B is used not just as a subject, but as a medium of instruction in some or all of the classes. An ongoing experiment in Montreal, under the supervision of Wallace Lambert, has shown that children from English-speaking homes can get their early grades in French without damage to their English and with the bonus of achievement in French. However, where the home language is dominated rather than dominant, the school with its sudden enforcement of the dominant language may cause a trauma which can be a serious setback to the pupils. This is the situation of most immigrant minorities in the United

States, above all those whose visibility makes them liable to social exclusion and segregation.

The school situation that most of us are familiar with is that in which the adolescent meets language B at a time when he is so far advanced in A that B can rarely become anything but a supplementary language, if that. It is usually only a subject, not a medium, and therefore doomed to be learned largely through the first language. This is what Weinreich called a 'subordinate bilingual', whose meanings are mediated through another language, i.e. if he wants the word for 'book' in another language, he can do so only by way of the English word. This, too, is a kind of bilingualism, in which all that is stored is a set of synonyms: next to the word 'book' is a string of equivalents such as *Buch* or *libra* or *livre* or *kniga*, each of which can be triggered by the English word. In this situation many experiences are reported of erroneous triggering: it is as if one drew words out of a bag by lot. While one is speaking a weak German, the French or Italian word comes out instead.

These systems may seem painfully inadequate, especially to foreign language teachers; but they exist, and they are worthy of study. Student bilingualism, with its often pidginlike structures, is an achievement of its own, which should be studied for other purposes than that of assigning the students their appropriate merit badges. Adolescence is a difficult period in more ways than one; the crossing of the puberty threshold comes close to ending the learners' possibility for acquiring a native phonology, whether this be due to neurological hardening, as Penfield (1959) maintains, or to character formation and the establishment of personality.

3. The adult learner is characteristically an immigrant, who has arrived in a new linguistic ambience for reasons of employment, at an age when he neither has the advantages of the child learner nor the handicaps of the adolescent. His primary badge of identity is his accent, which few succeed in losing after puberty. It is even questionable whether he should, for the result may be that he is expected to behave like a native in all respects. A Greta Garbo or a Charles Boyer would not have been the same without their exotic accents. There is of course nothing to prevent an adult from becoming fully fluent and grammatically accurate in his new language. But there is a high degree of probability that whole areas of experience will remain closed to him: his infancy and his childhood were lived in another language, so that all the nursery rhymes and the endearing terms of motherhood will be missing. Poetry in the new language may seem colder and less appealing, while work and thought may develop new structures within him. Meanwhile, what happens to his language A? This will depend on the extent to which he uses it. He is less likely than the child to forget entirely, but without practice it can

easily recede into the past. I have known adult immigrants who claimed to have forgotten their native tongue in two or three years' time, and whose halting attempts to use it showed extensive interference from English. I have also known people who have retained it to the end of their lives, a half century or more, with virtually no diminution.

The usual thing in American immigrant history has of course been that immigrants sought out friends and kinsmen and settled near them, either in rural or urban enclaves. Here the immigrant's shock was cushioned, allowing postponement of his functioning in English while the native language continued to serve some or even all needs. Here there was even the possibility of stabilizing the two languages in a balance of complementarity, language A being used for home, neighborhood, and church, language B for work, trade, and politics. In this situation, which has been the special object of my own researches, we now have a fairly clear picture of the normal curve of development. Language B is learned by those members of the group who have to deal with the outer world. It is spoken as well as need requires, usually with an accent. Language A is gradually restricted to the inner world, losing large parts of its vocabulary, which are then replaced by items from language B wherever this reflects more accurately and effectively the cultural realities of the new environment. For no matter how attached the immigrant remains to his language, he cannot rebuild in a previously established culture anything like a replica of the world he left. Even the French Canadians are not living in the world of France, however French they may think of themselves as being.

The linguistic result is a spectrum of intermediate structures, a set of variable competences which are keyed into the various groups and domains of the immigrant community. Bilingual norms arise which are accommodations between the two languages, reducing the effort needed to switch from language to language. When the Swedish naturalist Pehr Kalm visited his countrymen in Delaware in 1750, a century after their settlement there, he declared that their Swedish was already so mixed with English terms that it had become a new tongue. Nearly two centuries later a Norwegian immigrant to western Wisconsin recalled his consternation on arriving in a community where everyone spoke his native dialect of Suldal: 'There they were, talking genuine Suldal, and they all talked alike. But whether they talked Suldal or they talked French made no difference at all to me, for I did not understand a word. They were chattering about "baren" and "fila" and "sheden" and "malkeshantie", "vinnmøllo" and "pompo" and all those words. I couldn't understand a single thing they were talking about, even though I understood about ninety per cent of all the words they used. I couldn't understand it because all the names were half or wholly English. They talked about "mekar" (makes) and "fiksar" (fixes) and so forth. . . . But when I went to church, the preacher preached so fine, you see, just as they did in Norway, and I understood every word.' (Haugen 1953: 59). A series of doctoral dissertations on immigrant communities in America have confirmed the existence of bilingual norms, and also of deviances from them in response to variable speech situations.

We have now looked briefly at these three selected types and observed how in each case the bilingual accommodates his two languages to one another. He keeps them apart only to the extent that the communities demand it, and he uses the one to enrich the other. Wherever there is a stable situation, the two languages arrive at an accommodation in which both of them can express roughly the same distinctions, often by a word-for-word equivalence that leaves only the bare skeletons of the languages untouched. The ultimate example of this development is the pidgin and creole speech of disadvantaged learners. But wherever the situation is in flux, the learner is building one or both languages at the same time. The general profile is one that we can describe as either a learning or an unlearning. If we call the build-up of a language an *Aufbau*, we can call the restructuring that takes place in bilingual situations an *Umbau*. While language B is being built up, it is not unusual that language A is being dismantled and replaced with parts from B. I have hinted at some of the possibilities: we have children's systems, school learners' systems, and adults' systems, each of them somehow intermediate between the standard systems postulated for ideal monolingual speakers.

In studying these we need to get away from the notion of 'inter-ference' as somehow noxious and harmful to the languages. The bilingual finds that in communicating he is aided by the overlap between languages and he gets his message across by whatever devices are available to him at the moment of speaking.

## VI. The Fruits of Bilingualism

What is the value of studying what I have here called intermediate systems and variable competence? As I see it, there are aspects which should be of pedagogical, historical, and theoretical interest.

1. Pedagogical. It is necessary for the teacher of language to realize that even his students' mistakes may offer evidence of their learning. The mistakes in language B may be due to features of language A, but they may also be due to the formation of new rules on which the teacher need only build further. One of our major problems is precisely that we are usually teaching standard, i.e. arbitrarily fixed languages, so that a premium is set on the elimination of intermediate systems. Yet these systems are indeed a bridge over which most learners must go to reach

the other language, and sometimes they succeed quite happily without actually ever getting off the bridge. Perhaps we don't need to labor so hard to eliminate all traces of their bridgework.

2. Historical. In diachronic linguistics the study of intermediate and variable systems has long been of central concern. What is often called substratum influence can be identified quite simply as the result of adult bilingualism: a whole population subjected to the need of learning the language of their conquerors. Its opposite, the superstratum influence, as in the case of French on English, results from the resistance of a dominated population to language shift while admitting elements that make a new, bilingual dialect of the old language: consider the change from Old English to Middle English. While linguistic divergence results from isolation, convergence results from contact, and the study of bilingual systems is the key to convergence.

3. Theoretical. The fact that intermediate systems exist should be a matter of concern to all theorists of language. There are varieties of English that do not have /θ/ and /ð/, spoken by adult bilinguals who substitute either /t/ and /d/ or /s/ and /z/. There are bilingual systems of English which lack an alternation between /s/ and /z/, so that the allomorphs of the s-morpheme are not distinguished. There are creolized varieties of English that have no copula or pro-verb and some that do not distinguish a present and a past tense. Granted that none of these are 'standard', the fact remains that they are mutually intelligible with English. But the main point is that 'English' is not a monolithic structure, with only one possible form at every node. Throughout its grammar there are available choices, and any tags that are attached to these must enable the speakers to make the right switches when the triggering factor is present. Natural languages can be realistically described only if we recognize that their grammars and lexica are not rigid, but flexible, not fixed, but variable. What I have called 'intermediate' is therefore not necessarily 'intermediate'; it is a real part of human communication, and is intermediate only when considered in relation to some arbitrary standard. The standard is itself only an intermediate system which has been temporarily frozen by social or academic fiat.

### Notes

First published in *The Ecology of Language*, edited by Anwar S. Dil, Stanford University Press, 1973.
This paper was presented as a lecture at Brown University in 1970.

# Social factors, interlanguage and language learning
Jack C. Richards, Laval University, Quebec

The field of second language learning is shown to encompass the study of interlanguage phenomena, which reflect the conditions under which language is learned and used. These include the processes of language transfer, transfer of training, strategies of learning, strategies of communication, and overgeneralization. Five different contexts for language learning are considered and the results of language learning in each context related to the social context for learning through the notion of interlanguage.

## Introduction

A number of diverse contexts for second language learning are considered in this paper and the following questions asked: Under what conditions is standard English learned? What factors lead to the development of non-standard varieties of English, such as immigrant English? What accounts for the divergence of local varieties of English such as Nigerian or Indian English from British or American norms? Under what circumstances is more marked language divergence likely to occur, such as is found in Creole settings? More generally the paper focuses on the choice of appropriate models for the analysis of second language data. An area of research is illustrated which encompasses both psycholinguistic and sociolinguistic dimensions. The concept of *Interlanguage* is proposed for the analysis of second language learning and illustration is drawn from the processes affecting language learning in the following contexts: immigrant language learning, indigenous minority varieties of English, pidgin and creole settings, local varieties of English, English as a foreign language.

## Immigrant varieties of English

Despite the huge numbers of immigrants settled in the English-speaking world in the last century, relatively little is known about the learning of English by immigrants. The linguistic dimensions of immigrant assimilation have tended to arouse interest only in instances of unsuccessful adaptation. Some immigrant groups have developed functionally adequate but socially unaccepted or non-standard varieties of English, and these are the focus of analysis here. In isolating the generation of non-standard varieties of immigrant English, we are separating the initial language learning problems confronting all immigrant groups from those which persist and result in the development of distinctive non-standard varieties of English. Studies of immigrant communities in the initial stages of contact have referred to the emergence of particular dialects of English, such as Swedish English, Norwegian English, and German English, many of which have been transient and short lived (Haugen 1953). We do not hear any longer of Norwegian English or German English as a group phenomenon arousing educational concern. Yet Puerto-Rican and Mexican-American English have not had the same history. How may we characterize these varieties of English and under what circumstances do they arise? To answer these questions we will consider both the social and the linguistic dimensions of immigrant English.

## The social dimension

One of the best accounts of the general factors involved in the preservation of the immigrant's mother tongue, which may be used as a guide to assimilation into the majority language group, is given by Kloss, who emphasizes that the factors involved are so variegated that their interplay cannot be summarized by a single formula (Kloss 1966). Clearly much is dependent on the pattern and area of settlement. Immigrants not inhabiting a compact area are less likely to develop non-standard dialects than those in a compact area. The fate of an individual immigrant arriving in an English-speaking city will provide data on how the individual acquires English, but this is of less general concern here than the fate of an interacting group of immigrants concentrated in a given place, where the outcome of the contact between the immigrant group and the dominant culture is not so much a result of *individual* solutions, depending on motivation, intelligence, perseverance, aptitude, learning strategies, personality, socialization, etc., but a result of the social and economic possibilities made available for the group. Besides numerical strength and distribution, a number of other factors can affect immigrant assimilation. These have to do with educational level, cultural and linguistic similarity to the mainstream culture, color, race and other general factors which may determine the attitudes towards the majority group and vice versa.

The evolution of lasting non-standard varieties of a standard language is a consequence of the perception by the immigrant of the larger society, and a reflection of the degree to which the immigrant groups have been admitted into the mainstream of the dominant culture. Psychologists have been able to distinguish between instrumental motivation, where the dominant or new language is acquired primarily for such utilitarian purposes as getting a job, and integrative motivation, which demonstrates a desire for or the perceived possibility of integration with the dominant group. The former may lead to a functionally adequate but non-standard dialect of English. We can predict for example, the sort of English likely to be acquired by an immigrant who mixes exclusively with his own language group and who opens a food shop catering largely, but not exclusively, to that language group. He will probably learn first to reply to a limited set of questions in English, to manipulate a closed class of polite formulae, the vocabulary of some food items, and perhaps the language of simple financial transaction. Whether he goes on to learn standard English or develops a functionally adequate but non-standard personal dialect of English will depend on the degree of interaction and integration he achieves with the English-maintained societal structures. He may have very little control over the degree of interaction possible. If 100,000 such immigrants in similar situations reach only a minimum penetration of mainstream power structures, begin to perpetuate their semi-servile status, and begin to use English among themselves, the setting for the generation of an immigrant variety of English might be present.

Where the learning of English is not associated with societal penetration and upward mobility, but rather with occupational and economic subservience, we can expect language divergence to be the outcome of contact with standard English. As an illustration of the two extremes it may be useful to refer to the fate of German and Puerto Rican immigrants to America. A recent account of the fate of German immigrants to Texas emphasizes that the German immigrants there are not poverty stricken (Gilbert 1971). They do not live in ghettoes. They suffer under no handicaps whatsoever. They thus learn English easily and well. Although a certain amount of German interference is present in their English, it results in no obvious social discrimination. The people of German descent are thus well-off and pursue the whole range of occupations open to Americans of purely Anglo background. The Puerto Ricans however arrived in New York at a time when economic patterns were already well established, hence the melting pot which they were invited to join was one which applied to the lower rather than the upper end of the social and economic spectrum (Hoffman 1968). For those immigrants with limited access to social and economic channels the immigrant mother tongue becomes one marker of second-class citizenship; the other is the dialect of English generated and maintained as a consequence of these very same social limitations.

Immigrant varieties of English are the product of particular settings for language learning. There are said to be two levels of communication in society—the horizontal level, which operates among people of the same status—and the vertical level, which is predominantly downward (Hughes 1970). In the case of non-standard immigrant English we are presumably dealing with the language of horizontal communication, and the contexts in which it occurs are those where there are few informal or friendship contacts with speakers of standard English and no intellectual or high culture networks in English. It may also become part of the expression of ethnic pride. It is a dialect resulting from low spending power, low social influence, and low political power. It reflects not individual limitations, such as inability to learn language, low intelligence, or poor cultural background, but rather the social limitations imposed on the immigrant community. Favorable reception of the immigrant group leads to temporary generation of an immigrant variety of English. This has been the case for many European immigrant groups in the United States (Fishman, *et al.* 1966). Favorable conditions include fluidity of roles and statuses in the community. Unfavorable social conditions lead to maintenance and perpetuation of the immigrant dialect of English. The economic and social possibilities available for some immigrants do not make the learning of standard English either possible, desirable or even helpful. The non-linguistic dimension of the immigrant's task has been emphasized by Leibowitz (1970):

> The issue is indeed a political one. Whether instruction is in English or the native language makes little difference; rather what is important are the opportunities that are thought available to the ethnic group themselves . . . Educators have provided the most significant evidence to demonstrate this. Increasingly, they have studied the relationship between a pupil's motivation and performance in school to his perception of the society around him and the opportunities he believes await him there . . . The crucial factor is not the relationship between the home and school, but between the minority group and the local society. Future reward in the form of acceptable occupational and social status keeps children in school. Thus factors such as whether a community is socially open or closed, caste-like or not, discriminatory or not, has restricted roles or non-restricted roles and statuses for its minority group segment, become as important as curriculum and other factors in the school itself, perhaps more important.

The difficulties of some immigrant groups thus result from more than simple questions of language learning but depend on the type and degree of interaction and acceptance available in the community.

*The linguistic dimension*

Having looked at the social background to immigrant varieties of English we may turn to the linguistic problems associated with the description of their particular form and characteristics. The simplest approach is to begin with the source language (LS) and the target language (LT) and to describe instances where the learner's speech differs from the target language as interference. This approach is inadequate, however, and obscures the nature of the processes involved. Nemser (1970: 116) proposes a three part approach, adding the learner's approximative system as the intermediate stage between the source and target language:

> An approximative system is the deviant linguistic system actually employed by the learner attempting to utilize the target language. Such approximative systems vary in character in accordance with proficiency level; variation is also introduced by learning experience ... communication function, personal learning characteristics etc. ... Our assumption is threefold: (1) Learner speech at a given time is the patterned product of a linguistic system, *La*, distinct from *LS* and *LT* and internally structured. (2) *La*'s at successive stages of learning form an evolving series, *La*i ... n' the earliest occurring when a learner first attempts to use *LT*, the most advanced at the closest approach of *La* to *LT* ... (3) In a given contact situation, the *La*'s of learners at the same stage or proficiency roughly coincide, with major variations ascribable to differences in learning experience.

Nemser proposed that learner speech should thus be studied in its own terms (Corder 1967, 1971).

I propose to use Selinker's concept of *Interlanguage* to characterize these approximative systems, and to interpret immigrant varieties of English as interlanguages generated from the social circumstances under which English is acquired in particular settings. Selinker's (1972) definition of interlanguage focuses on the psycholinguistic processes presumed to contribute to interlanguage.

> If it can be experimentally demonstrated that fossilizable items, rules and subsystems which occur in interlanguage performance are a result of the native language then we are dealing with the process of *language transfer*; if these fossilizable items, rules and subsystems are a result of identifiable items in training procedures, then we are dealing with *transfer of training*; if they are a result of an identifiable approach by the learner to the material to be learned, then we are dealing with *strategies of second language learning*; if they are a result of an identifiable approach by the learner to communication with native speakers of the target language then we are dealing with *strategies of communication*; and finally if they are the result of a

clear *overgeneralization of target language*, then we are dealing with the *overgeneralization of linguistic materials*.

These concepts are discussed and illustrated in Selinker (1972) and Richards (1971a).

In using this model as a framework for the analysis of immigrant varieties of English, we begin with the premise that the acquisition of a new language by an immigrant group is always a developmental creative process. In the case of a non-standard immigrant interlanguage we have to account for the generation of a subsystem of rules which are at the same time linguistic and social in origin.

... Within a large and stable bilingual community like the New York City Puerto Rican community, bilinguals interact and communicate with each other, using both languages far more frequently than they interact and communicate with members of the surrounding monolingual community. In such a community, speakers generate their own bilingual norms of correctness which may differ from the monolingual norms, particularly when there is a lack of reinforcement for these monolingual norms (Ma and Herasimchuk 1968).

These norms of immigrant English are illustrated by the speech samples given in Fishman, Cooper, Ma *et al.* (1968). One subject for example, when asked to say where he did his shopping, replied:

No make any difference, but I like when I go because I don't have too many time for buy and the little time we buy have to go to someplace and I find everything there.

When asked about trips to Puerto Rico, he gives:

I go there maybe about one and half and I find too many job for me. But I can't work over there if I go alone and I have the family here. I work I think 7 or 8 months in Puerto Rico ...

The concept of interlanguage as applied to this data would lead to a focusing on it as the learner's 'approximative system', and to the isolation of examples of language transfer, strategies of communication, strategies of learning, transfer of training, and overgeneralization. Language transfer is illustrated in the second sentence, which closely follows the structure of Puerto Rican Spanish. In the first example however the syntax used cannot be exclusively attributed to the effect of language transfer, since translating the English back into Spanish does not render the sentence directly into Puerto Rican Spanish. To further characterize the interlingual features of the first sentence, we need to refer to the concepts of communication and learning strategies, and to overgeneralization.

Under communication strategies we may characterize interlingual features, derived from the fact that heavy communication demands may be made on the second language, forcing the learner to mold what he has assimilated of the language into a means of saying what he wants to say, or of getting done what he wants to get done. The learner, isolated from close interaction with speakers of the target language, may 'simplify' the syntax of the language in an effort to make the language an instrument of his own intentions. Such strategies affect both first and second language performance in English. A child, not possessing the rule for nominalization in English, gave as a definition for *fence*:

> to keep the cow . . . don't go out of the field (Labov, in Hymes 1971: 455).

This process is seen in many of the constructions produced by second language learners (Richards 1971b). Referring to a study by Coulter (Coulter 1968), Selinker (1972) notes:

> Coulter reports systematic errors occurring in the English inter-language performance of two elderly Russian speakers of English, due to a tendency on the part of second language learners to avoid grammatical formatives such as articles, plural forms, and past tense forms . . . Coulter attributes it to a communication strategy due to the past experience of the speaker, which has shown him that if he thinks about grammatical processes while attempting to express in English meanings he already has, then his speech will be hesitant and disconnected, leading native speakers to be impatient with him . . . this strategy of second language communication seemed to dictate to those speakers of English that a form such as the English plural was not necessary for the kind of English they used.

Strategies of learning and communication refer to the language contact phenomenon, whereby due to the circumstances of learning and the uses required of English, the learner generates a grammar in which many of the marked-unmarked distinctions of the target language are removed, where inflected forms tend to be replaced by uninflected forms, and where preposition, auxiliary and article usage appears to be simplified. Simplification is one way in which speakers of different languages can make a new language easier to learn and use. Ferguson (1971) emphasizes the theoretical importance of such processes, and notes that

> . . . many, perhaps all speech communities have registers of a special kind for use with people who are regarded for one reason or another as unable to understand the normal speech of the community (e.g. babies, foreigners, deaf people). These forms of speech are generally

felt by their users to be simplified versions of the language, hence easier to understand, and they are regarded as imitation of the way the person addressed used the language himself . . . The usual outcome of the use of foreigner talk is that one side or the other acquires an adequate command of the other's language and the foreigner talk is used in talking to, reporting on, or ridiculing people who have not yet acquired adequate command of the language. *If the communication context is appropriate however, this foreigner talk may serve as an incipient pidgin and become a more widely used form of speech* (italics added).

In addition to these processes, overgeneralization is frequently observable in interlingual speech. Overgeneralization of target language rules is seen in the sentence *have to go to someplace* (above) where previous experience of *infinitive + to + adverb* is overgeneralized to an inappropriate context. Overgeneralization as a feature of interlingual speech is extensively illustrated in Richards (1971a and 1971b).

In describing immigrant interlanguage, important questions will arise as to the degree to which norms actually exist, since there is always a cline from minimum to full proficiency in English. Writing of *Cocoliche*, an immigrant interlanguage once spoken extensively by Italian immigrants in Argentina, Whinnon notes that the interlanguage was completely unstable in given individuals, since there was almost invariably continuing improvement in learning the target language, and that acquisition of lexical, phonological and syntactic items must have been subject to chance, so that the speech of any two individuals was never identical. 'Nevertheless, the system as a whole, however ephemeral in given individuals, and however broad a series of spectra it encompassed, was fairly clearly *predictable*, and was continually renewed in recognizable form from year to year and from generation of immigrant to generation of immigrant.' (Whinnon, in Hymes 1971: 98). In analyzing such interlanguages, language transfer, overgeneralization, strategies of learning and communication, and transfer of training (see below) would appear to account for the basic processes involved, and allow for the analysis of language learning in terms of the social conditions, under which learning and communication takes place.

## Indigenous-minority varieties of English

In examining the social and linguistic dimensions of immigrant English, we have seen that the size of the immigrant group and their characteristics, on dimensions of status, power, mobility, prestige and wealth, can influence the variety of English acquired. All language learning, whether the child learning his mother tongue, or an adult acquiring a second language, proceeds in terms of approximative systems, but under certain conditions in second language learning this interlingual stage may become the end point in the learning process, taking on a new role in in-group communication and hence in ethnic identity and solidarity. The conditions under which such non-standard interlanguages are the outcome of culture/language contact are present to a greater or lesser extent in a number of related situations. The language, educational and economic problems of many Mexican-Americans in the western and southern United States are well known, as well as the particular problems of certain American and Canadian Indian groups. Ornstein analyzes Spanish and Indian language questions, and notes the varying and often clashing social systems which have contributed to mother-tongue maintenance in the southwest. Ornstein suggests that an interlingual Hispano-Spanish and probably a Hispano-Anglo-Indian interlanguage exist in certain areas of the southwest. Among the forms of English he includes in his taxonomy are Spanish-Indian English pidgin, Spanish-English border pidgin, other Spanish-English pidgins, occupational English and teenage English (Ornstein, in Perren and Trim 1971: 87).

I should like to isolate for consideration here however the varieties of English which result from contact between standard English (i.e. the English of the dominant economic, social and cultural group) and culturally displaced and economically underprivileged indigenous minorities in a number of countries. Evidently a decision to isolate, say, North-American Indian groups for separate consideration and the classification of Mexican-American English as an immigrant variety, depends on whether one wishes to emphasize sociological, historical, or linguistic characteristics. The language performances reported for certain American and Canadian Indian and Eskimo groups, for Australian aborigines, and for some rural New Zealand Maoris, suggest sufficient historical, sociological and interlingual similarity to justify their inclusion here. Linguistically and socially, we are dealing with the same phenomenon isolated as operating in the immigrant language setting—the development of an interlanguage generated from the limited opportunities for social and economic advancement often associated with membership of an indigenous minority group. Typical descriptions write of loss of or decreasing fluency in the native language, and an inadequate command of English, and local terminologies have evolved from the particular dialects of English encountered: Cree English, Pine Ridge English, Dormitory English, Aborigine English, Maori English and so on (Darnell 1971, Wax, et al. 1964, Rubin 1970, Alford 1970, Benton 1964). Regretfully, there are virtually no adequate or even partial descriptions of any of these dialects. The closest I know of to an account of such a dialect is that given by Benton for the English of certain rural New Zealand Maoris (Benton 1964).

Traditionally the so-called 'broken speech' of many children from these cultural groups was attributed to poor learning backgrounds, such as bad speech patterns in the home, lack of adequate English reading materials, limited general experience together with self-consciousness resulting from poor language control. Cultural deprivation was seen as the key to poor language development. Of course failure in the school means alienation from the school and the early drop-out levels reported for many native children reflects an early awareness by the child of the school's non-acceptance of his culture and its values (Ashton-Warner 1963). The school's failure, rationalized as the child's failure, generated such concepts as cultural deprivation, restricted language development, and even cognitive deficiency, all of which are symptomatic of analysis that fails to recognize the real ingredients of the child's experience.

Recently emphasis has been placed on the inter-dependence of social and linguistic variables. Plumer points out that 'the relation between knowing English and the ability to perform in school is clearly much more vital and complex for these groups but the general point of view is the same. If they see themselves locked out of society anyway, then their motivation to learn English will be understandably low, especially if in so doing they risk cutting themselves off from associations they already have, namely their peers and families.' (Plumer, 1970: 270). Wax *et al.* describe the progressive withdrawal for Sioux Indian children from the white environment represented by the school. They refer to the existence of Pine Ridge English, and point out that few Indian children are fluent in the English of the classroom (Wax, *et al.* 1964). Darnell (1971) describes an Indian community in Alberta, Canada, and the interaction between Cree and English:

Interference of Cree with the learning of English is too simple a model to account for the actual behaviour of speakers. English mistakes cannot be accounted for directly by attributing them to differences between the structures of the two languages. Rather it is necessary to define the linguistic repertoire of Calling Lake in terms of at least four, not merely two languages.

She refers to Standard English, Cree English, anglicized Cree and traditional Cree.

Recent work by Philips highlights the role played by conflicting learning styles and behavioral expectancies between the Indian child's home environment and the school, which explain his reluctance to participate in many normal school activities (Philips 1970). Benton (1964: 93) notes the role of the non-standard dialect as an instrument of self and group identification and of social perception:

While the type of language spoken by children as reflected in their performance on reliable verbal tests, is often a guide to their likely educational performance, it may be only one of several factors which retard both the growth of language ability itself, and general scholastic achievement. Ethnic differences also play an important part. Very often children from a minority or low status ethnic group may feel less able to control their own destiny than children from a dominant group. They may find it more difficult to work with a teacher whose ethnic background and general outlook is different from their own, either because they feel less secure with someone in whom they can find no point of common identity, or simply because they do not know how to communicate with this stranger. Many children consciously relate their mode of English speech to their ethnic identity. One teacher reported that a Maori child had told her 'Maoris say *Who's your name*, so that's what I say.' Maori English is often an important sign of group membership and a source of security for these children.

The notion of interlanguage is again basic for a description of these dialects of English, which manifest (a) rules which are linguistic in origin, derivable from the mother tongue and from limited exposure to the target language and (b) rules which are social in origin, derived from what we have broadly referred to as communication and learning strategies. Many of the characteristics of these dialects stem historically from the limited functions required of English in the early stages of contact between the indigenous and colonizing groups. Initial uses of English would have been mainly in non-prestige domains, such as trading, and these dialects are characterized by the same structural and morphological simplification observable in immigrant speech. Examples from Benton's Maori English data are:

'Yesterday we going by walk. I shoot one deer and the other deers running away and I saw another deer up on the hill.'
'All her friends going up to her place.'
'She went down to her Nanny's and see if her mother was there.'

Other examples from Benton illustrate features historically derived from limited exposure to English, fossilized through lack of reinforcement from native speakers. For example, *by walk* (from *by foot*); preposition overgeneralizations such as *on their car*, *we ate dinner on the table*; features derived from transfer of grammatical features of Maori are also noted: *Who's his name*? and absence of the copula: *They in bed*—though copula omission, as Ferguson suggests, may be related to language simplification in certain types of language contact situations. That the distinguishing features of such a dialect serve as signs of group membership and solidarity is illustrated by the use of *you fellows* among rural Maoris, which is a solidarity and 'mateship' marker, though historically derivable according to Benton, from an attempt to parallel a singular/plural *you* distinction in Maori.

The following samples of aborigine English from Australia suggest that this dialect is closer to the 'incipient pidgin' end of the cline of bilingualism, reflecting sharper social and economic segregation of Australian aborigines than for comparable groups elsewhere. As well as omitting certain structures (verbs, auxiliaries, plural *s* and the copula), constructions such as the following are observed:

'He bin go bump in you.'
'We bin give you a lot of shell, eh?'
'He big one, eh?'
'Ufla (we) got tee vee.'
'You know ufla (our) dog name?'
'Youfla (you) can have one.'
'Oh look at crocodile-la.'
'Look here-la. Him find this-la.'
'You mook mine-la.' (Alford 1970).

In studying the history of Cree English, Pine Ridge English, Dormitory English and so on, it may be possible to use the framework proposed by Fishman for unstable bilingual societies, where language domain separation gradually disappears (Fishman 1967). In the initial stages of contact between the native community and the colonizing group, domain separation of languages obtains, and English is required in certain limited roles and capacities that are not conducive to the acquisition of a standard form of it (Leachman and Hall 1955). These are the conditions for the generation of a pidgin or a non-standard form of English characterized by structural and morphological simplification and by communication and learning strategies and interference. As domain separation in language use gradually disappears, English becomes an alternative to the mother tongue, especially in family and friendship domains. The non-standard form of English now has functions related to intimacy, solidarity, spontaneity and informality. The standard language, encountered in the school and through contact with outsiders, has formal functions, thus the characteristics of a diglossic setting may obtain where complementary values L(low) and H(high) come to be realized in different varieties of English. This would appear to apply to some members of the Cree community described by Darnell and is found with some monolingual Maoris, where the frequency of Maori English features increases according to the appropriateness of the domain. Features attributable to inter-language processes can thus achieve stabilization through identification with ethnic roles. More detailed studies however are needed of the native communities sharing these cultural, economic, social and linguistic features, to determine the degree to which interlanguage features in non-standard dialects are related to the social, economic and political status of the community.

## Pidginization and creolization

We have seen that certain non-standard varieties of English may be viewed as interlanguages derived from particular patterns of social interaction. Hymes suggests that the extremes to which social factors can go in shaping the transmission and use of language is seen in the processes of pidginization and creolization (Hymes 1971: 5). The concept of pidgin and creole languages owes much to Hall's distinction between a pidgin as a lingua franca spoken as a second language, and a creole as a first language which has developed out of an original pidgin and expanded its resources and functions through becoming the mother tongue of a speech community (Hall 1966). Not all linguists however see a pidgin as a necessary base for a creole. Mafeni notes that in some cases a pidgin may be a lingua franca for some members of the community and a mother tongue for others, which is the case for the English-based pidgin spoken in Nigeria, for Krio in Sierra Leone, and of pidgin English in parts of the Cameroon Republic (Mafeni 1971).

For our present purposes we will define a pidgin as an interlanguage arising as a medium of communication between speakers of different languages, characterized by grammatical structure and lexical content originating in differing sources, by unintelligibility to speakers of the source languages and by stability. A creole is a similarly derived language spoken as a mother tongue.

English-based creoles are found in such areas as the Bahamas, Jamaica, Barbados, Trinidad, the English-speaking Windward and Leeward islands, in Guyana and Belize in South America, and in Sierra Leone and the Cameroons in West Africa (De Camp 1968, Hymes 1971). In many settings an internationally acceptable standard variety of English is the official language, but the majority of the population speak an English-based creole for the normal purposes of communication. Stewart suggests that in creole settings one tends to find monolingual creole speakers, monolingual standard speakers, and bilinguals, each of the languages having particular functional distributions in the national communication network and being associated with quite different sets of attitudes about their appropriateness (Stewart 1962). In describing the Jamaican situation, Craig proposes a model with a creole component, an interlanguage, and the standard local variety of English. He uses the interlanguage concept to describe the area between the creole and the standard which is the end point for the majority of young people in Jamaica (Craig n.d.). When the population is given educational, economic, and social opportunities the creole thus loses its distinctive features and becomes more like the standard. The future history of the creole hence 'depends on the social status of the creole vis-a-vis the standard, and the variability of the language and the culture' (De Camp 1968). Cave gives details of this interlingual continuum in a creole setting (Guyana), the spectrum of speech varieties he illustrates ranging from that used by the aged East-Indian grandmother on a sugar estate, to that used by the educated middle class urban dweller, to that of the speaker of RP at the University (Allsopp 1958).

| Form | Used by |
|------|---------|
| 1. /ai təold hɪm/ | Britons and a small number of persons in higher administrative posts imitating white talk for social reasons. |
| 2. /ai to:ld hɪm/ | Important middle class in administrative positions in government and commerce and also professional men. |
| 3. /ai to:l ɪm/ | Ordinary middle class such as clerks, commercial employees, and teachers who have had secondary education. |
| 4. /ai tɛl ɪm/ | Careful speech of non-clerical employees, shop assistants, hairdressers, who have had primary but no or negligible secondary education. |
| 5. /a tɛl ɪm/ | Alternative for 4. |
| 6. /ai tɛl i/ | Relaxed form of 4. |
| 7. /a tɛl i/ | Relaxed form of 5. |
| 8. /mi tɛl i/ | Rural laboring class—tradesmen, servants, carters, etc.—who have had probably a primary education but are often underschooled, semiliterate and sometimes illiterate. |
| 9. /mi tɛl æm/ | Older generation of East-Indian laboring class with no schooling. |

Pidgin, creole and post-creole phenomena pose typological questions and more general questions as to the circumstances under which languages reduce and expand in structure and lexical resources. What factors account for the intelligibility of the immigrant interlanguage as opposed to the evolution of a new linguistic code in the case of a creole? Are the processes of language adaptation and creative generation seen in pidginization similar to the processes of interlingual generation in other language learning contexts?

One of the earliest to recognize that non-standard forms of English and English-based creoles should be related to factors in the social environment, rather than attributed to individual limitations, such as low intelligence, sloppiness, laziness, etc., was Reinecke, who wrote a sociolinguistic history of Hawaiian creole in the 30's, under the influence of Park's sociological account of dialect and language change (Reinecke 1969, Park 1930). Reinecke (1969) emphasizes that most creoles have in common the fact that they are derived from situations where an imported laboring and indentured servile class were under the subjection of European masters. The difference between the integratively motivated immigrant and the plantation worker is that

> the immigrant comes to a country having the ideal of assimilation of the various immigrant stocks into a fused new nationality . . . the immigrant is usually of the same race and culture. The plantation laborer is of a different race and culture from his master. He is typically held in a servile or semi-servile economic and political status, and is at any rate, completely dependent upon his master.

Reinecke's thesis is that creoles are the result, not merely of linguistic processes, but of the interplay between language, and economic, social, educational and political factors, deriving from what we have called 'communication strategies'. The communication structure of a plantation is an important factor, since the plantation environment furnished neither the opportunity nor environment to learn standard English. The disproportion between English and non-English-speaking groups resulted in limited interaction networks with native speakers. The division between creole speakers and standard speakers was a consequence of the deliberately maintained servile or semi-servile economic status for the laborers, which afforded them little chance to rise into the middle class.

The degree and nature of contact with the upper language differs in the creole setting from that of the immigrant and indigenous minority examples we have looked at. The immigrant and native interlanguages are characterized by settings where the target language dominates, leading to continued opportunity for the learning of English. Complete social assimilation is theoretically possible whereas, in the pidgin setting, English was the language of a resident or transient minority who were socially inaccessible, hence the target language was not considered as a model for learning. Occupational, racial and social stratification, the powerlessness and restricted mobility of the slaves or laborers, meant that there was no solidarity between speakers and addressees, and no suggestion that they were to become a single community. The relative presence of these factors in the other learning contexts we have considered leads to interlingual generation which remains, however, intelligible to speakers of English (Mintz 1971, Grimshaw 1971).

*Problems of Description*

Our basis for the analysis of immigrant and indigenous interlanguages has been the learner's approximative system, or interlanguage. Related concepts have been made use of by creolists in their work, though we lack a complete illustration of the process of creolization due to a relative lack of first hand data. The process of linguistic adaptation as a product of language contact which is the basis of pidginization and creolization, has however been illustrated from second language learning examples by a number of linguists interested in the explanation of creolization. Samarin (1971) illustrates what we have referred to as communication and learning strategies in discussing the grammatical adaptation and reduction seen in creoles, drawing comparative examples from second language learning. Whinnom (1971) illustrates how certain essential features of pidgin—simplification, and impoverishment in terms of the source languages—could come about if a German and English school-boy were forced to use French as a medium of communication in a context where no other models for French were available. Cassidy (1971) looks at contextual needs in the learning situation and the use of linguistic adaptation to meet these needs. The need for grammatical change and lexical borrowing is thus related to the social needs for language. Problems of process description are heightened however by the very nature of most creole settings.

Settings where creoles exist in a clearly defined diglossic relation to a status language would presumably allow for a description of learning according to the separate contexts in which each language operates. Speakers themselves however cannot be so clearly compartmentalized. Le Page observes that the term interference may be appropriate to describe certain elements of a foreign language learning setting, where the L1 and L2 represent the languages of two sociologically and psychologically distinct speech communities, such as the learning of English in France (Le Page 1968). In many creole settings, as in the other interlingual cases we have looked at, there is no such clear cut dividing line between L1 and L2. If the child's *native language* is indeed an interlanguage derived from exposure to creole and standard English problems arise in deciding what is known and what is unknown, since unlike the foreign language setting, increased knowledge of standard English adds to the learner's *native language repertoire*, rather than forming a new independent linguistic code. Linguistic competence in such cases cannot be described by reference to the abstract representation of the corporate rules of the speech community but must be seen as the rules governing individual interaction at a variety of social levels, some of these rules belonging to what linguists call L1 and others to L2. There is, however, no homogeneous and clearly defined group speaking only either L1 or L2 (Lawton 1964). Likewise the distinction between standard and non-standard English cannot be unequivocally correlated with the absence or presence of particular speech forms, since individual speakers vary according to the distance they have moved from one norm to another. The speech communities involved are not independent sociologically, culturally, or linguistically. There is no sharp break in social communication but a series of approximations which are represented by successive interlanguages generated according to the degree of social mobility achieved.

The complex and little understood process of pidginization and the related creole and post-creole interlingual continuum hence suggest a field of research which can both illuminate and be illuminated by the study of second language learning. While the social conditions characteristic of pidgin and creole settings are not those of typical language contact situations, our understanding of interlanguage processes will surely be clarified by the expanding field of creole studies, illuminating the factors involved both in the learning of a standard language and the dimensions that need to be accounted for in analyzing the development of interlingual varieties of English. Typological description of the different settings involved and detailed study of interlanguage processes in contact situations should enable us to predict in instances where English comes in contact with another language, whether the outcome will be a standard form of English, a non-standard form, or a new English-based language.

## Local varieties of English

The interlanguages we have looked at so far reflect differing degrees of social, economic and political penetration of societal structures, these structures being controlled by native speakers of the standard language. Another related phenomenon must be considered in reference to the generation of different dialects of English or of English-based languages —the situation where these societal structures are maintained by non-native speakers of English. This is the phenomenon associated with countries where English is not spoken natively but is widely used as a medium of instruction and of official and informal communication. It is the case of English as a second language in multilingual areas such as commonwealth Africa, India, Pakistan, Malaysia, the Philippines, Fiji and so on. In areas where English is widely used outside of native-speaking environments, local varieties of English have developed; Filipino English, Educated Nigerian English, Indian English etc. We do not have this phenomenon inside a political area where English is widely spoken natively. Thus we do not have 'French-Canadian English' as an alternative to Canadian English. Deviations between French-Canadians' use of English and Canadian English are always considered idiosyncratic, just as the immigrant varieties of English are said to be characterized by errors or by poor learning of English. But the educated Nigerian's or Indian's use of English, though it differs from British or

American English, is regarded as a standard acceptable way of speaking.

In these countries English serves a variety of formal and informal uses (Jones 1968, Brosnahan 1963, Fishman *et al.* 1967, Hunt 1966, Laver 1970, Prator 1968, Spencer 1971). It may be used often or rarely, but no one has recourse to English for all his language needs. It is reserved for use with specific individuals in a narrowly restricted and clearly defined range of situations. In many of these countries English is the language of commerce, law, politics, administration, education, and of culture at all levels above the local. It exists alongside a complex of local languages, with English functioning as an important auxiliary and sometimes national language. It is invariably learned after the mother tongue in the somewhat artificial environment of the school, consequently it is not often the language of intimacy. It has few emotional connotations. It is largely an urban phenomenon, knowledge of English being correlated with distance from an urban center. It has the important role too in many settings of being the key to social mobility. In West Africa for example, it is through English that an individual breaks the bonds of West African traditional life and enters into some kind of relationship with the westernized sectors of society (Spencer 1971).

In such settings the concept of interlanguage can be used to describe the processes by which local varieties of English have emerged in many parts of the world. Kachru suggests that the process of Asianization of English in those areas where English functions as a second language 'supplies a rich data for language contact study in a cross-cultural and multilingual context . . . and raises many typologically interesting theoretical and methodological problems about the new Englishes which have developed from the L1 (mother tongue) varieties of English.' (Kachru 1969). Similar problems of description arise in some settings as exist in creole areas, since in any area where English is a second language we find a range of local varieties of English varying from an upper level 'intellectual' to a lower level 'market' English. At the lower end we may find a pidgin or an English-based creole, hence the Caribbean examples discussed above become special instances of the general trends noted here.

Kachru writes of the cline of bilingualism in India and defines three measuring points—a zero point, a central and an upper (ambilingual) point. He defines the zero point as competence in some very restricted domain such as counting. African examples would be the market woman whose English is limited to *customer buy here; my friend buy from me; look tomatoes; what of oranges; Madam I have good pawpaw O!* (Spencer 1971: 37). In the Philippines this is presumably the level of the 'halohalo' (mix-mix) speech (Llamzon 1969). There is no 'rule-governed creativity' in English. A minimal knowledge in Indian usage is the register of postmen, travel guides and bearers. The central point, in

India, is the register of the law courts, administration, and of a large number of civil servants and teachers who learn English as their major subject of study and who are able to make use of English effectively in those restricted fields where English is used in India. The extent to which English is required in prestige settings as opposed to purely functional settings is important as a standardizing factor in these countries, as it is of course in the other contexts we have considered. English trade pidgins represent the effects of purely utilitarian roles for English, and trade or market English likewise represents limited functions for English, where it is not needed as an instrument to manipulate social behavior or the speaker's prestige. The upper level in Indian usage Kachru defines as the language of those who are able to use English effectively for social control in all those social activities in which English is used in India. In other settings the upper level may be defined by the educated uses of government and government officials, the middle level as that which might be heard in and around the secondary school, and the lower level as out-of-school uses. In West Africa the informal out-of-school language may be a local pidgin. There is of course much variety from one country to another but the overall pattern of a cline of bilingualism with the local standard at the upper level (Standard Filipino, Educated Nigerian etc.) is general. There thus appear to be quite distict feelings of appropriateness in particular contexts for the different levels of English usage, as there are in creole settings for the appropriate use of creole or English. Ure (1968) notes that in Ghana the kind of English that is used as a *lingua franca* in the market places is not likely to be used in the classroom, and likewise no one is likely to use classroom English in the market.

Studies of the local varieties of English suggest the insufficiency of the concept of *interference*, and confirm the usefulness of an approach which includes interference as but one element of the learner's interlanguage. Kirk-Greene, writing of African varieties, suggests the need for study of the social role of language in the second language setting: 'Only by understanding both the structure of the first language and the method by which English is acquired as well as the purposes for which it is used can we account for the deviant forms in bilingual usage.' (Kirk-Greene 1971: 61). Halliday suggests of the local varieties 'their grammar remains that of standard English, with few important variations; their lexis too differs little from normal usage; but the accent is notifiably and identifiably local.' (Halliday 1968). He is of course writing about the upper end of the cline of bilingualism, but his description needs modification. Kachru makes a useful distinction between *deviations* and *mistakes*, a distinction which reflects an interrelating of socio-cultural and linguistic factors in the analysis of local dialects of English. He thus distinguishes between *mistakes* which are outside of the linguistic code of English, and which are consequently not part of the English code of speakers of educated Indian English, and *deviations* which can be explained in terms of the socio-cultural context in which English functions. A mistake in Indian English would thus be *He can to speaks* for example, but *this all* as opposed to *all this* is part of the English code of educated Indian speakers. In Nigerian English *He go work* is not representative of the level of usage in English language newspapers, but sentences like *All of the equipments arrived*, and terms like *motor park* for *parking lot* represent the local standard (Walsh 1967). Of Indian English Kachru (1965: 408) notes that

> . . . the linguistic implications of such acculturation of Indian English are that the more culture-bound it becomes the more *distance* is created between Indian English and other varieties of English. This is well illustrated by the extended domain of the kinship terms of the natively used varieties of English in Indian English, or by contextually-determined Indianisms which are deviant as they function in those contextual units of India which are absent in British culture . . . the distance between the natively used varieties of English and Indian English cannot be explained only by comparative studies of phonology and grammar. The deviations are an outcome of the Indianization of English which has gradually made Indian English culture-bound in the socio-cultural setting of India. The phonological and grammatical deviations are only a part of the Indianization.

All of the central processes of interlanguage can be seen in local varieties of English. While we do lack detailed descriptions of any of these dialects, and do not have rigid criteria by which interlingual features can be identified the following examples are representative. In general the concept of language transfer may be used to characterize geographically defined varieties of English as a second language, such as differences between the pronunciation of English in different parts of Nigeria or the Philippines, of differences between mother-tongue based idioms in Filipino and Indian English. Differences between standard Nigerian English and regional Nigerian English are seen in the contrast between Nigerian English and Yoruba, Ibo, or Hausa English. Examples of mother-tongue transfer in standard Filipino would be:

'I will pass by for you at 4' (*for* I will call for you).
'How are you today? Fine. How do you do to?'
'Close the light / open the light' (*for* turn off the light).
'Go down the bus' (*for* Get off the bus).
'to lie on bed' (*for* to lie in bed) (Llamzon 1969).

Examples of this sort of mother-tongue / local-variety-of-English relationship can be found in many settings where English is a second

language. Many of the grammatical characteristics of local usage however must be seen as the results of overgeneralization or rule simplification and redundancy reduction etc. Examples would be the extension
of *isn't it* as a question tag in *Your brother was on holiday isn't it*, and
such Indianisms as:

    'I am doing it since six months.'
    'It is done' (*for* it has been done).
    'When I will come' (*for* when I come).
    'If I will come' (*for* If I come).
    'for doing' (*for* to + verb) (e.g. imprisonment for improving his
    character).

These reflect general tendencies observable in the acquisition of a
second language, and I have described them elsewhere in terms of
*interlingual interference* (Richards 1971a), that is, as English-based sub-
systems, derived not from the mother tongue but from the way English
is learned and taught.

    Many other characteristics of local varieties of English reflect
assimilation of English to the cultural mores of the country. Kachru
describes these in terms of transfer, collocation-extension, collocation-
innovation, and register-range extension, and gives many examples
from the Indian setting. All these factors operate to make English part
of the socio-cultural structure of the country, hence it is not surprising
that those who would use an overseas standard instead of the local
standard are regarded as affected and artificial and subjected to ridicule
and criticism.

    The evolution of local varieties of English is thus an illustration of the
adaptation of an overseas variety of English to meet the requirement
that a second language in use as a medium of both formal and informal
communication and not native to a country, should be capable of
expressing the socio-cultural reality of that country. Some of this
reality is expressed through modification of the phonological and
grammatical system of standard overseas English and description of
this modification in terms of the processes of interlanguage illustrates
how a second language reflects the contexts in which it is learned and
used. The generation of new lexical and grammatical extensions to either
reduce some of the unnecessary complexities of English or to accommodate some areas of the local culture which cannot be covered by existing
uses of English, are reflections of this interlingual creativity.

## English as a foreign language

The final context I wish to consider for the study of interlanguage
phenomena is the learning of English in countries where English is

studied as a foreign language in formal settings (such as the school), and where English is not normally a language of instruction but simply a branch of study. English in Japan, France, Indonesia, Russia and so on, is a purely cultural object of study (though it may serve the country's economic plans) and is not involved in societal functions. What are the differences between the learning of English in these settings and in areas where English is a viable second language? There are basic motivational differences. In a foreign language setting there is always an effort to acquire an overseas standard form of English, and not some local form of English. Hence Japanese, Russians, Germans etc. are bilingual in the popular sense when they cannot be distinguished from native speakers of English by their uses of the language, though no such demands are made in the case of English as a second language, where local varieties are accepted as standards. These motivational differences are reflected in the course books in use in foreign language and second language settings. In foreign language contexts, the English lesson is the occasion to bring a sample of American or British life into the classroom, and the lessons are about life and people in English-speaking countries. In second language contexts the content of the school course is usually local, and learners begin to learn English without necessarily knowing or caring what life is like in England or America.

These different learning goals influence the nature of the learner's interlanguage. In the foreign language setting all differences between the learner's use of English and overseas English are *mistakes* or signs of incomplete learning. There is no room here for the concept of *deviancy*, since the socio-cultural basis for deviancy does not exist in the foreign language setting. The learner is generally not satisfied until he has 'eradicated' traces of his foreign accent, though for practical purposes, this may not be possible due to the limited time available in the school course. Limitations to the acquisition of standard English in the foreign language setting are hence not socially imposed limitations, which we encountered with the analysis of domestic dialects; in the foreign language setting limitations are rather *individual*, reflecting personal differences in motivation, perseverance, aptitude and so on. There are no societal limits to the learner's progress in English. In reality those who do acquire accentless English in a foreign language context probably do so because of unique personal opportunities, rather than because of the school program.

These motivational factors have been emphasized by Reinecke (1969: 94). The desire to acquire an overseas model of the foreign language rather than a variety which is influenced by the conditions of acquisition was

. . . followed by the Japanese at the two cultural crises of their history, when in the 6th and 7th centuries A.D. select classes learned to read and speak Chinese in order that they might have access to the cultural riches of China, and again when in the 19th century, the educated classes learned Western languages so that they might compete on equal terms with the Occident. The same phenomenon was seen in the Hellenictic age, when the oriental peoples, that is, certain classes, among them, administrators, gentry, priests, litterateurs, and traders, learned the Greek Koine or common language. By 'learned' we are not to understand that all orientals who set themselves to write and speak Greek came to use the language without an admixture of native Greek elements . . . the point is that there was an effort on the part of the well equipped classes really to learn the foreign speech, to get at its cultural treasures, as well as to use it as a mere instrument of communication with the foreigner. There were limitations in the use of the foreign language, but these were due to individual limitations, not social limitations.

In analyzing the English language performance of students in a foreign language setting all differences between the students' performance and an overseas model may be regarded as transitional or undesirable. While in the second language setting the generation of an interlanguage may become institutionalized at the group level, through socio-cultural adaptation of English to the local setting, and through purely linguistic processes such as overgeneralization and interference, in the foreign language setting these characteristics are not institutionalized at the group level but remain a normal part of the learning process. In a foreign language setting, where the major source of the input for English is the teaching manual and the teacher, the concept of transfer of training may be a basic analytic approach, since many of the errors observable are directly traceable to the manner of presentation of the language features in the school course. Selinker illustrates transfer of training as a feature of the learner's interlanguage, through reference to an observed difficulty in distinguishing between *he / she* by Serbo-Croatian learners, although the same distinction occurs in the mother tongue. Textbooks however invariably present drills with only *he* and it is this aspect of the teaching process which influences the learner's interlanguage performance (Selinker 1972). Language transfer will also be a basic concept, since many of the techniques used to teach English in a foreign language setting will depend on translation from the mother tongue to English. The concept of interlanguage thus differs according to the setting in which English is being learned. James' (1970) description of learner's interlanguage is appropriate to the foreign language context:

The learner of any L2 has a propensity to construct for himself this interlingua, an act of linguistic creativity so natural that it would be unrealistic to expect learners to circumvent it and proceed directly from his L1 to the native speaker's version of the L2. A further reason for allowing the learner to construct the interlingua is that it is immediately usable by him in the context in which he is learning; his classmates have the L1 in common so will converge in tacit agreement on the form of the interlingua. With this they will be able to communicate while they are learning, while the conventional approach, which proscribes the interlingua as a 'corpus of error' either stifles the learner's communication drives altogether, or requires that the linguistically mature student becomes as a little child, practicing perfectly well-formed native-speaker's sentences, which are, however, often idealized and usually trivial. Accepting the interlingua, like accepting a child's non-standard speech, avoids the necessity to halt the communication process for the sake of the learning process.

We have seen that the nature of a particular interlanguage will depend on the particular context under consideration, which will define whether the feature is to be considered a *deviancy* or a *mistake*, a marker of transitional or terminal competence, the result of interference, simplification, overgeneralization, collocation extension, collocation innovation, register-range extension, or to strategies of learning and communication.

## Conclusions

I have tried to suggest here that a number of different contexts for language learning can be studied with a common model of analysis. The notion of interlanguage focuses on the learner's systematic handling of the language data to which he has been exposed, and the particular form of the learner's interlanguage will be determined by the conditions under which learning takes place. Standard English will be the outcome of language learning when the learner learns in order to become a member of the community who speak that form of English (e.g. the successful immigrant), or in order to invite perception of the learner as a person of equal status to standard speakers (e.g. the foreign student motivated to learn accentless English). Non-standard English will be the outcome of learning when the learner learns under circumstances which hinder his becoming a member of the community of standard speakers. Self-perpetuating social stratification correlated with color, race and other ethnic indicators, leads to the non-standard dialect taking on a new role of ethnic identity and solidarity. Educational planning which ignores this dimension of non-standard English is unlikely to achieve success. Partial learning, resulting from a lack of integrative interaction with standard speakers is reflected in modifications to the grammar of standard English, and these are best described as aspects of interlingual generation, that is, as either language transfer, transfer of training, communication strategies, learning strategies, or overgeneralization. The extreme case of nonintegrative motivation affecting language learning is seen in pidgins and creoles, where the learning process contributes to the separateness of the groups in contact, while maintaining solidarity at the lower level. Non-standard dialects differ from pidgins in that in the former, the target language is closer to the learner. There is no sharp break in social communication but rather a gradual merging. Progress towards standard English in a creole setting reflects changing perception of class and status as a consequence of social mobility. A local variety of English such as Indian English is influenced by the perception of English as a tool for nationhood, and reflects the modification of overseas English as the social and cultural mores of the country are accommodated. In a foreign language setting, while many of the interlingual processes are comparable to those seen in other contexts for language learning, they are always considered as indicators of partial learning. They have no social role to play for the learner. The study of interlingual phenomena in language learning thus leads to a focusing on the central processes of second language acquisition, and to a study of the circumstances which give these processes significance.

**Note**

First published in *Language Learning* 22, 2, 1972.

# The linguistic dimensions of a
# bilingual neighbourhood
Roxana Ma and Eleanor Herasimchuk

## Linguistic diversity in bilingual behavior

This report is primarily concerned with the structure of stylistic variation of Spanish and English in the linguistic behavior of a Puerto Rican
bilingual community located within the greater New York metropolitan
area. The theoretical and methodological orientation of this research
project draws heavily on recent work by Fishman, Labov, and Gumperz
in their investigations of linguistic diversity within various speech
communities. A common theme, and one which is fundamental to our
study, runs through these investigations, namely, that variation in
linguistic behavior is patterned variation, a lawful behavior whose
manifestation reflects and accompanies other social patterns within the
speech community itself. Whether one is dealing with 'monolingual' or
'multilingual' communities, the conclusions are similar: choice among
linguistic alternatives (which can range anywhere from choosing between two 'equivalent' pronunciations of the same word to choosing
between two or more different languages to express an idea) is largely
conditioned by a complex interrelationship of factors present in the
social organization of the community and in the social setting of the
speech act. The key concepts of this sociolinguistic orientation are
*diglossia* (Ferguson, 1959), *language domain* (Fishman, 1964), *linguistic
repertoire* (Gumperz, 1965), *communicative competence* (Hymes, 1971)
and *linguistic variable* (Fischer, 1958; Labov, 1964 c, 1966 a). A discussion of these general notions will help to place our study in proper
sociolinguistic perspective.

Ferguson's article was one of the first to delineate the pattern of a
complementary distribution of usage between the two languages of
bilingual (and bidialectal) communities. This distribution is associated
with complementary sets of attitudes and cultural values held by
members of these communities. Choice of language is a function of the
set of values (designated as 'high' and 'low') and social situations operating in any given social interaction such that one language is typically
considered more appropriate for certain kinds of linguistic behavior

(be it written or oral) than the other, and vice versa. In addition, he set forth a typological description of the linguistic features which respectively marked the H and L language varieties. Other studies illustrating this diglossic relationship have been carried out for such language pairs as French/Haitian Creole (Stewart, 1962) and Spanish/Guaraní (Rubin, 1962). Even though Stewart's study dealt with the formal/informal axis whereas Rubin plotted usage according to the power/solidarity dimension, these studies succinctly illustrate the basic functional interrelationship holding between usage of a language and its social value.

Fishman (1964, 1965b, 1968a) has developed this concept further by formulating a hierarchical set of sociological constructs which relate language choice behavior to domains of social interaction, such as the family, neighborhood, and occupational spheres of activity. Where the complementary, non-competing sets of 'value clusters' are each associated with a different language or language variety, and where the value clusters are realized in different sets of domains, the maintenance of stable intra-group bilingualism becomes possible. The intersection of language usage and domains of social interaction forms a matrix called a 'dominance configuration'. The value of this approach is that it permits one both to assess the degree of bilingual usage within the community and to plot the direction of any possible trend from bilingualism to monolingualism. We shall return to this point of view later on in our discussion.

The next two concepts, linguistic repertoire and communicative competence, are closely related. Gumperz' work on small group interaction in diverse speech communities has emphasized the need to recognize that speakers choose from a range of linguistic options to express their communicative needs. The totality of these available linguistic forms can be considered as a verbal repertoire and may consist of a range of different speech styles (for monolingual groups) or separate languages (for multilingual groups). Each of these 'varieties' (to use a more neutral term) is associated and used, through community-known rules of appropriateness, with specifiable social relationships and communication networks. Bilingualism per se is merely a more salient extension of the general phenomenon of variation in code repertoire and code switching, so that bilinguals switch languages for many of the same reasons that monolinguals shift styles (Gumperz, 1967). The question is the same for mono- or bilingual communities: How do the language varieties function to fulfill the total range of different communicative needs of the society?

Hymes emphatically states the case for the functional separation of diverse codes:

'No normal person and no normal community is limited in repertoire to a single variety of code, to an unchanging monotony which would preclude the possibility of indicating respect, insolence, mock seriousness, humor, role distance, etc.', by switching from one code variety to another.' (1967: 9).

He has argued that a native speaker's ability to know when to use which variety can be regarded as his communicative competence (or performance competence). Rules of usage are in some sense comparable then to the rules of grammar. He thereby urges linguists to give more serious consideration to the role which factors in the social setting play as determinants of linguistic behavior.

Approaching the same conclusions from a slightly different point of view, Labov's work has consistently sought a social explanation for the phenomenon of 'free variation' and its importance as a predictor of linguistic change. With the exception of the pioneering article by Fischer, structural linguists had largely ignored the problem of variation. This was because they accepted de Saussure's theoretical dictum of the fundamental separation between *langue* and *parole* (more recently reiterated by Chomsky as the distinction between 'competence' and 'performance'), namely, that there is one underlying abstract linguistic structure which exists and coheres in spite of the ephemeral fluctuations in usage which speakers of a language bring to it. It is this inherent idealized structure (transformed into actual speech by a corresponding ideally homogeneous community of speakers) which the science of linguistics must seek to characterize (Chomsky, 1965: 9). Labov and Hymes have both questioned the narrow scope of the structuralists and noted that widespread linguistic variation is not completely random, not on the individual level and much less so in the community context. Labov dismisses the simplifying assumption that linguistic communities are homogeneous. Linguistic divergence and change have long been studied as separate sub-disciplines, namely, dialectology and historical linguistics. Labov has contributed a third dimension by looking into the dynamics of linguistic change, not just the static results of change. What is the genesis of such change? Are changes due only to pressures and to shifting relationships within the linguistic systems themselves (Martinet, 1955) and to no outside factors? Are speakers of a language merely literal mouthpieces of their languages, or do they play an active (if unconscious) role in guiding the direction of lingustic change? By systematically relating the quantitative data of linguistic variants on the one hand to stylistic and sociological variation on the other, Labov has provided a model of the sociolinguistic structure of language change which is at once explanatory and predictive (1965; with Cohen and Robins 1965).

To Labov is due the credit for introducing and developing so thoroughly the concept of 'linguistic variable' as the major linguistic unit by which the sociolinguistic structure of a language can be studied and measured. His earlier work on phonological variation showed that the traditional analytic units of 'phone', 'allophone' and 'phoneme' were inadequate to explain the patterned phonological variations found both within and between speakers, since these patterns cut across both phonetic and phonemic categories, thus defying definition. He posited a new non-discrete categorial unit, the 'linguistic variable' (1964c). This unit had scale-like properties, such that a distribution of its variants could be plotted as points on a scale, these points being correlatable to such other axes of variation as stylistic variation and social stratification. Labov's theoretical assumptions and methodological orientation have been adopted quite wholly in our study, as will be seen later.

This brief review points out that all of these investigators, whatever their methodological differences, agree on one basic theoretical premise: they take it as given that speakers interact in speech communities of varying degrees of linguistic diversity and social complexity. Whether monolingual or multilingual, these communities are characterized by distinguishable speech varieties such that their distribution of usage is intermeshed with and signaled by various factors in the social communicative systems of the community.

## 1. Bilingualism: norms vs. variation

In light of the above discussion on code diversification, how have past linguistic studies treated bilingualism as a form of social behavior? The emphasis in most studies (Weinreich, 1953; Haugen, 1954; Mackey, 1962, 1966) has been on the purely linguistic aspects of the problem, dealing primarily with the analysis of the structural perturbations (phonological, grammatical, and lexical) which one language causes in another when the two of them come into contact. The usual working assumption has been to treat one language as primary or P (i.e., the mother tongue) and the other as secondary or S (the foreign language) and to focus on those sub-systems within P which undergo influence from increasing exposure to S. Although bidirectional influence has also been recognized (see Weinreich, 1953; Diebold, 1961), the usual studies deal with one-way influences from S into P (for example, see Haugen, 1953; Seaman, 1965; Kriedler, 1957). The sub-systems are affected due to processes which are strictly linguistic in nature, involving interlingual identification of 'similar' elements, resulting in the phenomenon known as 'structural interference'. Interference has been variously defined as:

'The use of elements of one language in speaking or writing another.' (Mackey, 1966: 239).

'Instances of deviation from the norms of either language which occur in the speech of bilinguals as a result of their familiarity with more than one language.' (Weinreich, 1953: 1).

In keeping with the traditional structuralist bias regarding the autonomy of linguistic structure, interference studies have not been primarily concerned with the community context of bilingualism but have assumed that the two ideal linguistic systems must correspond to two ideally homogeneous speech populations. Although it was early recognized by Weinreich that extra-linguistic factors (e.g., psychological and socio-cultural) do play a definite role in the effects which bilingualism has on a person's speech habits, linguists have been content to locate and describe the purely linguistic aspects and to view the others as merely reflections of degree of exposure of P to S. However, recent studies of multilingual communities provide evidence that several past assumptions about language contact are possibly incorrect or at best oversimplified. For example, it has been assumed that members of one speech community automatically have access to the linguistic norms of the other speech community and that they usually attempt to apply these norms. In fact, however, within a large stable bilingual community like the New York City Puerto Rican community, it is more likely the case that *bilinguals interact and communicate with each other*, using both languages, far more frequently than they interact and communicate with members of the surrounding monolingual community. In such a community, speakers generate their own bilingual norms of correctness which may differ from the monolingual norms, particularly where there is a lack of reinforcement of these monolingual norms (Gumperz, 1967; Ervin-Tripp, 1967). It has also been observed that, given certain social conditions, speakers may choose not to apply the norms even though they may be aware of them. If this is so, then interference per se can no longer be assumed to be either constant or uniform through the bilingual community. Mackey (1962) has pointed out that

'In the speech of bilinguals, the pattern and amount of interference is not the same at all times and under all circumstances. It may vary with the medium (reading vs. speaking), the style (narrative vs. conversational purpose of the interaction), the register (social role of the speaker), and the context (topic of the discourse).' (69) . . . In the last analysis, interference varies from text to text.' (70).

In any meaningful analysis and measurement of bilingual interference he concludes that it is necessary to know

'. . . not only the sort of interference but also the extent of each inter-ference, quantify it, and find out where it predominates.' (82)

Thus interference is a continuum and varies with other factors in the speech situation. Some of the most interesting sociolinguistically oriented studies are those of Ervin-Tripp on Japanese-American bilinguals (1964, 1967). She shows that co-variation of language, topic and listener have rather startling effects on the linguistic structures themselves, and the phonological and syntactic fluency in discussing a particular topic in a particular language depend on whether the topic, language and listener constitute a congruent or admissible combination. This suggests very clearly that ability to talk about typically American content and ideas may be part of the competence to be acquired along with the English language, i.e., that linguistic competence is itself dependent upon social contextualization.

If we are to study adequately the speech patterns of any bilingual community, we must go beyond merely describing how well speakers know the linguistic norms of both languages, i.e., their abstract linguistic competence. What they know is only important in relation to how they use it. Many bilinguals speak and use standard as well as non-standard varieties of both languages. The more significant fact is their socio-linguistic or communicative competence (also considered to be a single set of patterned speech habits) for knowing how and when to use what-ever varieties of each language they may command (Hymes, 1967; Fishman, 1968a). It is only after we have understood the reasons (both social and psychological) for the existence, extent, and diversity of linguistic varieties that we can proceed to study the exact nature of the linguistic differences which characterize these varieties. A study of code diversity is thus one of the major tasks of a sociolinguistically oriented approach to bilingualism. Such an approach does not make an *a priori* assumption that these linguistic varieties necessarily conform to the abstract 'standard' norms of either 'language'. Nor does such an approach automatically consider interference phenomena as always and only 'deviations' from these norms. Sometimes interference can be considered as a functional variety or norm in and of itself. Haugen has admitted that 'if it [interference] is frequently repeated, it may itself become part of the norm' (1957b; 777). Thus the linguistic norms of any speech community must always be empirically (and quantitatively) discovered for that community.

## 2. Intragroup bilingualism and degrees of bilingual usage

As we have noted earlier, the languages and language varieties of stable bilingual communities have been found to co-exist in a relation of diglossia. If a functional separation of languages is not maintained, then intragroup bilingualism is likely to die out. In the past, this has been the case with numerous immigrant languages in America. As new cultural patterns have to be assimilated and learned, a linguistic means for expressing these new ways and values has to be found. The first stage is usually extensive borrowing on the lexical level from the dominant language, English; subsequent stages affect higher orders of complexity, such as the grammatical and semantic levels. Borrowing, or linguistic acculturation, is a three-stage cycle which Haugen has characterized as code-switching, interference, and integration (1954). This cyclic process continues in direct proportion to the shift in cultural context which the immigrant community continually experiences. A period of widespread intergroup plus intragroup bilingualism reflects the ongoing acculturation process. Haugen's early (1953) study is a massive documentation of the results which linguistic acculturation and shift have produced in the Norwegian language in America. Simultaneously with progressing acculturation, the immigrant language becomes more and more restricted in its social usage and functions. When assimilation becomes so complete as to render the mother language no longer useful in any contrastive functions, a language shift will occur and bilingualism may then cease to exist at the community level, although it may still be retained on an individual or small group basis. Fishman has pointed out that, to the extent that immigrant languages have survived and retained some unique functions in American life, this has been largely a result of institutionalized intragroup forces at work, such as religious organizations, private bilingual schools, bilingual mass media, and social-cultural community programs, all of which emphasize the traditional and ethnic values associated with the immigrant languages. Language choice (or intragroup bilingualism) often persists long after the requirements of mutual intelligibility (or intergroup bilingualism) have been met precisely because languages are in fact not considered 'equivalent' by their speakers.

Of course, this is because bilingualism as such is never only 'native-like' control of both languages (Bloomfield's definition) nor is it only a minimum proficiency in the other language (what Diebold calls 'incipient' bilingualism). Bilingualism is a continuum between these two extremes, and one can properly speak about degrees of bilingual usage within a community corresponding to speakers' differing linguistic proficiency and social usage of the two languages. To ask the question 'which language is dominant?' is to look for mere dichotomy where a much more complex situation exists. We have to modify the question to '. . . dominant with respect to whom and when?' If it is true that choice of language or language variety and type of social situation are interdependent, then we must look for what Fishman calls the 'domain appropriateness' of each variety. In our Puerto Rican community, the domains of family and neighborhood friendships create social pressures which tend to work in favor of maintaining Spanish, whereas other domains such as public education, occupational activity and public mass media create favorable contexts for English. One Spanish variety may be dominant in an informal conversation between friends, another in an interview with a prospective employer; or an English variety may dominate in formal conversations with co-workers, etc. Thus a multiplicity of social and linguistic factors must be considered before we can arrive at a total picture of language usage and language choice; only from this total configuration can the degree of bilingual usage be described and measured. As we mentioned earlier, the extent to which this 'dominance configuration' changes over time should reflect the changing social functions of the language varieties.

## 3. Stylistic variation as a measure of degree of bilingual usage

What correlations exist between the degrees of bilingualism among various Puerto Rican speakers and the linguistic varieties of Spanish and English which they use? We have hypothesized that if one were to sample the actual range of social situations involving language choice, he would find a corresponding range of linguistic varieties and that these two repertoires co-vary. It is therefore reasonable to assume that, as changes occur in the patterns of language usage and choice, shifts will likewise occur in the verbal repertoire. In other words, range of bilingual usage (as measured by domain analysis) will correlate with range of stylistic variation. We would expect that speakers who differ in degree of bilingual usage also differ in the linguistic varieties they control. If both are indeed true scales, we will find correlations for corresponding points between these scales. To put it more succinctly, our hypothesis is that speakers who show greater sensitivity to Spanish than to English, i.e., use Spanish more frequently over a wider range of social interactions, will reflect this fact linguistically by having more varieties in Spanish than in English. Similarly, the reverse should hold for speakers who are closer on the bilingualism scale to English usage and dominance. We can depict this relationship in Figure 1. Our general problem is to empirically test this hypothesis by describing in detail the respective repertoires involved.

*Figure 1. Correlation between repertoire of language choice domains and linguistic repertoires*

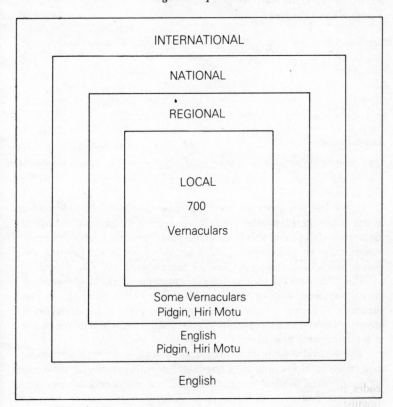

INTERNATIONAL

NATIONAL

REGIONAL

LOCAL

700

Vernaculars

Some Vernaculars
Pidgin, Hiri Motu

English
Pidgin, Hiri Motu

English

**Note**

First published in *Bilingualism in the Barrio*, edited by Joshua A. Fishman, Robert L. Cooper, Roxana Ma et al.

# Language use in a Chicano community:
# A sociolinguistic approach
Lucía Elías-Olivares

## Introduction[1]

The goal of this paper is to discuss the different linguistic varieties in use in the Chicano speech community of East Austin, Texas as well as the attitudes toward them.

In the last few years interference—how two 'pure' or independent codes influence each other—has been a great concern of traditional linguistics. In spite of this interest, linguists have not asked when or by whom these so-called 'pure' codes are used, nor when the linguistic forms which have undergone interference are used.

Most linguists (of various schools and approaches) have considered actual linguistic usage of no real interest. The notion that only the ideal structure of the pure code underlying speech usage and speech corpora deserve attention has especially dominated recent work in generative-transformational grammar.

The general view has been that speech communities are homogeneous, that, in the words of Chomsky, 'linguistic theory is concerned primarily with an ideal speaker-listener, in a completely homogeneous speech community, who knows its language perfectly and is unaffected by such grammatically irrelevant conditions as memory limitations, distractions, shifts of attention and interest, and errors (random or characteristic) in applying his knowledge of the language in actual performance.'[2]

If we take this theory strictly as a framework to study language, then there is no room left for variation in language or language interplay. We know that language does not come in a vacuum but is used by speakers in the course of social interaction. If one pursues this theory one is left with the image of 'an abstract and isolated individual, not, except, contingently, of a person in a social world.'[3]

Sociolinguistics analyzes this problem from a different angle. A sociolinguistic approach to the study of language diversity in a bilingual community means that instead of starting with such abstractions as two pure codes or two distinct languages that happen to be in contact, one takes as a starting point the bilingual speech community as a whole, in order to determine the structure of the different varieties of each language coexisting in that community. Thus, one investigates if those varieties are used by a particular subset of speakers in particular situations and for particular purposes.

This approach to the study of bilingual communities goes beyond the usual interest in the standard variety and the single informant. It is concerned with the description of the other varieties of the language and with the question of how these varieties function to fulfill the total range of different communicative needs of the population.

The notion of speech community, defined by Hymes as 'speakers sharing rules for the conduct and interpretation of speech and rules for the interpretation of at least one linguistic variety'[4] is not only useful but almost impossible to avoid in linguistics, if we think of languages as instruments of communication, constantly adapting themselves to the needs of the different groups who use them.

The concept of the language repertoire of a community (introduced by Gumperz), as opposed to the more limited notion of a language, means the totality of linguistic forms available to the speakers. This concept allows us to describe the speech behavior of the speakers in terms of their selection within particular sets of grammatical systems of linguistic options. The native speaker's ability to know when to use which variety is regarded as the speaker's communicative competence.

A basic sociolinguistic principle is that in a heterogeneous speech community, with varying degrees of linguistic diversity and social complexity, speakers interact using different speech varieties drawn from a repertoire of choices which for the most part are not random. On the contrary, the distribution of usage of these choices is determined by several factors in the social communicative systems of the community.

The data for this paper have been collected from field work done in the Chicano speech community of East Austin, a section of this city that comprises over half of the Chicano population, a community in which this researcher lived for two years. The area referred to, hereafter, as East Austin extends from East 7th Street to East 1st Street and from the Interregional Highway to Broadway Street. It is a section of the city of Austin where the majority of working class and lower class Chicanos live. It is a practically segregated urban neighborhood and somewhat isolated from other ethnic influences. Over ninety-five per cent of the people in this area are Chicanos, the only Anglos are those who own some shops in the area, but live elsewhere. It is important to consider this fact in order to understand why Spanish has been maintained here and why acculturation has not yet taken place completely.

The community, as a socio-cultural group, is very heterogeneous contrary to the opinion of those who still talk about the 'traditional

Mexican culture'. In every family one can see how opinions and ideas differ in regard to language attitudes, bilingual education, male-female roles in the community, ethnic labels, etc. Young and old members of the families do not agree in their judgments. Neither the Mexican-American family nor this Mexican-American community can be considered as a monolithic entity. Every family includes different types of people as one can see in the following opinions concerning the ethnic label 'Chicano'.

> *(Tape 20A45)*
> 'I can't stand the word "Chicana". Chicano means a very low class sort of . . . Chicano means animal, or say, really, the definition is bandido, embustero, traicionero and things like that and I don't consider myself that type of person.'

> *(Tape 15B83)*
> 'I say Chicano and I feel very much that the word itself connotates more than just an ancestral background, it connotates a belief in yourself, your race, a certain pride in your race whereas when I say "Mexican-American" it's more in the sense that I have an ancestry that comes from Mexico, that now I'm an American and all this.'

Being 'Chicano' or 'Mexican-American' or 'Mexicano' depends on the age, the educational background and the environment of the speaker. It also depends on who he or she is talking to when they refer to themselves. By the same token, one finds in each family a continuum that ranges from speakers who do not speak Spanish at all to those who are able to function in several varieties of the language.

## Language varieties in East Austin

Data on language varieties of East Austin gathered from ninety-two persons interviewed indicate that East Austin speakers have access to a language repertoire that includes English and four varieties of the Spanish language. The four varieties of Spanish which can be distinguished are: *Northern Mexican Spanish*, *Popular Spanish*, *Español Mixtureado*[5] and *Caló*. These reflect to a certain extent the ones that Rosaura Sánchez (1974) has proposed for a general Southwest Spanish and Jacob Ornstein (1974) for El Paso Spanish.

These four varieties are listed below, together with the names that the speakers themselves assign to them. Speech samples are included to illustrate them.

| *Language varieties* | *Native terms* |
|---|---|
| 1. *Northern Mexican Spanish* | Español formal, Español |
| a) Se fue a la escuela en su bicicleta. | bueno, Español correcto, Español político (polite), |

b) Pásame los zapatos.

Straight Spanish.

2. *Popular Spanish*

a) Se fue [hwe] a la escuela [ehkwéla] en su bicicleta.

b) Pásame los zapatos. [páhame lohapáto]

Mejicano, Everyday Spanish, Español de East Austin, Español mocho.

3. *Español Mixtureado*

a) Se fue [hwe] a la escuela [ehkwéla] en su bycicle [báysIKɛL]

b) Pásame los shoes. [páhame ločúw]

Spanglish, Tex-Mex, Español revuelto, Español mixtureado.

4. *Caló*

a) Se fue [hwe] al escuelín [ehkwelín] en su yonca (or chisca).

b) Pásame los calcos. [páhame lohkálko]

Pachuco talk, Barrio language, Pachuquismos, Hablar al modo loco, Vato language.

*Northern Mexican Spanish* is the formal variety of the language, spoken by educated northern Mexicans.

*Popular Spanish* is a variety which shares all of the phonological and morphological characteristics of the variety of Spanish used by some educated Latin American speakers in informal situations and by workers and peasants in most situations. It is a variety of the Spanish language many of whose features have been described by Spanish and Spanish-American dialectologists in works that go as far back as 1919.[6]

I have not been able to find a single phonological or morphological feature that cannot be traced back to forms that belong to informal varieties of Spanish all over the Spanish-speaking world and, of course, to other dialects proposed for the Southwest.[7]

Among these features one finds those of the examples given above such as: 1. Aspiration of the voiceless fricative /f/ especially before the glides /we/ and /wi/, afuera: [ahwéra]; fuimos: [hwímos]; etc. 2. Aspiration of sibilants even in intervocalic position, pásame: [páhame], before consonants, escuela: [ehkwéla]; los niños: [lohníño]. 3. Deletion of /s/ in final position, especially in plurals, calcos: [kálko]; le decimos en inglés [leihémoheninglé]. 4. Labial and velar voiced fricatives are frequently interchangeable before a high back vowel such as /u/ and the glides /wa/ and /we/, aguja: [aɣúha]~[aƀúha]~[aúha]; envueltos: [embwéltos] [engwéltos]~[enwéltos]. 5. Laxing of affricates, muchachito [mušašito] [mušito]. Alternation between [č] and [š] is very common in this community, expecially among youngsters. A process of change seems to be in progress in which there is a reduction of [č] to [š].

All the phonological changes present in this variety, including the aspiration of the sibilants, the reduction of voiced stops to fricatives, the deletion of unstressed syllables, the reduction of consonant clusters, are features that this variety shares with varieties of informal Spanish throughout the Spanish-speaking world.

The syntax of this variety is predominantly standard and most of the structures that deviate from the formal variety have been also documented in some of the works mentioned in note 7. Some of the structures are the following:

1. Omission of the 'personal' preposition, that is to say, the direct object marker when this is a person, in pre-noun position: *Jueron a guachar los chavos* instead of *Jueron a guachar a los chaves* or *Fueron a mirar a los muchachos*, in variety 1.

2. Use of the possessive determiner instead of the definite article: *Se puso su suera*, instead of *Se puso la suera*, or *Se puso la chamarra*, in variety 1.

3. Use of reflexive pronouns with intransitive verbs: *Se sale de la casa*, instead of *Sale de la casa*.

4. Deletion of reflexive pronouns in verbs that require them in the formal variety: *Va (a) gradar next year* instead of *Se va a gradar next year* or *Se va a graduar el próximo año*, in variety 1.

Some recent works[8] have considered these cases to be calques or loan translations from English. I believe they should be included as part of the variety Popular Spanish since some of them are very common in the informal variety of the language, such as numbers 1 and 2. Examples 3 and 4 are probably less common, but they have also been documented in the literature.

An utterance like *Insistí que viniera*[9] instead of *Insistí en que viniera* where the preposition *en* that follows the verb *insistir* in the formal and literary language is deleted, should not be considered as favoring an interpretation for integration of English rules in Chicano Spanish, as this change is rather common with educated speakers of Spanish and is certainly present in my speech. The same thing happens with such cases as *Vamos a ir después que tú vengas* instead of *Vamos a ir después de que tú vengas*. These examples should not be explained, it seems to me, as loan translations paralleling such English constructions which do not take a preposition, as *I insisted that he came*, *We are going to go after you come*, but as examples of internal change in the Spanish language.

By the same token, the use of the possessive determiner rather than the definite article, a common feature in Chicano Spanish, has been documented in Spanish-speaking areas which do not experience an English-Spanish language contact situation. Examples such as *Sus ojos*

*se llenaron de lágrimas* or *Metió su mano a su bolsillo y sacó su pañuelo*[10]
are certainly common throughout the Spanish-speaking world.

We should also note that very often Spanish speakers use the possessive determiner to indicate a stronger or more direct command. To say, *'Ponte tu abrigo inmediatamente'* is not the same as *Ponte el abrigo, por favor'*. The use of the possessive determiner has a different socioexpressive meaning.

It would seem then that in analyzing data for the Spanish of any Southwest area or speech community we should keep in mind not only its relationship to English but also to all of the informal varieties of the language present in Latin America.

*Español Mixtureado* is the third language variety. Socio-historical circumstances have created in this community as well as in other Spanish-speaking communities in the United States, a speech variety which is rich in the use of loan words and shows a certain degree of grammatical interference from English. It should be stressed, however, that the differences between this variety and the rest of those that belong in the verbal repertoire of the community are mainly of a lexical nature rather than morphological or syntactical.

Lexical items which have undergone the process called relexification, and calques have become a part of the Spanish repertoire of speakers who for the most part do not recognize their English source. When the speaker says *la mira* (the meter) or *la jira* (the heater) or *Ella me ticha español* (She teaches me Spanish) and has no notion of the origin of the word we no longer have interference but integration. When a speaker says *Lo puso patrás* (He put it back) instead of *Lo regresó a su lugar* or *Lo volvió a poner en su lugar* we are not in the presence of a bilingual who is experiencing interference from English when speaking Spanish but in the presence of a variety which is the habitual system of communication of a number of speakers who sometimes do not speak English. Español Mixtureado ought to be recognized and accepted as an important speech variety for purposes of research as well as for educational purposes. There are also certain syntactic constructions that parallel English structures as is the case of *Una mexicana maestra* in which the standard Spanish word order Noun + Adjective has been shifted to the English Adjective + Noun order. Or the case of *El chango estaba muy frío* in which the speaker uses the verb *estar* paralleling the English construction *The monkey was very cold* instead of using the verb *tener*. Finally, in a sentence such as *Lo que me ayuda es jugando escuelita* a gerundive verbal complement has been used instead of the infinitive on the pattern of English. All these examples, however, are present only in the speech of four- to nine-year-old children. I do not think these should be considered representative of the community as a whole.

The fourth variety is called *Caló* in the literature, and *Pachuco* language among other names by its speakers. Again, this variety shares morphological, phonological and syntactic features with the other three but has a unique vocabulary of its own. It is used predominantly by young male Chicanos for intra-group interaction, although there are some other instances, which we will discuss later, when *Caló* can be used.

There have always been problems in classifying lexical items as either *Caló* or *Popular Spanish* due to the fact that *Caló* changes in a relatively short time. Some of these terms are being accepted by a larger segment of the population. Such is the case for the term *chota* for example, for any policeman. The new *Caló* term is *la jura*. There are four terms in East Austin for police or policeman: *La polecía*, *la ley*, terms used by older speakers, *la* (or *el*) *chota* and *la jura*.

The use of these varieties together with English results in another mode of communication known in linguistics as *code-switching*, the constant alternation of the two languages in the middle of the sentence or in between sentences. This way of speaking is the rule rather than the exception in the everyday language of the community.

In the language repertoire of an East Austin speaker then, a statement such as *He went to school on his bicycle* may be expressed as:

1. Se fue a la escuela en su bicicleta.
2. Se [hwe] a la [ehkwéla] en su bicicleta.
3. Se [hwe] a la [ehkwéla] en su [báysIkɛl].
4. Se [hwe] al [ehkwelín] en su yonca.
   chisca.
5. He went to school on his bicycle.

As Labov (1970: 19) has shown in his studies in New York City, we see that there are no single-style speakers. But, what is more important, in this community we find that despite the opinions of laymen in the sense that Chicano speakers speak only one form of Spanish, called Tex-Mex and considered corrupt, there exists a language repertoire composed of a wide range of varieties of styles which might not conform to the rules of the formal variety of the language but which serves to fulfill the communicative needs of the speakers.

## Language use in the community

A language repertoire usually includes a wide range of styles or varieties in one language and a narrow range of styles in another. The speakers in East Austin possess these varieties with different degrees of fluency. One of the informants, a 55-year-old first generation speaker possesses the standard variety to a certain degree, she is fluent in Popular Spanish and has a receptive competence of Español Mixtureado and Caló; she has a very limited command of the English language and therefore of code-switching. This pattern is usually reversed in second- and third-generation speakers. Youngsters interacting among themselves use Caló and code-switching if they are males; their parents address them in Spanish and they respond to them in English or code-switching.

These language varieties are not used in a vacuum but through community rules of appropriateness. If a speaker commands several varieties or ways of speaking he knows when to use them and how.

The variety called Caló in the literature used to be restricted to lower class male Chicanos, but many of its forms and expressions are now understood and used by people of all ages in informal situations. It is still, however, used predominantly by young male Chicanos, in the course of intra-group interaction. As a female student put it:

(*Tape 32B69*):
Conocí a una señora y usaba esas palabras, se oyían muy feas, that's not the kind of language . . . coming from una mujer, no se oye bien. It's all right for them [the men] pero en una mujer se oye feo.

The only women who use *Caló*, and seem to be accepted by their audience, are the ones that frequent the cantinas in the barrio.

It is inappropriate for youngsters to use this variety in the presence of their parents. There are times however when a change in the type of interaction may trigger the Caló variety. A change from varieties 1, 2 or 3 to *Caló* may signal anger, or a jocular turn, or it may be used by a couple who are in the middle of a heated argument; it may be used to show disrespect. The following example illustrates the social function of this variety in the expression of anger, and how one speaker understands this expression in the other.

(*Tape 38B90*)
FW: So if you go home y no puedes encontrar los zapatos y le llamas a tu mamá, ¿qué le dices?
I: ¿On tan mis zapatos?
FW: Would you ever say ¿on tan mis calcos?
I: Pos cuando te enojas, you know, hablas más juerte.
FW: What would she say?
I: Pos ella se va a nojar patrás cause ya sabe que toy enojao.

This would be one of the few instances in which this variety is appropriate to address an elderly person; in other instances it would not be accepted as it is expressed by the following comment made by an 18-year-old Chicana concerning her use of the Caló term *trolas* (matches):

(*Tape 37A88*)
Not in front of my parents! I would say that among my friends but with my parents I wouldn't, cause that's showing disrespect.

By the same token, if several young men are talking among themselves at work, telling jokes, it would be highly inappropriate to use the standard variety even if they did command it. Speakers make very interesting remarks about the general communicative situations that they encounter with Mexican aliens who are closer to the Standard variety than to Español Mixtureado, Caló or code-switching. The use of the formal variety by the Mexican aliens determines a change in the situation from informal to formal, and this makes Chicanos uncomfortable. The use of these 'polite' forms conveys distance rather than intimacy. We note this in the following excerpt of an interview with a 25-year-old Chicano.

> (*Tape 38B90*)
> Con los mojaos yo pueo hablar pero lomás no me gusta pa mí como ellos hablan. Se me hace que hablan muy recio. Y lo dicen too al revés. Usan las palabras muy formal. Se me hace que toy con alguien completely stranger. Hablan muy formal pa mí, muy polite.

One should point out that, contrary to the opinion that contact with Mexico and Mexican aliens could influence the speech of Chicanos, the reverse situation is true at least in this community. Once the aliens learn enough English vocabulary they follow the trend and pick up the ways of speaking of the community.

East Austin is then a speech community by itself in which speakers share rules regarding language usage; basing themselves on these rules they interpret the social meanings of different linguistic choices.

Bilingual speakers in this neighborhood express ethnic membership by using the mode of communication known as code-switching. In general one could say that to be a bilingual means precisely to be able to switch rapidly from one language to the other. The social psychologists' ideal or coordinate bilingual who controls his choice of language according to topic and interlocutor is impossible to find in East Austin.

Speakers switch languages among other things because they do not want to give the impression that they do not speak one or the other language, or that they have become anglicized, as a 28-year-old female secretary explains:

> (*Tape 10B82*)
> Porque si hablas puro inglés, después dicen 'válgame, se cree muy americana, you know'. Y loo si hablas puro español, dicen 'pos no sabe ni inglés'. And then, if you mix a little of each, you know, and they say 'pos ah, she's all right, she knows how to talk Spanish, and yet she knows how to talk English'.

Code-switching is the mode of communication more often used in East

Austin especially among third- and fourth-generation speakers as they feel more at ease using it.

Although informants declare that the standard Northern Mexican Spanish variety does not play any role in the everyday interaction of the community, it is nevertheless present in the speech of a great number of the speakers. However few of them use it, except to clarify a point. This is shown by speakers whom I asked, as part of a class project for a sociolinguistics course at the University of Texas at Austin, to repeat previous statements. It was found that in almost seventy-five per cent of the cases the repetitions included more standard forms than the original utterances, given as indicated:

1. *Reduction of consonant clusters.* (/nd/>/n/)
   O: Está nomás toma*n*o.
   Q: Mande . . .
   O: Nomás toma*nd*o.
2. *Alternation of phonemes.* (/i/>/e/)
   O: Su hija no d*i*cía nada.
   Q: Mande . . .
   O: Nunca me d*e*cía nada.
3. *Obsolescent forms of the present tense.*
   O: Será que así *semos*.
   Q: ¿Que dijiste?
   O: Será que así *somos*.
4. *Borrowings.*
   O: *Mistió* el bos.
   Q: Mande . . .
   O: *Se le pasó* el bos.

   O: Vende el *aiscrín*.
   Q: Mande . . .
   O: Aiscrín, ¿nieve, no?

Aside from the fact that the relationship of the original statement to the repetition reflects the existence of particular linguistic subsystems or varieties shared by the speech community of which the two persons are members,[11] we see that at all levels of language, the speakers possess many of the standard forms, which were elicited by asking them to repeat original utterances. This pattern is especially consistent for phonology and morphology. This seems to show that within a paradigm of varieties people are conscious of standard and non-standard or different forms.

Most people in this community recognize the existence of a more formal variety, differing from that of their normal use. Some, especially first generation speakers, claim control of this variety, others do not. Second-generation speakers in particular deny that they speak or understand 'el español correcto' and say 'hablamos mocho, reveulto'. This shows the effect which the prejudiced opinions of outsiders, especially Spanish teachers and Latin Americans, have had on these speakers, who always minimize the command they may have of the standard variety.

Those who speak the standard variety are the school teachers of the area, protestant preachers, catholic priests and some community and welfare employees who have taken Spanish in college or have lived in Mexico for some time.

Some of the studies done previously in this area (Sánchez, 1974) have maintained that English is always the language with non-Chicanos even if they are from Latin America, and that English will always be chosen if the topic under discussion involves technical or specialized terminology.

In the first case, personal observation indicates that non-Chicanos who are addressed in the barrio are talked to in Spanish (if they look Latin of course). The situation will be different in another setting, outside from the community, where all communication tends to be or to start at least, in English, until the outsider uses a Spanish word that triggers the switch. It is the outsider however that signals this change. At any rate one must be very careful not to make categorical statements, as the linguistic situation is very heterogeneous and bilingualism is a phenomenon that varies from individual to individual.

I do not think that it is always true either that topics which deal with subjects related to barrio experiences require Spanish and other topics related to the anglo world require English. In general it would seem that the category of participant is more crucial in language choice than other components of speech, such as setting and topic.

## Attitudes of the speakers towards their own speech

In this community, English, the language of the dominant society, has an instrumental value. This makes it superior to the vernacular, especially for second- and third-generation speakers. This determines that people who belong to the lower class oppose the vernacular outside the community and in the teaching of students. Nobody questions, however, the use of Spanish as a means of communication inside the barrio. It seems that those Chicanos with more economic problems tend to reject the teaching of this language, while those who enjoy a better economic situation have more positive feelings about the language. The desire of a better socio-economic situation is linked to the learning and use of English. Poverty is linked to Spanish and therefore as something not to be maintained, except in the case of militant Chicanos, who try to make people aware of the necessity of maintaining their language.

Those who are experiencing upward mobility prefer to speak

English, and look down on the local varieties, and declare they do not use them, which is hardly true, of course.

In general, however, one finds that the negative attitudes towards the East Austin speakers found in Anglo and Latin American speakers is also found among the speakers themselves, a fact which is easy to explain since their history is one of socioeconomic and therefore linguistic oppression.

This feeling of linguistic inferiority is particularly strong among older informants. But it is not so with younger speakers, who seem to express ethnic pride in their ways of speaking. This is especially true of the young activists in the community.

The following are some of the most general comments about the different varieties:

(*Tape 30A60*)
El español de México es más perfecto, formal y aquí nosotros no hablamos ese español.

A thirty-year-old teacher-aide speaks in the following terms about rhe school principal's Spanish:

(*Tape 11B84*)
El español d'ella está tan elevado y tan bonito y tan correcto, que me da vergüenza hablar con ella. Ella pasaría por una mexicana del otro lao.

As with other cases in which there is a prestige variety involved, East Austin speakers recognize the prestige variety, which is in their terms 'el español puro', 'el español correcto' but the community also shows a strong sense of loyalty to the local varieties, especially those of lower class and young speakers. The standard variety is characterized by them as a Spanish which is not mixed with English, a variety in which syllables are not deleted. The local varieties are characterized as 'el español mocho', 'el español revuelto', 'un español rápido, acortando palabras, mal pronunciado', etc.

The propensity to use Español Mixtureado or code-switching is condemned by first-generation speakers, who think that 'están echando a perder el español'.

Young people on the other hand, do not see the need for the standard variety, and they even make fun of school children who attempt to speak this way. This proves that children in bilingual programs get very little reinforcement of the standard variety from the barrio. A 25-year-old Chicano thinks that:

(*Tape 38B90*)
Yo creo que deben enseñar el que hablan aquí porque lo que hablan en México, el correcto, aquí no si oye nada. Viene un chavalío y te

habla asina como habla en clasia, yo me vo a rir, yo sí sé qué ta ijiendo pero me vo a rir porque nootros no hablamos eso.

The reverse pattern, that is to say, a rejection of the Caló variety is found among older speakers, who regard Caló as a language spoken by 'gente baja'.

(*Tape 2A3*)
Sí sé cuales son (the words) pero no me gusta, es muy corriente ese modo de hablar, como una gente muy baja, de a tiro p'hablar, una gente que no tienen nada de educación, las palabras que hablan los pachucos.

There may be another reason why older speakers do not like this variety: This is because it serves as an intra-group mode of speaking for the youngsters when they do not want the elders to understand something.

(*Tape 2A3*)
Agarran ese modo de hablá pa que la otra gente no los conozca, no sepan qué es lo que quieren decir; un estilo vulgar, muy bajo.

## Conclusion and pedagogical implications

I have attempted to show here that the language situation of a Chicano speech community such as East Austin is not simple. On the contrary, it is rather complex. Instead of looking at one abstract language one must take into account the language repertoire of the community and the varieties that this language repertoire encompasses, as well as some of the different social functions that these varieties serve. Furthermore an understanding of the language situation in these communities should help us to apply some of the findings to concrete educational problems, such as the implementation of bilingual educational programs. The aim of research in this field should always be to benefit the community.

An important task in describing the language situation of Chicano speech communities should be therefore to describe not so much the referential function of the language varieties the speakers command and use but the socio-expressive functions of these varieties. This would enable us to see if they convey seriousness or joking, distance or intimacy respect or disrespect, concern or indifference, and we could then describe 'the relationship between the structure of language and the structure of speaking'.[12]

One of the speakers has summarized in the following terms the general situation concerning the language repertoire of the community:

(*Tape 11A21*)
If you're gonna make anything, you know, or do anything you have to know how to communicate and you're never gonna have the same

group. You may be talking to an anglo, so you have to learn to speak English. You may be talking to the poor white then you talk the slang or the hippie; then you talk to the mexicano professional que avienta puras palabras grandes, you have to speak that way, los viejitos otra manera y de ai a la gente de tu edad, mexicanos, el estilo de nosotros [pachuco] y ai está.

What educational implications does the language situation of this community, and perhaps other communities as well, have? How do we relate these findings to the bilingual education effort?

It is clear that bilingual education programs have taken into consideration neither the heterogeneous linguistic situation of this speech community nor how people feel about this issue.

Very often self-appointed experts on bilingual education design programs for bilingual children of different communities without considering the linguistic situation of the speakers. Hardly anybody has considered whether the community feels that the teaching of the standard variety would serve any purpose for the community. Undoubtedly, one must consider the question of the practicality of teaching the standard variety to people that do not see a need for it, for whom 'standard Spanish' is nothing but an abstraction at this moment, something that they would like to speak but do not know for what purposes.

One definitely needs to take into account the linguistic make-up of the community. Then we should select the variety or varieties to be used in the program. Another issue is whether a combination of varieties ought to be used not only as a medium of instruction but also in the developing of educational materials.

One should also consider the possibility of using the mode of communication labelled as code-switching to teach some of the school subjects. If used, it could probably be conducive to a more relaxed atmosphere and to better learning.

Much work has to be done in the area of the attitudes of teachers toward the different varieties. Even some Chicano teachers in some schools in East Austin look down on the local ways of speaking because most of them come from areas such as Laredo or the Valley in which the standard variety is highly valued and plays a role in the everyday interaction of those communities, and because their linguistic background in standard Spanish is stronger than that of the East Austin population.

The general attitudes of teachers show very clearly that there is a need for the implementation of basic sociolinguistic principles in teacher training, particularly those that deal with language varieties and their use in the communities. A valid sociolinguistic description of these varieties would enable teachers and pupils to recognize the varieties that local communication appropriateness presupposes and also to recognize the

norms that the community has for the use or non-use of a variety between particular types of persons in particular types of situations.

## Notes

First published in *Working papers in sociolinguistics No. 30.*

1. An earlier version of this paper was presented at the Southwest Areal
   Linguistics Workshop in 1975. This paper has benefited from the
   helpful suggestions of Joel Sherzer and Rosaura Sánchez.
2. Noam Chomsky. *Aspects of the Theory of Syntax.* 1965: 3.
3. Dell Hymes. 'On Communicative Competence'. Ms. 1971: 2.
4. Dell Hymes. 'Models of the Interaction of Language and Social
   Life', in *Directions in Sociolinguistics.* 1972: 54.
5. *Español Mixtureado* is one of the terms used in the community for the
   variety of Spanish influenced by English in various ways.
6. See for example, Rufino José Cuervo. *El Castellano en América.*
7. For an analysis of some of the phonological and morphological features
   of this variety, see Aurelio Espinoza. 'Estudios sobre el Español de
   Nuevo Méjico', *Biblioteca de Dialectología Hispanoamericana.* Vol. 2.
   1946; Rosaura Sánchez. *A Generative Study of Two Spanish Dialects.*
   1974; Eduardo Hernández-Chávez et al. *El Lenguaje de los Chicanos.*
   1975. For a description of similar features in other areas see among
   others: Laura Arguello Burunet. *El habla de Santa María de Zompa,
   Estado de Oaxaca, México.* Universidad Iberoamericana, 1965;
   Tomás Navarro Tomás. *El Español en Puerto Rico.* Río Piedras:
   Universidad de Puerto Rico. 1948. Pedro Henríquez Ureña. 'El
   Español de Santo Domingo; *BDH.* Vol. 5.; Luis Flórez. 'El Español
   hablado en Colombia', *OFINES.* Vol. I. 1964; Rodolfo Oroz. *La
   lengua castellana en Chile.* Santiago: Universitaria. 1966; Angel
   Rosenblat. *El Castellano de España y el Castellano de América.*
   Caracas: Universidad Central. 1965; Berta Vidal de Battini. 'El
   Habla Rural de San Luis', *BDH.* Vol. 7. 1949.
8. See for example: Yolanda Solé. 'Sociolinguistic Perspectives on
   Texas Spanish', *Southwest Languages and Linguistics in Educational
   Perspective.* San Diego: Institute for Cultural Pluralism. 1975. 171–
   185; Anthony Lozano. 'Grammatical Notes on Chicano Spanish'.
   *La Revista Bilingüe.* Vol. 1. No. 2. 1974: 147–151.
9. Anthony Lozano. *Op. cit.,* 149.
10. I have taken these examples from the book *Interferencia Lingüística
    en el Español Hablado en Puerto Rico*, by Paulino Pérez Salas.
11. Joel Sherzer. 'Semantic Systems, Discourse Structure, and the
    Ecology of Language', *Working Papers in Sociolinguistics.* Southwest
    Educational Development Laboratory, 1974: 10.
12. Dell Hymes. 'Introduction.' *Functions of Language in the Classroom.*
    New York: Teachers College Press. 1972: xiii.

# Designing the language curriculum

# Primary French in the balance
Clare Burstall, Deputy Director, NFER

## Summary

During 1963, arrangements were made by the then Ministry of Education for a national experiment in foreign-language teaching to be carried out in selected primary schools in England and Wales. The main purpose of the experiment, which came to be known as the Pilot Scheme for the teaching of French in primary schools, was to discover whether it would be both feasible and educationally desirable to extend the teaching of a foreign language to pupils who represented a wider range of age and ability than those to whom foreign languages had traditionally been taught. Under the Pilot Scheme, French was to be introduced into the primary school curriculum on an experimental basis from September 1964 onwards. The choice of French as the language to be taught was virtually inevitable, since it would have been impossible to provide an adequate teaching force for the implementation of the experiment if any language other than French had been chosen. In most of the schools taking part in the Pilot Scheme, French was to be taught throughout the primary stage of the experiment by class teachers who had received special inservice training, rather than by specialist teachers of French. Arrangements were made to provide continuity of teaching at the secondary stage, so that all the pupils taking part in the experiment would be able to continue learning French without interruption for at least five years.

Once the experiment had been set up, it was agreed that its effects should be evaluated over a period of years by the NFER. In the event, the NFER evaluation spanned the period 1964–1974, taking the form of a longitudinal study of three age-groups or 'cohorts' of pupils attending the schools taking part in the experiment. The sole criterion on which pupils were chosen for inclusion in one of the experimental cohorts was their date of birth. In the first instance, French was to be taught to all eight-year-old pupils in the selected primary schools from September 1964 onwards; thereafter, the teaching of French was to be extended to a further year-group each autumn, until it involved all pupils in the 8–11 age-range. Thus, the first cohort to come under study was composed of all pupils in the large primary schools taking part in the experiment who fell within the age-range 8.0–8.11 on 1st September 1964 and all pupils in the small primary schools who fell within the age-range 8.0–9.11 on that date: this provided a sample of approximately 5,700 pupils. (A wider age-range was sampled in the small primary schools, to avoid the creation of unworkably small groups). The second cohort was composed of all pupils in the large primary schools in the sample who fell within the age-range 8.0–8.11 on 1st September 1965: this provided a sample of approximately 5,300 pupils. Pupils in the small primary schools were not represented in the second cohort, since most children of an appropriate age had already been included in the French classes set up for the first cohort.

Originally, the NFER evaluation was to have been based entirely on a longitudinal study of the pupils forming the first two experimental cohorts. It was hoped that the results of this study would provide sufficient information to enable valid conclusions to be drawn regarding the feasibility and advisability of teaching French at the primary level. As the experiment progressed however, it became clear that the pioneer status of the first cohort had entailed an atypical introduction to French. During the first year of the Pilot Scheme, for instance, difficult staffing problems were encountered which had not always been foreseen: in some primary schools, French teachers were absent without replacement for a whole term in order to attend intensive language courses in France; in others, no trained staff were available to teach French during the first term of the experiment, with the result that the first cohort pupils in these schools started to learn French one term later than the others in their age-group. The first year of the experiment could therefore be regarded with some justification as an essentially exploratory period, calling into question the validity of using the results obtained from the study of the first cohort as a basis for future comparison. In view of these circumstances, it was considered advisable to extend the evaluation to a third cohort of pupils: those who would begin their study of French in September 1968. The third and final cohort to come under study was thus composed of all pupils in the large primary schools still taking part in the experiment who fell within the age-range 8.0–8.11 on 1st September 1968 and all pupils in the small primary schools who fell within the age-range 8.0–9.11 on the same date: this provided a sample of approximately 6,000 pupils. Inclusion in the experimental sample was again determined solely by the age of the pupil. This meant that the sample was drawn from all the socioeconomic strata normally represented within the national educational system and, in consequence, was characterized by a wide range of ability.

The time-span of the evaluation did not allow all the pupils taking part in the experiment to be studied for an equal period of time. The pupils in the first and third cohorts were under study for a total of five years: three years in the primary school and two years in the secondary school. The pupils in the second cohort were under study for a longer period: three years in the primary school and five years in the secondary school. During the ten-year period of the evaluation, the main aims of the study were: (i) to investigate the long-term development of pupils' attitudes towards foreign-language learning; (ii) to discover whether pupils' levels of achievement in French were related to their attitudes towards foreign-language learning; (iii) to examine the effect of certain pupil variables (such as age, sex, socio-economic status, perception of parental encouragement, employment expectations, contact with France, etc.) on level of achievement in French and attitude towards foreign language learning; (iv) to investigate whether teachers' attitudes and expectations significantly affected the attitudes and achievement of their pupils; (v) to investigate whether the early introduction of French had a significant effect on achievement in other areas of the primary school curriculum.

The main findings to emerge during the earlier years of the evaluation were published in two interim reports (Burstall, 1968, 1970); the recent publication of the final report (Burstall *et al.*, 1974) brought together both the earlier and the later findings and provided an overall view of the effects of the experiment during both its primary and secondary stages. What follows is an attempt to review briefly the research evidence presented in the final report, but it must be borne in mind that limitations of space will inevitably impose a certain selectivity on this review.

## Findings

### 1. *An optimum age for foreign language learning?*

The belief that young children are better equipped than older children or adults to learn foreign languages with speed and efficiency underlies the recent expansion of foreign language teaching at kindergarten and elementary school level. Much of the impetus for the early introduction of foreign language study can be attributed to the influence of Wilder Penfield's work. Penfield has frequently reiterated the view that the young child's brain is uniquely well-adapted for language learning and that there is an 'optimum age' during which 'multiple languages may be learned perfectly, with little effort and without physiological confusion' (Penfield, 1953). Penfield situates this 'optimum age' for language learning within the first decade of life, after which period a 'built-in biological clock' inexorably records the lost educational opportunity (Penfield, 1964). Further attempts to acquire foreign languages will be crowned with only modest success. The age of the learner is thus the most critical factor in the language learning process; if it is to be successful, foreign language learning must take place before the age of ten, 'in accordance with the demands of brain physiology' (Penfield and Roberts, 1969).

The findings of the evaluation are not in harmony with this view. Other things being equal, the older children tended to learn French more efficiently than the younger ones did. Pupils taught French from the age of eight did not show any substantial gains in achievement, compared with those who had been taught French from the age of eleven. By the age of 16, the only area in which the pupils taught French from the age of eight consistently showed any superiority was that of listening comprehension. Even there, the differences between the various groups of pupils, although statistically significant, were hardly of a substantial nature, being of the order of two to four points difference on a 28-item test—a fairly minimal return for the extra years spent learning French in the primary school.

Where the pupils taught French in the primary school did appear to gain was in attitude rather than in achievement. When they were successful in their efforts to learn French, they maintained a more favourable attitude towards speaking the language than did those who were not introduced to French until the age of eleven. However, this more positive attitude was not reflected in a correspondingly higher level of achievement. The most conservative interpretation which the available evidence would appear to permit is that the achievement of skill of a foreign language is primarily a function of the amount of time spent studying that language, but is also affected by the age of the learner, older learners tending to be more efficient than younger ones. Penfield's contention that the first ten years of life constitute a 'critical period' for foreign language learning remains unsupported by direct experimental evidence.

## 2. Sex differences

Throughout the period of the experiment, the girls in the experimental sample scored significantly higher than the boys on all tests measuring achievement in French. From the age of 13 onwards, the low-achieving boys in the sample tended to 'drop' French to a significantly greater extent than the low-achieving girls did, with the result that the sample of girls still learning French at the age of 16 represented a considerably wider range of ability than the corresponding sample of boys did. However, in spite of this disparity, the girls still continued to score significantly higher than the boys on each of the French tests. If the composition of the original experimental sample had been maintained until the end of the secondary stage of the experiment, there can be little doubt that sex differences in achievement in French favouring the girls would have been even more prominent.

The attitudes of the girls towards learning French were also con-

sistently more favourable than those of the boys. This finding is similar
to that reported by Nisbet and Welsh (1972) in their evaluation of the
teaching of French in schools in Aberdeen. Differences in attitude undoubtedly stem partly from the different employment expectations of
boys and girls and the extent to which foreign language learning can
be perceived as relevant to their occupational requirements. Other studies
have reported that adolescent pupils of both sexes tend to view the en-
hancement of vocational success as the primary function of education
and, in consequence, place a high value on school subjects, such as
English and Mathematics, which have an obvious relevance to their
future employment prospects. Girls and their parents are also reported
to accept the vocational value of foreign language learning, whereas
boys and their parents are reported not to do so (Schools Council, 1968;
Sumner and Warburton, 1972). Where achievement in a particular area
of the curriculum can be shown to vary systematically with the sex of the
pupil, it seems highly probable that parents are transmitting to their
children the accepted values of the wider society. The findings of both
the primary and the secondary stages of the evaluation would support
this view.

3. *Socioeconomic factors*
During the early stages of the evaluation, it rapidly became apparent
that the pattern of results emerging from the inquiry pointed to a linear
relation between the pupil's socioeconomic status and his level of achievement in French. On each occasion of testing, high mean scores tended to
coincide with high-status parental occupation and low means scores with
low-status parental occupation: this was equally true for both boys and
girls and for the pupils in each of the experimental cohorts. This
association between socioeconomic status and level of achievement
in French became even more prominent during the early years of the
secondary stage of the experiment, when the pupils in the experimental
sample were distributed unevenly among the different types of secondary school. Disparities in the socioeconomic composition of the different
types of school were closely paralleled by significant differences in the
pupils' level of achievement in French: the highest level of achievement
was reached by the grammar school pupils, the lowest by the secondary
modern and bilateral school pupils, while the comprehensive school
pupils occupied an intermediate position.

Similarly, during the early years of the secondary stage of the evaluation, there was a positive tendency for the percentage of pupils with
favourable attitudes towards learning French to increase with social
status. This tendency was clearly illustrated by significant differences in
attitude between pupils attending the different types of secondary
school: whatever the specific point at issue, favourable attitudes were

most characteristic of the grammar school pupils in the experimental sample and unfavourable attitudes of the secondary modern school pupils, particularly of the boys. The secondary modern school boys were characterized by the growing conviction that they were unlikely ever to speak French in after-school life, linked with the diminishing belief that their parents were in favour of their continued study of French.

After their second year in secondary school, the secondary modern school boys 'voted with their feet', 'dropping' French in such large numbers that, by the end of the secondary stage of the experiment, the tendency for the percentage of pupils with favourable attitudes towards learning French to increase with social status was barely discernible. By that stage, the attitudes of the pupils attending the different types of secondary school were remarkably uniform, reflecting the restricted socioeconomic range represented in the attenuated experimental sample.

### 4. *Achievement in the small schools*
The primary schools involved in the experiment had a wide geographical distribution and varied greatly in size. The experimental sample included a number of small rural schools, the smallest of which had 16 pupils on roll, the largest 160 pupils. Throughout the primary stage of the experiment, the pupils in these small rural schools consistently maintained a higher level of achievement in French than did those in the larger urban schools. This finding was an unexpected one. The classes in the small schools usually contained pupils differing widely in age and ability, and classroom conditions were often inimical to the teaching of French by audio-visual means. In spite of these apparently adverse circumstances, however, the test performance of the pupils in the small schools was consistently superior to that of the pupils in the large schools. At first it was thought possible that this superiority might be partly attributable to the small size of the classes in which the pupils attending the small schools were taught French, but this did not prove to be the case: further analysis of the data revealed no association between size of class and level of achievement in French. The possibility remains that the high level of achievement in the small schools stems partly from the heterogeneous nature of their classes. If a given class contains pupils who vary greatly in age and ability, the individual pupil is not in direct competition with others of his own age-group: the concept of a 'standard' of achievement, which a pupil of a given age 'ought' to be able to reach, is difficult for either teacher or pupil to acquire. The classroom situation in the small school tends to encourage co-operative behaviour and to lack the negative motivational characteristics of the competitive classroom in which success for a few can only be achieved at the expense of failure for many.

The differences in achievement in French between pupils in small primary schools and those in large primary schools proved to be of an extremely persistent nature. A follow-up study of the pupils who had formerly attended small primary schools showed that, even after two years in the secondary school, these pupils continued to achieve significantly higher scores on the French tests than did their classmates who had formerly attended large primary schools. There is some evidence (Dale, 1969, 1971; Sumner and Warburton, 1972) that pupils in small schools tend to form closer relationships with their teachers than pupils in large schools do and, in addition, are more responsive to evidence of 'teaching effort'. The higher level of achievement in French of the pupils in the small schools may thus be at least partly attributable to the early establishment of good teacher-pupil relationships and the subsequent development of positive attitudes towards further learning.

### 5. *Achievement in other areas of the primary school curriculum*
Since the introduction of French into the primary school curriculum inevitably reduced the time available for other school activities, the possibility arose that this reduction in time might be sufficient to exert a detrimental effect on the experimental pupils' acquisition of the basic skills of literacy and numeracy. It was equally possible that the stimulus of learning a foreign language might serve to increase the pupils' understanding of their own language and so exert a generally beneficial influence on the development of their skills. In order to investigate these possibilities, it was necessary to assess the experimental pupils' level of attainment in the 'basic' areas of the curriculum before they began to learn French and to repeat this procedure three years later, at the end of the primary stage of the experiment, comparing their test performance with that of control pupils who were not exposed to any foreign language teaching during their period in primary school. This assessment was carried out by means of a battery of general attainment tests, designed to measure both verbal and mathematical skills.

The results of the general attainment survey revealed that the introduction of French had not exerted any significant influence on achievement in other areas of the primary school curriculum. Variations in test performance were always accompanied by corresponding variations in the social composition of the groups concerned: there were no indications of a major trend in either a positive or a negative direction. It must be emphasized, of course, that these findings are specific to the tests used in the evaluation and cannot be generalized to areas of the curriculum which fall outside their range, but they are, nevertheless, in harmony with findings reported over the years by a number of other investigators.

### 6. *Attitudes and achievement in co-educational and single-sex schools*
The findings of the secondary stage of the evaluation largely support

those reported by Dale (1974) in his study of attitudes and achievement in co-educational and single-sex schools. Dale found that boys in single-sex schools tended to have a more favourable attitude towards learning French and to reach a higher level of achievement in French than did boys in co-educational schools. He also found some evidence of a reverse trend for girls, but differences in attitude and achievement were less marked for girls than they were for boys. However, Dale did note a tendency for girls in co-educational schools to show a greater reluctance to 'speak out in class'.

With regard to achievement in French, the findings of the secondary stage of the evaluation are clear-cut: both boys and girls in single-sex schools reached a higher level of achievement in French than did pupils of either sex in co-educational schools. With regard to pupils' attitudes towards learning French, the findings indicate greater differences for boys than for girls: boys in single-sex schools had markedly more favourable attitudes towards learning French than had boys in co-educational schools. It is interesting to note, however, that a significantly higher percentage of boys in co-educational than in single-sex schools enjoyed being at school. Dale had also found that boys in co-educational schools expressed greater 'happiness' in school than did those in single-sex schools.

Girls in single-sex schools showed a slight tendency to adopt a less favourable attitude towards learning French than did girls in co-educational schools, but girls in co-educational schools were significantly more fearful about speaking French in class. This latter finding is similar to Dale's evidence regarding the greater reluctance of girls in co-educational schools to 'speak out in class' and is no doubt attributable to the stresses of adolescent sexuality. There were no sex differences in pupils' attitudes towards speaking French in class during the primary stage of the experiment, even though the majority of the pupils were in co-educational schools. It was only during the secondary stage of the experiment that the girls revealed an ever-growing anxiety about speaking French in front of other members of the class.

Limitations of space prevent a fuller review of the evidence, but the interested reader may care to note that the final report also contains a wealth of teachers' and pupils' comments on various aspects of the experiment, some evidence regarding regional differences in attitude, the effect of contact with France, the influence of teachers' attitudes on pupils' achievement in French, and the impact of early success or failure on later achievement in French and attitudes towards learning the language.

## Notes

First published in *Educational Research*, Vol. 17, No. 3, 1975.

# Bilingual education: The 'immersion' model in the North American context

Andrew D. Cohen and Merrill Swain

> Although non-English-speaking minority groups have largely attributed school difficulties to an inability to learn both English *and* subject matter at the same time, recent experiences in North America suggest that it is possible to do so successfully. The purpose of this paper is to account for these apparent contradictions by examining first characteristics of 'immersion' education for the majority group child. The possibility of programs based on the successful model of immersion education for several target groups is then considered. It is suggested that the advent of successful immersion education may motivate bilingual teachers to reconsider their methodology for creating bilinguals.

Non-English-speaking minority groups have often struggled and even failed to successfully complete their education in North American schools. This has been attributed in large part to an inability to learn both English *and* subject matter at the same time. However, recent experiences in North America suggest that it is possible to learn both a second language and subject matter at the same time. The purpose of this paper is to account for these apparent contradictions by examining first the characteristics of 'immersion' education for the majority group child. The possibility of programs based on the successful model of immersion education for several target groups is then considered.

The school experience of minority groups not receiving any form of bilingual education has tended to include the following characteristics:

1. The students were grouped indiscriminately with native English speakers for all or most of the school day. Whereas heterogeneous language grouping is valuable at the right time and place, such grouping may be counterproductive at the outset. The child acquiring a second language has initial difficulties in communication and consequently may have a sense of insecurity or even one of failure in the presence of native speakers of that language. Sometimes native English speakers—even from the same ethnic background (e.g., third-generation Chicano)—may tease the non-native speaker because of his imperfect English.

2. If English as a second language (ESL) lessons were offered, the programs were of a pull-out nature, that is, the students were segregated for ESL instruction. Pulling students out for ESL classes has often resulted in stigmatizing the students as possessing a 'language handicap' or a 'cognitive deficit', labels which are damaging to student self-esteem.

3. The ESL lessons were of a formal, structured nature, generally from kindergarten or from first grade on. The value of explicit teaching of ESL syntax at such an early age has been questioned (Dulay and Burt 1974). Furthermore, such classes have often produced only mixed results in English acquisition,[1] at the expense of progress in the content subjects.

4. The teachers of both the ESL classes and of the regular academic program were unilingual English speakers. Thus even the simplest of requests from a student in his native language were misunderstood or ignored.

5. The students were not permitted to speak their native language in school. The U.S. Commission on Civil Rights (1972) has documented beyond reasonable doubt that such practices existed.

6. The teachers had low expectations for the success of the students, particularly those from certain ethnic groups. For example, two separate studies (Carter 1970; U.S. Commission on Civil Rights 1973) found that Mexican American teachers had lower expectations for the academic success of Mexican American pupils than for Anglos. It is quite possible that these low teacher expectations for minority student success academically—partly a reaction to their imperfect English—have been passed on to the students such that they performed accordingly (the self-fulfilling prophecy syndrome).

7. There was little effort to provide reading or subject matter instruction in the student's native language. The lack of instruction in and through the native language may have heightened minority student feelings of linguistic insecurity already present in a majority society where English is the dominant and more prestigious language.

8. Parental involvement in the school program was limited. The lack of parental involvement in the school program has worked to the detriment of the students. Recent experiences in bilingual education have demonstrated that such parental involvement, even from low-income homes, can be engendered.[2]

The form of school language experience described above has often been referred to as 'immersion'. The reality of the situation for the non-English speaker in English-medium schools is perhaps better reflected in the term 'submersion' than 'immersion'. Submersion reflects the sink-or-swim nature of the school experience for the minority group student. Another form of school language experience, also referred to as 'immersion', has begun to appear in many parts of Canada (Swain 1974) and in several schools in the United States. These carefully planned immersion experiences have led to considerable success in that the students involved acquire a high level of competency in a second language, while keeping up with peers (schooled in the native language) in native language development. They also make normal progress in the content subjects although these are taught primarily, or exclusively, in a second language. Their cognitive or intellectual development shows no signs of a deficit. The students develop a healthy attitude toward the second language and toward their own language and culture. Furthermore, they enjoy school and are motivated to continue studying rather than dropping out (see, for example, Lambert and Tucker 1972; Cohen 1974, 1975; Cohen and Lebach 1974; Barik and Swain 1975 (b); and Swain 1974).

What are the characteristics of immersion education that have led to such positive results? Below we have listed some of the important characteristics. L1 refers to the student's native language and L2 refers to his second language.

1. All instruction initially (i.e., in kindergarten and grade 1) is in L2.[3]
2. In second, third or fourth grade, L1 language arts (reading, writing, etc.) are introduced in L1.
3. By fifth grade, content subjects such as Geography or History may be taught in L1.
4. All kindergarten pupils are unilingual in L1. In essence, the successful program starts as a *segregated* one linguistically. This segregation eliminates the kinds of ridicule that students exert on less-proficient performers. In immersion education, all learners start off linguistically 'in the same boat'. In later grades other children with more advanced L2 abilities can be brought into the class with positive effects.[4]
5. In first grade, native speakers of L2 may be introduced into the classroom to provide native peer models of L2, to foster interethnic interaction and friendship, and, in essence, to make the program a two-way bilingual education program. For the native speakers of L2, it may be in actuality a native language program.
6. The learners are selected without special attention to social class, intelligence, personality factors (such as shyness) or any language disabilities they may have.[5]
7. The teachers are bilingual, although they only speak L2 in the classroom. They need not be native speakers of L2, but must be perfectly fluent in it and possess the appropriate adult-speaking-to-child register. (Particularly if it is intended that the students get the

message that it is desirable for everyone to be bilingual, then there are advantages to having a blond-haired blue-eyed teacher as the Spanish-speaking model in a California Spanish immersion or bilingual education program.)

8. The students rarely hear the teachers speaking L1 to each other. If L1-speaking visitors wish to address the teachers in the classroom, the teachers use students to interpret for them. At the kindergarten level—before the children can perform this task well—the teacher may step outside with the visitor. Outside the classroom, the teacher is also careful to use L2 whenever the students are around. Although this procedure may appear to be excessive, it *does* emphasize to the students that L2 is a language the teachers use—not just when they 'have to' in the classroom.

9. In kindergarten, the children are permitted to speak in L1 until they are ready to speak in L2. The teacher makes it clear that she understands L1 by responding appropriately. The teacher will often repeat the children's remarks or comment on them in L2. (For a description of teaching strategies used in response to the use of L1 by the students, see Stern and Swain 1973.)

10. In first grade and beyond, the teacher requests that only L2 be spoken in class, except during L1 medium classes (see nos. 2 and 3 above). Ideally, a teacher other than the immersion teachers teaches L1-medium classes so as to keep the languages separated by person, at least at the early grade levels.

11. The program follows the regular school curriculum. Sometimes this is difficult if L2 materials are not available in the same series that the school is using for L1 instruction. Careful curriculum planning and development are essential.

12. In the early grades, there are no structured L2 lessons (pattern practice drills, etc.) in class. This avoids the selection and sequencing of structures in a way that is inconsistent with how children actually learn language. L2 is the medium of instruction rather than a separate subject. Formal discussion of persistent problem areas in pronunciation (e.g., aspiration of voiceless stops) and grammar (e.g., gender agreement) may be introduced in later grades.

13. The teacher has the expectation that the children will learn L2 and content material through immersion.

14. When attrition occurs, new unilingual L1-speaking children may or may not be permitted to enter. Programs allowing replacements have varied in the procedures they adopt, some only allowing new entries at the kindergarten level and some at various points up through the grades.

15. The program is optional. Students participate in the program voluntarily and only with the consent of the parents.

16.In many cases the program has been initiated because of parental pressure. Support of both the community and the educational administration is essential.
17.Some programs elicit and receive parent volunteer support in the classroom.

The above 17 characteristics typify the recent wave of successful immersion programs in North America. Yet as suggested at the outset of this article, it would appear that many of these characteristics are not found in the education of minority group students. In review, they are points 2, 3, 4, 7, 9, 12, 13, 15, and 16 above.

The successful immersion program as described above has generally only included children whose L1—English—is the majority or dominant language in North America. In Canada many French immersion programs have been initiated in recent years. One has only to read through the November 1974 issue of *The Canadian Modern Language Review*, which was devoted to immersion education, to see how widespread the phenomenon of French immersion education for English Canadians actually is. Total immersion programs exist in almost all the provinces of Canada, including New Brunswick (Fredericton, Moncton), Nova Scotia (Dartmouth), Quebec (Montreal), Ontario (Toronto, Ottawa, Cochrane, Brampton), Manitoba (Winnipeg), and British Columbia (Vancouver, Victoria, Coquitlam).

Immersion education for majority group English speakers in the United States is still much more limited. There is the Spanish immersion program (K–4) at El Marino School in Culver City, California (Cohen 1975), and there is a French immersion program going into its second year at the Four Corners Elementary School in Silver Spring, Maryland. The Culver City program began in 1971 with one kindergarten group. The Silver Spring program began in 1974 on a multigraded basis, grades 1–3.

Paulston (1975b) suggests that there are not adequate socio-structural incentives for U.S. parents to want their children to become bilingual and that the success in Culver City can be attributed largely to the idealism and dedication of the parents. Tucker and d'Anglejan (1974) also see little incentive in the United States for the middle class to enroll their children in bilingual instruction. There is no doubt that the language policy at both the federal and provincial levels of Canadian government is helping to provide incentive for English-Canadian parents to enroll their children in French immersion programs (see Lambert 1974, for example). In the United States the majority group English speakers have not been the target group of federal and state bilingual programs, and this has both limited the majority group's participation[6] and generated only a moderate concern for becoming fluent in a minority language. Perhaps as English-speaking parents begin to appreciate the benefits of having their children comfortably fluent in a minority language such as Spanish and likewise comfortable interacting with native Spanish speakers in that language, the number of U.S. immersion programs for the majority-language child may increase.

But what about immersion education as described above for the minority group child? Concerning the minority non-English speaker, it may not be possible to create a comfortable English immersion environment for these students, nor may it be socially or politically feasible, given the prevailing educational climate which favors vernacular-language as the initial medium of instruction. For immersion to be successful in the case of the non-English-speaking minority student, it would be necessary to provide most or all of the positive factors lacking in what we termed submersion education above.

For the minority group child who has already learned English—perhaps as an L1—immersion education might be an appropriate model. For example, Spanish immersion education might be an appropriate model for English-speaking Chicanos, just as French immersion education might be an appropriate model for English-speaking Francophone minority groups. For those Chicanos with some or even substantial skills in Spanish already—but skills that have been passive or dormant—Noonan (1975) suggests that a concurrent approach[7] to bilingual schooling would be most appropriate.

It is important to note that total immersion for minority groups would have as the intended outcome functional literacy in both languages. What the total immersion model does is reverse the usual *order* in many bilingual education programs from L1 first/L2 second to L2 first/L1 second as far as the medium of instruction and the introduction of reading are concerned.

To date, there is little conclusive evidence that one order is inherently superior to any other (Engle 1975; Paulston 1975a; Cohen and Laosa 1975). Proponents of U.S. bilingual education may take issue with such a language reversal, but advocates of the English-first/minority-language-second approach include experienced minority educators (see, for example, Valdés-Fallis 1972). Ironically, many programs that have supposedly been providing primarily Spanish schooling in the early grades have actually been hurrying the introduction of English to the point where English reading is introduced simultaneously in English and the minority language anyway (in about 52 per cent of the U.S. Federal Title VII projects started in 1969 and 1970; see Shore 1974). Such an approach may be less effective than that of L2 reading first, provided there has been an adequate pre-reading period in L2 (Barik and Swain 1974). Furthermore, some projects that indicate in their proposals that teachers use Spanish 80 per cent of the time in kindergarten are in reality employing a model where the teacher uses *English* more than Spanish. Shultz (1975) found English used considerably more than Spanish in a first/second grade bilingual classroom. He described Spanish as a 'marked' language in that classroom. Phillips (1975) studied the language switching behavior of teachers in a bilingual project in California. During designated Spanish-medium lessons, teachers frequently switched to English, primarily for disciplinary-manipulative purposes. Phillips concluded that such behavior was inadvertently attributing more 'importance' to communication in English.

Perhaps one of the more important side-effects of immersion education is the double standard it points to: People applaud a majority group child when he can say a few words in the minority language and yet they impatiently demand more English from the minority group child. Undoubtedly, both groups merit praise for their accomplishments in L2. Furthermore, the immersion approach appears to have a beneficial message for staff involved with other models of ongoing bilingual education: 'Be consistent'. For example, the Culver City Spanish Immersion Program has had notable positive spin-off effects on bilingual programs in Southern California. After visiting or viewing videotapes of the immersion approach, teachers in bilingual programs have become more conscious about consistently using Spanish, rather than slipping into English. Some teachers have even abandoned the concurrent method in favor of A.M.-P.M. or alternate days approaches so that they use only one language at a time.[8] They have also moved away from formal second-language lessons in the early grades in favor of the immersion approach.

These consequences are promising. If nothing else, perhaps the advent of successful immersion education will simply motivate bilingual teachers to reconsider their methodology for creating bilinguals. Undoubtedly, there is a long way to go in the design, execution and evaluation of innovative language programs. But, we are certainly beyond the point where bilingual education can be viewed as a simple entity. There are numerous approaches—of which the immersion model as characterized in this paper is but one—which should all be given consideration before the selection of any particular one is made in a given context.

## Notes

First published in *TESOL Quarterly*, 10, 1, 1976.

1. Few rigorous evaluations of such ESL programs have been conducted.
2. Cohen evaluated a bilingual program (Rosemead, California, 1974–75) which attracted a number of Spanish-speaking parent volunteers

from low-income homes. A community liaison person contacted parents by phone or in person, and arranged some English instruction for volunteer aides. One kindergarten classroom had at least five regular volunteers.

3. The form of immersion education described is that which has been referred to as early total immersion. Late immersion programs, consisting of total immersion at the fourth, fifth, seventh or eighth grade level, have also been initiated. In these instances, the students had been receiving second-language instruction (French) for at least one year prior to the program. Following the one year of total immersion, at least one content subject is taught via that language in subsequent years (see, for example, Barik and Swain 1975 (a) ). Another variation in immersion programs is that of partial immersion, whereby the students receive, for example, instruction for one half of their day entirely in the second language (see Barik and Swain 1974).

4. In 1974–75, the Culver City Spanish Immersion Program included a group of six native English-speaking first graders who had already had one year of immersion in Spanish in the same classroom as the new kindergarten pupils. Apparently this approach stimulated the kindergarten pupils to produce more Spanish sooner than had been the case with those kindergarteners grouped separately in previous years (Personal Communication with Irma Wright, the K-1 teacher).

5. Research results from a French immersion program for working class students indicated initial success (see Bruck, Tucker and Jakimik 1973) although the research had to be discontinued due to severe attrition.

6. Either because of the ethnic composition of the school or because of the bilingual schooling model employed (e.g., one-way bilingual education), majority group English speakers have been excluded from a number of programs.

7. Sometimes referred to as 'simultaneous translation', in the concurrent method the teacher uses both Spanish and English interchangeably in the same lesson, alternating languages for words, sentences or sections of the lesson. This approach is intended to remind the student of the Spanish at the same time that he is hearing the content in English.

# A proposal for the use of pidgin in Papua New Guinea's education system
Robert Litteral

## Introduction

The purpose of this paper is to discuss the relationship between the complex linguistic situation in Papua New Guinea and the problem of language use in education. First some sociolinguistic terms are introduced which provide a framework for the discussion that follows. Then an analysis of the linguistic situation in PNG is presented along with a summary of past governmental policy on languages and education. Finally a sociolinguistic view of the goal of education in a multilingual society is presented together with a proposal for multilingual education in PNG.

## Some sociolinguistic terms

Those in the discipline of sociolinguistics have done significant research on the relation between language and education in multilingual societies (Fishman *et al.* 1968). The analytical concepts of this discipline can enable us to see the linguistic situation in PNG more clearly. After understanding the situation better we will be in a better position to discuss education policy as it relates to the linguistic realities of the country.

The first term that it will be helpful to consider is *communication*. Communication can be defined as an act in which individuals make themselves understood to each other by means of a common code, or language. Communication involves both encoding (sending a message) and decoding (receiving a message). The important aspects of this definition for our discussion on education are understanding and a common code, or language. Certainly understanding is a *sine qua non* of education. And for understanding in education to be adequate there must be bi-directional communication: from student to teacher as well as from teacher to student. For this to occur there must be a language that both the student and the teacher understand. For initial education this means that the teacher must speak a language known to the student. If this is not the case, effective communication may be delayed for years until the student learns enough of the teacher's language to be able to communicate with him. In the meantime, his learning has been greatly restricted or made impossible altogether. Communication is further complicated when the teacher is teaching in a language foreign to him, i.e., English for Papua New Guinean teachers.

The role of language in communication will be pursued a little further. In a monolingual society only one language is used for communication. If one is to communicate with the people of that society, he must learn that language. On the other hand, in a multilingual society there are two or more languages that may be used for communication. The language used may depend on the degree of social distance between the speakers, the topic under discussion, the geographical location, or other factors. Each language is used with specific functions in specific situations so that the more languages a person knows, the more people he will be able to communicate with.

Another term of relevance to our discussion is *communicative network*. This term can have a wide as well as a more restricted meaning. In the restricted sense it refers to the totality of all those individuals that a person or social group communicates with. In the wider sense it refers to all those individuals with whom one could potentially communicate because they both know a common language. Those who know English can communicate in an international network. Those who know Pidgin or Hiri Motu can communicate within a basically national network whereas those who know only a vernacular are restricted to a local network.

In a wider sense, a communicative network includes not only oral communication but also written communication through letters, magazines, newspapers, and books. Two aspects of this wider definition are important here. First is the potentiality of the network. If a person knows Pidgin, the number of people that he could communicate with in PNG is much greater than those with whom he would actually use Pidgin. Being a part of a larger network gives an individual greater mobility and security outside his local area. The second important aspect of this wider definition is that one can receive communication in such a network without reciprocating. In the English communicative network most of us are more on the receiving end of communication than on the sending end as far as written communication is concerned. In like manner, it is more important for most Papua New Guineans that they be recipients in the international English network than that they be initiators of communication.

The last sociolinguistic term that we should consider is *linguistic repertoire*. This is a modification of the term verbal repertoire used by Gumperz (1964). A linguistic repertoire consists of all the linguistic forms that one uses for communication. In other words, it is all the skills that one has learned that enable him to communicate as he desires. This refs to both the languages that a person controls and the modes in which he uses them, i.e., speaking, hearing, reading, and writing. The bilingual or multilingual has a larger linguistic repertoire than the monolingual. Likewise the person who can read and write has a larger repertoire than the person who can only speak a language. From the individual viewpoint, the larger one's linguistic repertoire, the more communicative advantages he possesses. From a national viewpoint, the more people there are in the nation who have a national language in their repertoire, the wider the national communicative network is spread and the faster national development can proceed.

## The linguistic situation in Papua New Guinea

Papua New Guinea is a multitribal nation with one international, two national, several regional, and numerous vernacular languages functioning as codes in multiple networks in a complex communications system. Two significant features of the PNG situation stand out. One is the existence of two pidginised languages functioning in regional-national communicative networks. They are Pidgin (Tok Pisin) based on English and Hiri Motu based on Motu. The other significant feature is the linguistic fragmentation: approximately 700 languages in a population of under three million.

English is an international language that functions as both an international language and an official national language in PNG. Its most important function is in providing a link with an international communications network. This link permits essential communication with the outside world without which the nation's political, economic, and social development would be stunted. Because of its importance as an international language, English is essential as a subject and as a means of instruction for higher education. English also permits foreigners to communicate with educated Papua New Guineans so that their skills and knowledge can be utilised without the necessity of learning another language first. Papua New Guineans use English as an international language more as receivers of communication than as senders. Consequently, a reading and understanding knowledge of English is more essential to them than a writing and speaking knowledge of it.

In addition to its function in providing an international communications link, English also plays an important part in the communicative network within the country itself. As a national language it is supraregional transcending the regional connotations of Pidgin (New Guinea) and Hiri Motu (Papua). The upper levels of government basically operate using English, a politically neutral language available equally to Papuan, New Guinean, and expatriate. It is also used between educated compatriates in non-casual social situations or situations in which there is no common vernacular or regional language.

The communicative function of Pidgin[1] is largely complementary to that of English.[2] Whereas English functions primarily as the code for international-national network within PNG, Pidgin functions mainly in national and regional networks. As a national language it serves as an intermediary between the international communicative network and the local network and provides vertical communications between the governing and the governed, the more-educated and the less-educated. It is largely through Pidgin that government departments communicate and implement their policies in the local areas. Likewise, much of the information about the outside world, science, medicine, or theology that has reached the village level has been transmitted first via Pidgin, then via the vernacular.

As a regional language Pidgin provides a code for a horizontal communications network between tribal groups. This permits wider communication on the local level without one group being cast in an inferior social position by being forced to learn the language of another group. As a regional language Pidgin enables local government councils to operate in many multi-tribal contexts.

Pidgin has functioned primarily as a verbal code. However, several factors have contributed to make its importance as a written language increase rapidly. One is the importance the government is giving to written Pidgin for its communications. A second factor contributing to its importance as a written language is the emphasis given to it as a means of basic education and adult literacy, especially by missions. A third factor is the appearance of widely-read publications such as the *Nupela Testamen* and *Wantok* newspaper.

Regional languages are vernacular languages that are used in a communicative network outside their indigenous areas but they have not attained national significance as languages. Many of these languages gained their regional status because they were used by missions as a means of evangelisation and Christian education beyond the areas where they were originally spoken. The missionaries often learned one significant local language and translated portions of the Bible into it. Then they tried to establish communications with those in surrounding language groups by teaching them that language. Examples of regional languages are Kâte (Madang and Morobe districts), Jabem (Morobe district), Kuanua (East New Britain district), Dobu (D'Entrecasteaux Islands) and Gogodala (Balimo area of the Western district). Because some of these languages had parts of the Bible translated into them and were used for basic education they were significant as written languages before Pidgin. In areas where Pidgin is used, the regional communicative role of these languages is being displaced by it.

The function of the vernaculars is restricted mainly to communicative networks within the local social groups. However, they are the most effective means of communication within the local groups. When the topic is about everyday life in the village or things significant to the local culture, there is no substitute for the vernaculars. They are used mainly in personal, informal social situations whereas Pidgin or a regional language would be used where there is a more distant social relationship. For the large number of Papua New Guineans who remain monolingual the vernacular is their only means of communication. These monolinguals present one of the greatest challenges to the education system. They need to be made bilingual so that they can communicate within a national communicative network and become more active participants in national life.

Approximately 30 per cent of the vernaculars of PNG have orthographies.[3] However, few of them have any published materials or have established literacy programmes using them. As a result very few of them can be said to be used in the written form as a significant means of communication.

Chart I shows the relationship between communicative networks and languages in PNG. The inner local networks are the most restricted in area while the international is the largest. Networks are written with CAPITALS and languages are written with capitals and small letters.

*Chart I* Communicative networks of Papua New Guinea

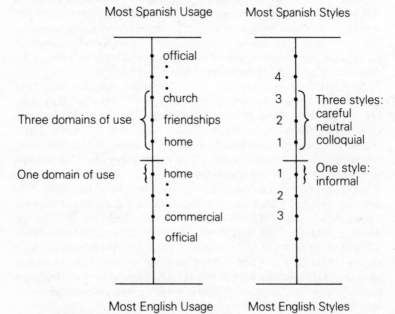

Most Spanish Usage     Most Spanish Styles

|  |  |  |
|---|---|---|
| | official | |
| | | 4 |
| Three domains of use | church | 3   Three styles: |
| | friendships | 2   careful neutral |
| | home | 1   colloquial |
| One domain of use | home | 1   One style: informal |
| | | 2 |
| | commercial | 3 |
| | official | |

Most English Usage     Most English Styles

In summary, the languages used in PNG can be classified into four groups according to their functions. They are largely complementary in function and provide the Papua New Guinean with entry into increasingly larger networks of communication starting with the local social group and extending to the international community. Each language has its unique role to play. The roles of some, e.g., Pidgin and English, are expanding whereas the roles of others such as the regional vernacular languages are contracting. However, the role of each is significant—otherwise it would cease to exist.

## Past education policy on language

Having discussed the types of languages found in PNG we shall now look at past education policy on languages and some of the results of this policy. The discussion will cover two periods: the period approximately to the end of the 1940's and the period from the 1950's to the present.

In the period to the end of the 1940's there was not a strong central education department and the missions provided most of the education for the country. Without a policy enforced by the government the missions were able to devise education systems suited to their needs. Their goals were generally to provide education for as many people as possible and to train leaders for the community and the church. These goals were achieved by providing basic education in the vernacular, a regional language, or one of the pidgin languages. There was then a transfer to English for those who were to advance in their education beyond the first few years. Many of the present leaders in PNG were educated in this type of system.

This system was fairly successful in that areas where it was used generally developed a higher rate of literacy than areas where only English has been used for education. Its success was due to several factors. One was that in most cases education was started in a language that the students understood so that it was meaningful and potentially motivating. Another factor contributing to the success of this system was that the system could be operated with little outside help and finance and without the extensive training of treachers required for an English education system.

By the 1950's the government began taking a more active role in determining education policy for the whole country. The education system was to be expanded greatly to provide education for a greater number of people with a goal of obtaining an educated elite who would be able to run and govern the country. This expanded system was to be uniform, and to meet the need of teachers more dependence was placed on expatriate teachers. Since it would be difficult to use vernaculars under these circumstances and since Pidgin was largely considered a debased language by the colonial education authorities, education in English only became the actual practice. With government assistance provided only for English education, missions using the vernaculars or

Pidgin in education were forced to drop or curtail these programmes and switch to initial education in English.

Another reason for the use of English was the view of national development held by the colonial government. National development meant becoming more like Western societies. Diverse cultures and languages hindered progress towards becoming westernised and so their development was discouraged. The best way to westernise the country was to introduce a Western education system with a Western language, English. As a result the Australian system was imported with only minor consideration given to local needs.

Considering the goals of this policy, it has been moderately successful. Many of the middle echelon of leaders in PNG were educated under this system. There is now an ample supply of educated persons to train for the manpower requirements of a developing nation.

However, this policy of education through only English has many disadvantages. The initial education experience of most PNG children is meaningless and non-creative as they are taught in a language they do not know. Together with the language, the content of the courses is also alien so that education is not relevant to the student's immediate situation. This alien English education has created social problems by emphasising Western values to the detriment of local values with the result that many students are alienated from their local societies. This system is also very expensive for providing basic education as expensive training and relatively high salaries are required to give a minority an education while the majority receive none. One can ask a troubling question about education through English only: Would not the country be more advanced today if more emphasis had been given to universal basic education in vernaculars and Pidgin rather than to basic education in English?

## A sociolinguistic view of education in a multilingual society

Using our sociolinguistic analysis of the linguistic components of a multilingual society, we shall now formulate a goal for education as it relates to languages in a multitribal developing nation, specifically, Papua New Guinea. A minimal goal of education would be to extend the linguistic repertoire of every person so that he can read and write in his mother tongue (UNESCO 1965) and that as many people as possible become participants in a national communicative network. This implies universal literacy with most people able to use a national language (Pidgin or Hiri Motu). From the viewpoint of the nation, this goal involves spreading its communicative network as extensively as possible throughout the nation. The maximal goal for languages in education would be to extend the linguistic repertoire for the largest number of students possible to include the effective use of English. This would strengthen one national communicative network as well as strengthen the link with the international network.

There are a number of implications related to attaining the above goals that need to be specified. The first is that reading and writing are the first skills to be added to the linguistic repertoire. This is best done in the vernacular. Where this is not possible, a regional or pidgin language known to the student should be used. As these literacy skills are learned only once, after they are acquired they can be readily applied to new languages that are learned. The second implication is that since effective education involves effective communication, the initial language used must be one that is understood by the students and not a foreign language. For education to be relevant to the immediate situation the language of the playground must be the language of the classroom. The third implication is that languages unknown to the students should be added to their repertoires by means of second language teaching. This applies equally for Pidgin, Hiri Motu, or English in the PNG context. And finally, widespread effective use of a national language is more essential for national communication and development than the wide-spread but ineffective use of an international language.

To summarise, one goal of the education system in a multitribal nation is to extend the national communicative network as far as possible. This is accomplished by expanding the linguistic repertoires of most or all of the nation's citizens so that they include the proficient use of a national language. This is best accomplished by first extending the repertoires to include the skills of reading and writing using a vernacular or known national language. Then the additional language or languages required to meet national needs can be added to the repertoires by means of second language teaching. The result should be more effective communication through increased literacy, a national communicative network that includes most of the nation's citizens, and an adequate number of people in an international communicative network to meet the needs of a developing nation.

## A proposal for multilingual education in Papua New Guinea

We have discussed the linguistic situation in PNG, past policies on language and education, and a sociolinguistic view of education in a multilingual society. We are now prepared to make a general proposal for the use of language in education in PNG. It is proposed that the best education programme for PNG's development is one that is multilingual and consists of four levels. These four levels are initial, primary, secondary, and tertiary. By making the system multilingual everyone would have an equal chance for a meaningful, relevant education. By including initial education in a national plan, vernacular and adult education would be given a legitimate status in education. Most of the discussion on the proposal will be on initial and primary education as secondary and tertiary education would remain in English as they are at present.

Initial education would be community oriented and would have as its main task functional literacy in the vernacular. In addition it would involve teaching a national language (Pidgin or Hiri Motu) and literacy in that national language. Initial education would be for both children and adults though conducted in separate classes.

The basic curriculum would include vernacular literacy, basic numeracy, social studies, hygiene, Pidgin or Hiri Motu as a second language (unless one of these languages is already known), and transitional literacy to Pidgin or Hiri Motu. Instruction would be in the vernacular. This would not require instructors trained in teacher's colleges if none were available but could suffice with people in the community adept at teaching and trained in literacy and basic education techniques. This curriculum would equip the child for entering primary school and provide adults with an adequate basic education while enabling them to become part of a national communicative network.

Initial education would be aimed primarily at the rural sector in order to remove some of the disadvantages the rural monolingual child has in comparison to the urban child who usually enters primary school knowing a national language. However, initial education would apply to urban areas also where there were large concentrations of vernacular speaking children or illiterate adults.

Primary education would use both vernaculars and Pidgin or Hiri Motu for the first year. In most urban areas only Pidgin or Hiri Motu would be used. English would be taught as a foreign language subject. From the second year on, the vernacular would be included as a subject in the curriculum. Most instruction would be in one of the two national languages with an increased emphasis given to English. By the fourth year English would become a medium of instruction also and by the final year almost all instruction would be in English. However, vernaculars and Pidgin or Hiri Motu would remain an essential part of the curriculum. This plan would need to be flexible and could be modified to meet local and changing situations. For example, some less-developed areas may need to continue using the vernacular for a longer period whereas in the larger urban centers instruction could begin in a national language and could probably switch to English earlier than in the rural areas.

There are two important differences between this proposed system and the one that has been in operation in PNG. First, because 'psychological and educational considerations clearly favor the learning of reading and writing in the mother tongue' (Bowers 1968: 385) the task of learning these skills is separated from that of learning a foreign language. The student would be taught to read and write a language he already knows using an alphabet that generally has a much better sound-symbol correspondence than does English. The second difference is that the student's initial education would be more meaningful in that he could communicate with his instructor and it would be more creative since he would be using a language he controlled. The temporal staging of this system would guide the student gradually from the vernacular which he knows best to English which is unknown at first. English would be used as a medium of instruction only after it had been taught as a subject for several years.

Chart II shows the roles of the different languages in the proposed education system for PNG for initial and primary education. The languages may be used either as a medium of instruction or as a subject. As a subject they are taught as a second language or in cultural and creative arts. The numbers refer to the years in primary school and the abbreviations are E(nglish), P(idgin), H(iri) M(otu), and V(ernaculars). P/HM indicates that either Pidgin or Hiri Motu is used in their respective areas.

*Chart II* Roles of languages in a proposed PNG education system

|  | Years | Language as medium | Language as subject |
|---|---|---|---|
|  | 6 | E | V, P/HM, E |
| PRIMARY | 4–5 | P/HM, E | V, P/HM, E |
|  | 2–3 | P/HM | V, E |
|  | 1 | V, P/HM | V, E |
| INITIAL |  | V | P/HM |

There are two practical problems related to introducing this system. One is providing teachers who know the vernaculars and the other is providing educational materials in the vernaculars and Pidgin and Hiri Motu. As for teachers, it is not essential that they have tertiary training to be able to teach in an initial education programme. Many of these teachers could be those who are already teaching in literacy programmes or those with primary education who could be trained as teachers. For primary schools the teacher need could be met by assigning enough teachers to their home areas to cover the needs for the first year of primary school. Capable teachers from the initial education programme could help where there were no trained teachers who knew the local vernacular.

The problem of materials could be solved by training individuals to write books in their own language or in Pidgin or Hiri Motu. Many of the larger language groups already have alphabets and reading materials. They also have educated people who could write the books needed for a vernacular program. For languages where there are no alphabets or written materials, educated members of these groups could work with linguists and educators to prepare alphabets and educational materials in their languages.[4] Preliminary efforts to produce written materials in this way have proved successful.

## Conclusions

PNG is a multilingual nation with many communicative networks based on the different local, regional, and national languages and English. Although early education took into consideration the reality of the different communicative networks, later education policy chose to ignore their relevance and use only English, an international language, in education.

One sociolinguistic view of education in a multilingual situation sees a main task of education to be that of expanding the linguistic repertoires of those in the country to include the skills of reading and writing and the use of a national language. Education requires communication so it must start with a known language with the linguistic repertoire of the student expanded first to include the skills of reading and writing. Then other languages can be added to the repertoire. In applying this principle to PNG it is suggested that initial education be in the vernacular and emphasise literacy and the introduction to a national language. Primary education would begin with both a vernacular and a national language with English being taught as a third language. Primary education would shift to the use of one of the national languages and then in the final stage to English. This system would permit the nation to approach universal basic education and at the same time provide enough people with an English education to meet its development needs.

## Notes

First published in *Kivung* Special Publication No. 1: *Tok Pisin i go we?* 1975.

1. This paper is a revision of a paper entitled 'What role should Pidgin and vernaculars have in Papua New Guinea's education policy?' read to the Pidgin Conference in Port Moresby in September 1973 and to the Eighth Waigani Seminar, also at Port Moresby, in May 1974. This paper was published under the title 'Pidgin and Education', *New Guinea* 9: 47–52 (July, 1974). I would like to thank Ger Reesink for reading and making valuable comments on an earlier

version of this paper. Research for this paper was provided in part by the Papua New Guinea Research Fund of the Summer Institute of Linguistics (PNG branch).

2. What is said here of Pidgin applies largely to Hiri Motu also but relates to a smaller part of the population.

3. A manuscript by J. Franklin entitled 'Towards a Language and Literacy Directory of Papua New Guinea' provides statistics on the languages of PNG with orthographies and published materials.

4. One proposal for such a program was given by Sarah Gudschinsky in a paper read at the Eighth Waigani Seminar in Port Moresby, May 1974 entitled 'Vernacular literacy as a base for formal education'.

# Bidialectal Education: Creole and Standard in the West Indies
Dennis R. Craig

## The definition and location of bidialectal situations

A bidialectal educational situation can be considered to exist where the natural language of children differs from the standard language aimed at by schools, but is at the same time sufficiently related to this standard language for there to be some amount of overlap at the level of vocabulary and grammar. Obviously, the amount of such overlap can be expected to vary with different situations. In some cases, the two forms of speech might possess sufficient common characteristics in phonology, lexis, and syntax for them to be mutually intelligible; at the other extreme, the relatedness of the two might be insufficient to produce mutual intelligibility in continuous speech, though some commonality of lexis might still be evident to speakers. In the latter case, a bidialectal situation would approach very closely to a genuinely 'bilingual' one.

Many of the West Indian countries where creole languages are spoken do not possess educational situations that may be regarded as bidialectal in the sense just stated since, in some of these countries, the Creole language bears no relationship to the standard language used or aimed at in schools. The latter is the case, for example in different places within the officially Dutch West Indian territories where Papiamentu (which is Spanish/Portuguese-based), Sranan (which is English-based) or Saramaccan (which is also English-based) are some of the Creole languages. In the latter territories, the educational situation, in the context of Creole language, has to be regarded as clearly bilingual.

Somewhat different from, though still relatively close to situations like the latter are those existing in West Indian countries such as Haiti and Martinique. In those countries, the base of the Creole is the same language that is accepted as the official standard and language of education: French. At the lexical level therefore there is a considerable relationship between Creole and Standard. Despite this, however, the phonological, morphological, and syntactic differences between the two forms of speech are wide enough to render them mutually unintelligible. There is some evidence, as discussed in Valdman (1969) for example, that in urban areas particularly, the occurrence of diglossia and the development of forms of speech intermediate between Creole and Standard might in time produce a situation equivalent to a bidialectal one; but at the present time, in the absence of large proportions of speakers whose habitual speech bridges the structural gap between Creole and Standard, the officially French-speaking West Indian countries, have to be regarded, like the Dutch countries, as giving rise to educational situations that are more bilingual than bidialectal.

In the officially English-speaking territories of the West Indies, however, where English-based Creoles either existed at some time in the past or still exist, processes of diglossia and the development of intermediate language varieties between Creole and Standard have proceeded much further than they have in the case of Haiti and Martinique just mentioned. In some of these officially English-speaking territories, as in the case of Trinidad and St. Vincent, for example, the original and extreme form of an English-based Creole has all but disappeared, and what remains are systems of linguistic items intermediate between Creole and Standard. DeCamp (1971) referred to such systems as the post-Creole speech continuum. The presence of this continuum led Stewart (1962) to suggest that the Creoles of Jamaica, Guyana, Belize and the non-standard speech of the other officially English-speaking West Indian territories may best be treated as regional varieties or dialects of English.

It can thus be seen that there is some justification for regarding the officially English-speaking West Indian countries as giving rise to bidialectal educational situations in a way in which the other countries do not; but it has to be noted that this difference between the officially English-speaking countries and countries like Haiti, for example, is one of degree rather than of kind. What has happened is that sociolinguistic history has caused countries like Jamaica and Guyana (both officially English-speaking) to have larger proportions of their populations speaking a language intermediate between Creole and Standard than Haiti has; but both of the former countries, however, still have considerable proportions of speakers whose habitual English-based Creole is just as incomprehensible to English ears as Haiti's French-based Creole is to French ears; and most of the remaining officially English-speaking countries, although they have no discrete Creoles like those of Jamaica or Guyana, possess just as complex a range of continuum variation.

The officially English-speaking countries that give rise to bidialectal educational situations involving Creole and Standard language in the way so far explained have a total population of about five million speakers and are as follows: the Caribbean mainland territories of Guyana and Belize, together with the islands of Jamaica, Trinidad and Tobago, Grenada, Barbados, St. Vincent, St. Lucia, Dominica, Montserrat, St. Kitts, Nevis, Anguilla, Antigua, The Virgin Islands, The Cayman

Islands, The Turks and Caicos Islands, and the Bahamas. Some of the mentioned islands, notably St. Lucia, Dominica, and Grenada have significant proportions of their populations who speak a French Creole exclusively or both a French and an English Creole.

In these countries, the monolingual speakers of Creole or Creole-influenced language, as will be further discussed subsequently, can be estimated to form about 70 per cent to 80 per cent of the total speakers. These Creole or Creole-influenced monolinguals would have a language that ranges from a basilect Creole to a mesolectal language intermediate between Creole and English. A social-class classification would put most of them within the levels of lower-working, working and lower-middle class. The language-education problem that they pose is experienced mainly in the public system of primary, all-age, and post-primary schools for which the governments of the respective countries are responsible.

## The neglect and rediscovery of Creole

One characteristic of educational policy in the countries mentioned is that, traditionally, Creole or Creole-influenced language has been treated in schools as if it did not exist, or as if it should be eradicated if it existed. One reason for the development of this attitude to Creole is to be found in the relationship, already mentioned, between Creole and Standard at the lexical level; because of this relationship, it was easy for educational planners in the past to feel that Creole was merely a debased form of the standard language, and that this debasement could be corrected merely by a sustained exercise of carefulness on the part of the learner. The fact that this attitude is caused by the apparent lexical relationship between Creole and Standard seems proved by the more favourable attitude towards Creole found in territories where there is no relationship between Creole and Standard. The favourable attitude towards Creole in the officially Dutch-speaking territories, is attested to for example in Stewart (1962: 53), as compared with both the officially French and English-speaking territories where the attitude tends to be the opposite.

Another reason for the traditional educational attitude of neglecting Creole or Creole-influenced language or attempting to eradicate it is to be found in historical factors. Stewart (1967) comments on some of these historical factors and shows that, by the seventeenth century, all the present-day distinctive features of Creole and Creole-influenced English had already developed in the Western hemisphere and that in the officially English-speaking territories especially, it was easy for the whites to consider Creole English to be 'broken' or 'corrupt' English and evidence of the supposed mental limitations of the black slave population. The historian Edward Long, for example, writing of Jamaica in

1774 pointed out that 'the language of the Creoles is bad English larded with the Guinea dialect', and this was obviously the pervading opinion, relevant to all the West Indian territories, which was handed down over the next two centuries. After the abolition of slavery in the 1830's the British Government made some attempt over the next century to develop public systems of education within the territories of the region, and early educational reports on the West Indies, like the 1938 Latrobe Reports for example, occasionally mention the role of English as a unifying force between the diverse language groups: aboriginals and Africans, French, Spanish, and Dutch speakers; and after the middle of the century Chinese, Indians, and other speakers who had come into the region. But Creole or Creole-influenced language as such was never regarded as one of the foreign languages to be reckoned with, except that in territories like St. Lucia and Dominica, where speakers of French Creole were to be found, the reports of the educational officials sometimes showed concern over the French Creole problem.

It was not until the 1940's at the earliest that the problem of English in what was essentially a bidialectal educational situation (although at that time it still was not recognized as such) began to receive some attention. An example of such attention, which comes from Jamaica, but which is relevant to all the similar West Indian territories is to be seen in the report of the educational commission under L.L. Kandel (1946) which endorsed the viewpoint expressed by the Norwood Committee (1943) in Britain that there was need for alarm over the deficiencies of school-leavers' English. The Kandel report then pointed out that the need for alarm was even greater in Jamaica as there was a much more serious problem than that being experienced in Britain. Even at this relatively late period, however, the dominant attitude of schools towards Creole or Creole-influenced language continued to tend either towards ignoring it or towards eradicating it by forbidding children to speak it within the hearing of teachers; the child was invariably made to understand that his speech in school had to be 'good' English.

This continued denial in the first half of the present century of the linguistic existence of the majority of West Indian speakers in the officially English-speaking territories occurred despite the fact that by the end of the 1920's, apart from general works on Creole like those of Van Name (1870), Schuchardt (1882–91), and the bibliography of Gaidoz (1881), there had been several studies and language collections, some going back to the previous century, and referring specifically to the officially English-speaking territories. These works are exampled in the writings of Russell (1868) relative to Jamaica; Bonkhurst (1888), Cruickshank (1916), Scoles (1885), and Van Sertima (1897, 1905) relative to Guyana; Cruickshank (1911) relative to Barbados, and Innis

(1910, 1933) and Thomas (1869) relative to Trinidad. Conditions in the remaining territories would have been closely similar to those represented in these works.

In the relevant countries, however, independent of and despite the educational system, there were factors at work that at the present time can be seen as contributing to a gradually more favourable attitude towards Creole and Creole-influenced speech. Such speech had long become codified in folk tales and vernacular humor, song and drama. In many territories, the daily and weekly newspapers (the only frequent reading for a majority of the literate population) had found it attractive, for many years, to present, written 'in the dialect' (i.e., in Creole or near-Creole language) regular humorous and satirical commentaries on daily local life. Within contemporary memory some examples of the latter, under their newspaper column-titles or writers' pseudonyms are Quow, Uncle Stapie (Guyana), Macaw, Boysie (Trinidad), Quashie (Jamaica), Lizzie and Joe (Barbados, Montserrat), Annie and Josephine (Grenada), and Chatty and Papsy (Nevis). This popular interest in the vernacular culminated in the late 1940's, at the same time as the first expressions of educational alarm (referred to above) over English language proficiency, in a growing number of Creole languages collections and commentaries like, for example, some of Louise Bennett's publications in Jamaica (e.g., Bennett, 1942, 1943, 1950), Frank Collymore's serialisations of 'Words and phrases of Barbadian dialect' (e.g., Collymore 1952), and in Guyana a series of articles on aspects of Creole language by D. A. Westmaas and Richard Allsopp, respectively, in the journal *Kyk-Over-All* between 1948 and 1953.

This growth of popular literary interest in Creole might have had, by itself, some influence on attitudes in education, but in any case it was followed closely by another, probably inevitable development which is the one that really made some educational change imperative. This development referred to is the beginning of modern grammatical studies of Creoles in the officially English-speaking territories.

Some of the first results of such studies are to be seen in Taylor (1945, 1952, 1955, 1961, 1963, 1968), LePage (1952, 1955, 1957; ed., 1959), Bailey (1953, 1962, 1966), Allsopp (1958a and b, 1962), LePage and DeCamp (1960), Cassidy (1961), Alleyne (1961, 1963), and Cassidy and LePage (1967). This body of work includes descriptions of the phonology, lexis and grammar of Dominican and Jamaican Creoles, some aspects of the morphology and syntax of Guyanese Creole, consideration of some sociolinguistic factors in relation to St. Lucia and Jamaica, some early thoughts on how language studies in the West Indies might be further promoted, and some general descriptive comments on Caribbean Creoles not yet substantially dealt with. In this work, Jamaican Creole gets the most comprehensive treatment in terms of its syntax, lexicology, and segmental phonology. Obviously, most of the relevant West Indian territories that have been earlier listed here, received no attention in these studies and, apart from the work on Jamaica, no one country received any wide-ranging study. Nevertheless, the work cited here was very significant for the West Indian region as a whole because firstly it created a scientific framework within which interested persons involved with language in the region could observe linguistic facts in the territories to which the work referred; secondly, it permitted such persons to make comparisons, within this scientific framework, between linguistic facts as described in this work and facts as known, merely through informal experience, relevant to territories not yet formally studied. As a result of this work, and the possibility just mentioned to which it gave rise, it became possible for educators within the region to view West Indian language-education problems in a manner comparable to how problems of bilingualism or multilingualism might be viewed in contemporary times; although the existence of this possibility does not necessarily imply its actual realization or achievement.

Work such as the preceding has continued up to the present, with some of the more recent additions to it taking on increasingly theoretical forms: Bailey (1971), for example, suggested that distinctions might be drawn between basilectal and mesolectal forms of Creole by measuring the quantity and complexity of the transformational rules that separated the respective forms from both Standard English and basilect Creole; and DeCamp (1971) showed that linguistic forms in the continuum between Creole and Standard were not just an ordered collection among which speakers shifted in response to social situations, but that the forms of the continuum were implicationally linked, so that the presence of specific forms rendered certain others obligatory. Subsequently, following the work of Labov (e.g., 1971) and C. J. Bailey (e.g., 1969, 1970) in Hawaii, Bickerton (1971, 1971a, 1972, 1972a, 1973) pursued further implications of DeCamp's thesis and suggested that in the West Indian Creole continuum, as presumably also universally in all speech communities, variation within and between idiolects existed as sets of implicationally linked characteristics that could not be described by static grammatical models. The developments apparent in these studies contribute to grammatical theory generally as well as to knowledge of Creole language situations of the bidialectal or multidialectal type; the implications of these developments for bidialectal education will be considered subsequently.

Concurrently with these developments, and additional to work appearing in Hymes (ed., 1971), there have been several studies within the West Indies, some of them unpublished, that describe specific aspects of English-based Creole or mesolectal language and thereby contribute further to the kind of information that the educator needs for work in relevant situations; among the latter studies are the following: Carrington (1967, 1969), Allsopp (1965), Reisman (1961, 1965), Hughes (1966), Lawton, D. L. (1963, 1964, 1971); Solomon (1966), Christie (1969), Warner (1967), and Winford (1972); in addition, a collection of papers currently in preparation for publication (Craig, ed., forthcoming) includes some relevant additional writing of Berry, Cassidy, Spears, Edwards, Allsopp, and Solomon (see references) that is of a descriptive or theoretical linguistic kind, as well as some other work of educational relevance that will be mentioned subsequently. The descriptive and theoretical writings just cited add the following information to that provided by the earliest set of Creole language studies already mentioned: additional information on the lexis and phonology of Jamaican, Cayman, Barbadian, and Guyanese creoles (Cassidy, Lawton, Berry, Allsopp, Spears); information on the distribution and structure of French creole in St. Lucia and Dominica (Carrington, Christie); tentative and very general statements on the linguistic and sociolinguistic situation in Belize (Allsopp 1965), Antigua (Reisman), and Grenada (Hughes); information on the syntactic structure of Creole and post-Creole language and the sociolinguistic situation in Trinidad (Warner, Winford, Solomon), and Guyana (Edwards). This work is not even in quality, and there is no comprehensive survey of the region as a whole, but it is sufficient to show the distribution of Creole and mesolectal language, the general nature of the language system in most territories, and some more detailed treatment of one or two situations sufficient to permit a degree of extrapolation to other situations where adequate work has not yet been done.

## The use of the vernacular in education

Growth of knowledge about Creole language situations, such as that outlined above for the West Indian Creole-English situation, coincided with the growth of new nations in the Third World and an international recognition of the need for these new nations to have educational systems that would be fully relevant in each case to the specific national identity, environment, and goals; part of this recognition implied the need for each child to receive at least his earliest education in the language that was most natural to him: his mother tongue. In the light of this recognition, the fiction, maintained for over a century, that Standard English was the mother tongue of West Indian Creole-speaking or Creole-influenced children could no longer be maintained. One of the first concrete reactions to this recognition was the proposal that the Creole or mesolectal language of children, in officially English-speaking West Indian territories should be used as the language of primary, even if for no other, education. An early example of such a suggestion is to be seen in the UNESCO (1953) monograph on the use of vernacular languages in education, where it was suggested that some of the officially English-speaking territories in the West Indies were among the areas of the world where creole languages might well be used in education. Up to the present, however, more than two decades after this suggestion, none of these territories has attempted to implement it.

The chief reason why the Creole or Creole-influenced language of West Indian children has not been used in education lies in deep-seated community attitudes to Creole. The old official attitude of ignoring its existence or advocating its eradication has already been mentioned. In the community at large, Creole language has generally been identified historically with slavery, and in more recent times with very low social status and lack of education. This feeling about creole exists even in the minds of its speakers, most of whom would attempt, if they can, to modify their speech in the direction of Standard English in the presence of an English speaker, and would feel insulated if a stranger who is obviously non-Creole-speaking attempts to converse with them in Creole. In this context, even the most Creole-speaking of parents tend to regard Standard English as the language of social mobility, and would tend to think that anyone who suggests the use of Creole or Creole-influenced language in education is advocating the socio-economic repression of the masses. This attitude of Creole and Creole-influenced speakers towards English has been mentioned in Bailey (1964) with reference to Jamaica, but it is an attitude that is to be found in all the officially English-speaking West Indian countries. It is not any way unique to these countries however, as it is very similar to that attitude of non-Standard speakers in the U.S.A. which Wolfram (1970: 29) describes, and which has been responsible for the non-acceptance of dialect readers in some 'black' English communities. Obviously, it is an attitude that can be expected in any situation which is essentially bidialectal in its nature, although there are some genuinely bilingual situations, like the Spanish/English situation in Puerto Rico and the Indian-languages/Spanish situation in Central America, where similar attitudes seem to be present.

In effect it is an attitude that represents a type of socio-psychological dualism in which the low-status language is stubbornly preserved by its speakers as a part of their identity and cultural integrity, but at the same time these very speakers resist any measures which, by extending the societal role of their own low-status language, might impede their children's acquisition of the accepted high-status language. At the base of the attitude is probably the very pragmatic realization that it is unlikely that the high-status language could ever be completely replaced, and that even if it is, its status in the wider world would still make it a very desirable acquisition.

Another very important reason why Creole or Creole-influenced language has not been used in education within officially English-speaking West Indian territories is to be found in the technical difficulties that would be involved. One such difficulty would be that of the standardization of the phonology and grammar of the non-Standard language and the choice of an orthography for it. It is possible, in the matter of phonology and orthography, that if the language of a territory is of a mesolectal kind without the existence of a basilect Creole, then solutions to the problem might be similar to those suggested in Stewart (1969) and Fasold (1969) for American black dialects where conventional English orthography is retained. In the latter cases, English orthography represents the underlying realities of the non-Standard 'dialects' to such an extent that it is easily possible to use the same orthography and incidentally benefit from having a single writing system for all speakers. However, in cases like those of Jamaica and Guyana, where there are basilect Creoles departing farther from English than mesolectal language does, the use of an English orthography might be somewhat more problematical, especially when relationships between phonology and grammar are taken into consideration, although it would be possible for teachers to use English spellings and permit a wide range of variant speech renditions as has been suggested in DeCamp (1972). In the matter of standardizing Creole or Creole-influenced grammar, there are still larger problems, however, occasioned by the range of continuum variation to which persons have become accustomed, and the difficulty of deciding on the point of the continuum at which the standard grammar will be selected. The selection of basilect Creole would exclude most mesolectal speakers, and the selection of a mesolect would not solve the most serious societal problems of Creole speakers; an idea of the extent of the problem can easily be gauged by an examination of the wide variation that is possible in the Creole and Creole-influenced versions of Standard English sentences discussed in Craig (1971a: 374).

Assuming, however, that the linguistic, technical problems just mentioned can be overcome, there are problems of implementation and costs of action programmes of the kind discussed in Bull (1955), that would by themselves tend to induce governments to avoid the use of Creole or Creole-influenced language in education. First of all, in the West Indian territories relevant here, it would be necessary for a relatively large percentage (probably about 50 per cent) of the professional people working in education to be taught the vernacular that is to be used. Textbooks and other educational materials would then need to be prepared in the vernacular in a situation where persons with the requisite skills would even in normal circumstances be very scarce. Even if the use of the vernacular is confined to primary education, with the prestige language being introduced subsequently as a second language and used later as the language of instruction in secondary school, the financial cost, to a newly developing territory, of the measures just mentioned would be enormous and, except in the absence of a viable and nationally respectable alternative, quite likely prohibitive. Apart from all this, a country with the bidialectal type of Creole-language situation that is relevant here would need to consider seriously whether the use of the low-prestige language in the public system of schools and at a low level of education might not accentuate social divisions within the society rather than remove them, especially in a context where most children already attend primary schools and acquire some amount at least of mesolectal language, and where there is a selective system of secondary schools geared to the production of an educated elite. It is obvious that these considerations would not apply with equal force in all territories with bidialectal situations, and might not apply at all even in those Creole-speaking countries which approach the bidialectal type very closely (like Haiti, for example, where the relatively small proportion of children completing primary education and the 90 per cent use of Creole within the society render such considerations inoperative). In the officially English-speaking West Indian territories, however, these considerations do apply and, together with what has already been said above about community attitudes, explain why governments have never seriously considered using the vernacular in education.

## Teaching the Standard by correction

When the educational use of Creole or Creole-influenced language is ruled out in a bidialectal situation such as the West Indian one, the most obvious alternative is for schools to employ a teaching strategy based on getting children to correct those characteristics of their own speech that differ from the language aimed at by schools. These are the characteristics which, in traditional school terminology would be regard-ed as resulting in language 'errors' or 'mistakes', and which the applied linguist would regard as contrasts between the native and target languages. The problem with this strategy of correction is that it leaves the learners completely at the mercy of the ad hoc and occasional inter-vention of the teacher, puts them in the position where they can learn only after they have made what they often come to regard as embarass-ing mistakes, and invariably makes them so aware of the possibility of mistakes that they become afraid and often incapable of expressing themselves in formal situations. In the older examples of the appli-cation of this strategy, some teaching of traditional English grammar would have formed a part of the classroom procedures, and in some ways this grammatical teaching was not altogether worthless, when carried out by intelligent teachers, as it gave the non-Standard speakers some logical framework within which they could systematize the 'corrections' that they learned, and within which they could see the Standard language as a whole; there is no denying, however, that in many, probably a majority of cases, learners acquired merely a rote knowledge of one or two inaccurate grammatical rules which in no way affected their ability to express themselves in formal situations.

With the gradual popularization of modern linguistics and the demonstration by teachers and scholars like C. C. Fries (e.g., 1940, 1952) that traditional grammatical rules often misrepresented English as it is actually spoken, and also with a better understanding, through child-development studies (see, e.g., Carroll, 1969), of how language is learned, the teaching of 'grammar' has declined in schools. However, present day survivals of the strategy of language-teaching by correction, with or without traditional grammar, can still be found in bidialectal classroom situations in the West Indies as well as elsewhere: in the U.S.A., for example, not so long ago, Crow *et al.* (1966: 124) showed the survival of this strategy when they stated:

> Some of the causes of speech problems of the socially disadvantaged children are similar to those of listening. For example, a deficiency in auditory discrimination may result from the failure of parents to correct mistakes in spoken language, owing either to lack of knowledge of correct speech or to sheer indifference. Faulty auditory discrimination can be illustrated by the child's confusing the 'th' sound with the 'f' sound in a word such as 'Mother' for which he may say 'Muffer'.
>
> Correct speech is learned through imitation in the home and elsewhere. Many parents of socially disadvantaged children do not realize that their speech is incorrect and that their children's poor speech patterns are formed in the home. In school, corrective help is given, but the time is too short for much progress, and when the child returns home, he is confronted again with the inferior speech.

Like all advocates of a teaching-by-correction strategy, the writers of this extract make no use of the concept that low-social-status speech is, for all practical purposes, a dialect with its own distinctive rules of phonology and grammar and that the problem of learning standard speech is that of learning a new dialect. However, the importance of the home environment is well recognized, and it is precisely because of this environment that the strategy of teaching by correction inevitably fails, since that strategy has within it no way of systematically teaching sets of new language structure in such a way that they have a reasonable chance of persisting parallel to the language of the home.

In the West Indies, first in Jamaica and from there to other territories, a movement away from the correction strategy began in the late 1950's.

It is well illustrated in this extract from Walters (1958), which it will be noted appeared fully eight years before Crow (*et al.*) already cited.

> The general attitude to this problem has been that Jamaican Creole structure is wrong and must be corrected. Training College syllabuses in English have begun the first and second year courses with 'Correction of common errors in speech', and 'A more formal application of the rules of grammar to common errors in English in Jamaica', while the Code For Elementary Schools does say: 'Spontaneity should not be discouraged by correction in the early stages' (Code of Regulations of the Education Department, 1938). A Training College principal recently announced, in a public discussion—'There is only one answer to the question of dialect—that is, it has no place whatever in our elementary schools', and a similar statement was circulated, in another territory, by the Inspector of Schools to all teachers. This attitude, that local speech is wrong and must not be allowed, held so firmly by educators and implemented in schools, has certainly had little effect on local speech, save to inhibit the spontaneous speech and writing in schools and produce a stilted and artificial style in the 'educated'.
>
> A gradual change of attitude is being noted, however, as above when teachers are warned not to begin corrections too early and stifle spontaneity. A further step takes us away from the concept of 'correcting wrong speech', towards learning a new way of saying things. A recently distributed directive on 'The Curriculum Of Primary And Post Primary Schools' states: 'The Jamaican vernacular is not the great obstacle to learning English it is generally supposed to be. It is a bridge to be used by the teacher to get to the use of the English language. There might well be the tacit understanding in our schools that English is the language spoken and written, but the Jamaican vernacular is understood.' A revised syllabus for Jamaican Primary Schools suggests—'Interest must be aroused in speaking correct English as soon as possible, not as a matter of correcting what is wrong, but as acquiring new skill.'

Enlightened as this change obviously was on the question of the 'correction' strategy, it did not however, and probably could not at that point in time, have within it an understanding of all the linguistic realities that would have made a systematic approach to the language and reading problem fully possible. The approach then advocated was an 'experience', approach which would get children to hear 'new ways of saying things', induce them to say things in these new ways, and get them to read and write the new language. What was lacking in this approach was an orderly structure for the children's acquisition and production of the new language; by it, children came into contact with the new language fortuitously and at odd moments, just as they would in a completely first-language, or mother-tongue, educational situation, and there were no procedures within the advocated approach whereby the patterns and structures of the new language could be learned in such a way as not to be suppressed by the dominant home-language environment.

## Teaching the standard language as a second dialect

As has been pointed out already, the growth of Creole language studies in the West Indies after 1950 brought forcibly to people's attention the fact that Standard English, if not actually a foreign language, was clearly in the nature of a second dialect to most West Indians. One result of this awareness can be seen in the appearance in the West Indies of a number of writings which looked in various ways at the language-education problem and made suggestions about alleviating it. Including Walters (1958) already cited, the earliest of these language-educational studies were concerned with documenting what happened when Creole-influenced individuals at different levels of education attempted to receive and produce English, both in speech and writing. A statement of some of these is to be found in the Faculty of Education (1965) Report of the conference on linguistics, language teaching and the teaching of English, convened at the University of the West Indies. Some of these studies, like those of Craig (1964) and Grant (1964), were not system descriptive in a linguistic sense, but were concerned with error analyses, occurrence frequencies of various types of linguistic items and the comparisons that could be made, in these terms, between different social-class types and age-groups of learners. Studies of this kind seem useful for the planning of language-education in the region for several reasons. Firstly, in the context of the Creole/Standard continuum, actual frequency distributions of specific linguistic items give a more practical picture of the competence of speakers than static system-description can alone and by itself; secondly, there is the pragmatic educational necessity for teachers to be able to compare different types of learners and to perceive quantitative as well as qualitative language differences where these occur; and thirdly, in the absence of language development and performance data relevant to the West Indies, of the kind that can be found relevant to other societies, well evaluated and summarized in sources like Carroll (1960) and Denis Lawton (1968), for example, studies of this kind seem well justified in the circumstances of the West Indies.

Additional to the preceding, there began to appear at this time (in the early 1960's) several analyses of the classroom implications of Creole language-studies, indications of the quasi-foreign language nature of the language situation, and general suggestions for necessary teaching programs in West Indian schools. Similar work has continued to appear up to the present and the relevant publications are Figueroa (1962, 1972), Gray (1963), Bailey (1963), Cuffie (1964), Jones (1966), and Carrington (1968, 1970). Some very recent additions to work of this kind are to be seen in Carrington (1971), Allsopp (1972), Edwards (1972), and Solomon (1972) where the language-teaching implications of specific phonological, lexical and syntactic characteristics of West Indian Creole or continuum language are examined. This most recent work differs from what preceded it by having its language-teaching considerations limited in each case to some single, specific aspect of linguistic form: implicational relationships in the continuum, prosodic features, morpho-syntactic variation in items like 'have' and 'be', and so on. It supplements the thesis of the foreign-language or quasi-foreign language nature of the language situation by a relatively in-depth analysis of the related linguistic form in each case, and what it would mean to teach an area of the Standard language that corresponds to or is related to that aspect of linguistic form. The problems of the total content of the language program for children, its classroom implementation, and wider educational issues such as valid goals and the strategies for achieving these are not objects of immediate concern in this work.

By the middle of the 1960's, the resemblance between the Creole language situations in the officially English-speaking West Indies and the non-Standard English problems in the United States of America had been perceived. Stewart, who in 1964 had participated in the West Indian conference responsible for the Faculty of Education (1965) Report already cited, edited in the same year the influential 'Non-Standard Speech and the Teaching of English'. In the latter, the Jamaican language situation received a significant treatment, and the point is strongly made that foreign language teaching methods seem necessary in the quasi-foreign language situations of Creole and other non-Standard speakers in officially English-speaking countries, including the United States of America. Appearing in the same year as the preceding, and of a similar import, was the publication *Social Dialects and Language Learning* (Shuy, ed., 1966) in which also appeared a contribution on the Jamaican situation (Bailey 1964).

It has already been shown in section three of this article that the community attitudes responsible for the failure of dialect readers in some parts of the United States of America are similar to the West Indian attitudes that made it impracticable for the vernacular to be used as the language of instruction in schools; and in the studies just mentioned the recognition of the similarity of the second-dialect characteristics of the language situations in the U.S.A. and the West Indies has also been cited. This basic similarity between the two situations means that much of the work done in any one is likely to have some relevance for the other. In this respect, work such as that of Labov (1964; *et al.* 1965, 1966, 1969), Shuy (*et al.* 1967), Wolfram (1969), and Fasold and Shuy (eds., 1970), which provides structural descriptions of language variation and of non-Standard speech in the U.S.A., and which suggests ways in which such descriptions need to be taken into account in school programs, gives an example of the kinds of factors that also apply in the West Indies; similarly, work on the teaching of reading in the context of non-Standard speech, like that of Baratz and Shuy (1969) have a corresponding import. In some instances, researches have been done expressly with both the American and West Indian situations in mind; this is the case, for example, in Shuy (1972) which discusses strategies for implementing sociolinguistic principles in schools and DeCamp (1972) which examines problems and possibilities in the use of Standard English books by Creole-speaking children.

In all of the work referred to in the present section of this article, as pointed out already, mention is made of the possibilities of using foreign-language teaching methods in the essentially bidialectal educational situations of the United States of America and the West Indies. In some cases, as in Stewart (1964), mention is also made of the fact that, to the relevant learners, Standard English is neither a native nor a foreign language. For a long time after the first proposals for the use of foreign-language teaching methods in the relevant situations, however, there were no clear statements of the adaptations that inevitably became necessary because the native language of the learner overlapped considerably with the target, and because also, particularly in the West Indian situation, most non-Standard speakers were capable of varying their performance along a stretch of the Creole/Standard continuum. The methods that were advocated varied from a formal English-as-a-second-language programme, with a strictly ordered set of procedures based on contrasts between English and the basilect, to the almost informal and fortuitous counselling described by Brooks (1964):

> . . . A trained volunteer now works with Carlos, often in this way. The boy picks up an interesting picture.
> 'I hab a tree, with leebs,' says Carlos.
> 'Yes, you *have* a tree, with *leaves*,' replies the teacher. 'Say *have—leaves*.'
> '*Have—leaves*,' replies Carlos, learning the /v/ sound in English. Because this boy already knows some English, he needs mainly to have someone take an interest in him to draw out what he knows, to involve him in the life around him, to help him share with others—

orally and in writing—his valuable contributions, and *to correct some speech difficulties*.

The differences in the emphasis and focus of the various suggested applications of foreign-language teaching procedures are such that it would obviously be beneficial to have some clear theory of the relationship between foreign language teaching and what is essentially second dialect teaching. In the West Indies, the first teaching experiment aiming at some formalization of the new methodology begain in Jamaica in 1965 and has been described in Craig (1969). Some theoretical principles underlying the methodology itself have been discussed in Craig (1966a and b, 1967, 1971a). In these studies it is shown that in a bidialectal situation of the kind relevant here, the learning of the new dialect proceeds as a mixing of newly learned linguistic features with older ones not yet replaced, so that in the case of the non-Standard speaker, the growing Standard repertoire that is being learned never appears separate and distinct until after prolonged learning when the acquisition of the Standard is quite complete. At each intermediate point of learning, the Standard tends to be produced mixed with survivals of the original non-Standard dialect. This does not mean that the speaker necessarily loses his original Creole or dialect, although this could happen with prolonged immersion into the cultural environment of the (high-prestige) Standard speech; but what happens is that the speaker acquires the ability to shift his speech closer to the Standard-language end of the Creole/Standard or dialect continuum; in other words, learning of the standard proceeds as a movement along this continuum.

In some cases during the acquisition of the Standard, a continuum can actually be seen in creation where none existed before, or rather, where no continuum items of a particular kind existed before. This was noticed, for example, in some of the children (7–8 years old) considered in the teaching experiment and related studies last referred to. Before these children became subjects of a modified second-language teaching program, they did not possess 'is' and 'has', and for the latter mentioned they used only the uninflected form of the verb 'have'. After a period of learning 'is' both as a copula and as AUX + 'ing'-form, and before they learned to use 'has', they regularly produced 'is have' wherever 'has' would have been appropriate. This habit passed away naturally, and without any special corrective, after the children learned to use 'has'.

Linked to the tendency of the children here being considered to mix newly acquired forms with their original language, to proceed in this way along the dialect or Creole/Standard continuum, and even to create a new continuum, was the ability to comprehend much more Standard language than they could produce. Wolfram (1970: 17) points out that such ability seems consistent with the viewpoint of Labov and Cohen

(1967) that the main differences between non-Standard and Standard language appear to be on the surface rather than on the underlying levels of language; Labov himself (1969: 24) refers to such ability as having been significantly proved by repetition tests given to subjects in some of his earlier researches; and Baratz (1969) found similarly through subsequent tests of the same kind in her own work. What is most significant in the Labov and Baratz evidence is that the non-Standard speakers, while being unable themselves to produce the Standard language, were able to restructure that language in non-Standard equivalents, showing indeed that it was the underlying structure that must have been comprehended.

These indications in the children in the West Indian experiment confirmed a basic principle that directed the teaching methodology. This principle was that, as far as the learner was concerned, the continuum between Creole and Standard consisted of four hierarchical strata of linguistic structures as follows: A, those common to both Standard and non-Standard speech and therefore within the production repertoire of the learner; B, those not usually produced in the informal, non-Standard speech of the learner, but known to him and produced under stress in prestige social situations; C, those which the learner would recognise and comprehend if used by other speakers (especially in a meaningful context), but which the learner himself would be unable to produce; and D, those totally unknown to the learner. As will be shown subsequently, it is sometimes convenient to regard elements of strata A and B as forming a single class, and similarly, those of C and D as forming a single class; but even when regarded in this way the four underlying strata show that in the class of second-dialect language known already to the learner, there is a set of items which he would use only in unusual or very formal situations, and in the class of second-dialect language not within the production repertoire of the learner, there is a set of items which can be recognised and comprehended.

The special implications of this stratification of language vis-à-vis the Creole or non-Standard learner of English has been discussed in Craig (1971: 378) where it is shown that, because of the B and C strata, the learner often fails to perceive new target D elements in the teaching situation, unlike the learner of a foreign language. Consequent upon this, the reinforcement of learning which derives from the learner's satisfaction at mastering a new element, and knowing he has mastered it, is minimal, unlike that accruing to the learner of a foreign language; and because of the ease of shifting from Standard English to Creole or other non-Standard speech and vice-versa, the learner, again unlike the learner of a foreign language, resists any attempt to restrict his use of language exclusively within the new language elements being taught to him.

In the light of these implications, it is not surprising if many non-

Standard speakers taught by foreign language methods continue to show a very low rate of acquiring Standard language. Kochman (1969: 87) in discussing this point, felt that the 'efficiency quotient' of Standard language teaching, i.e., the result that comes from an input of time and effort, is so negligible that the widsom of at all attempting to teach the Standard under conditions such as those relevant here has to be questioned. Usually, the reasons for such poor results have been ascribed completely to social factors and the unfavorable attitudes of learners as in, for example, Fasold (1968) and Abrahams (1970). There is no doubt that social and attitudinal factors are exceedingly important and obviously play a part, but slow or negligible acquisition of the Standard is not restricted to poorly motivated learners or to learners below the age of social awareness (vide Labov 1964: 91) at which some motivation might develop. The question therefore needs to be studied of whether the very nature of bidialectal situations does not produce strictly linguistic and non-attitudinal factors that have some additional bearing on the poor results of language teaching.

The teaching program dictated by the suggested stratification of language, vis-à-vis the learner, and by the considerations related to that stratification is structured as follows:

1. Topics for treatment in language are selected so as to reflect the interests, maturity and immediate cultural environment of the learners, but at the same time so as to permit adequate use of the specific linguistic structures that form the goal of teaching at the specific point in time.

2. The learners are led by the teacher to explore the topic fully in whatever language the learners possess. The teacher may either speak the vernacular, or speak some other type of language closer to the Standard or speak the Standard itself, so long as the learners are able to comprehend easily; and the teacher accepts whatever language the learners choose to respond in, including such new language as is infiltrating into the learners' competence. This part of the program is completely oral and may be designated 'free talk'. The purpose of this part is to promote normal growth and development of the learners in whatever language medium is most natural to them.

3. The teacher uses the selected topic, or aspects of the topic, as the basis of systematic quasi-foreign language practice. Because of the high rate of recognition and comprehension in the bidialectal situation, through the learners' possession of the language strata A, B, and C, teaching procedures do not usually call for a very intensive use of imitation drills, but rather more for substitution and transformation practices, controlled dialogues and dramas, and a heavy reliance on simulated situations for forcing learners into a creative use of the

specific linguistic structures that are aimed at. This part of the program may be designated 'controlled talk' and only Standard language is used.

4. For teaching in 3. preceding, linguistic structures are selected so that, relevant to the A, B, C, D classification of structures already discussed, the learners are forced to use a target structure or target structures selected from C or D (which for practical purposes may be combined into a single class), and at the same time to use incidental structures which come fortuitously from A and B (which, again for practical purposes, may also be combined into a single class).

5. Language learners who are also learning to read use material consisting only of such linguistic structures as at each given stage they have already learned as at 3. and that are relevant to the topics discussed at 2. Language learners who can already read may use materials that are linguistically unstructured (and the more such learners can be saturated with reading, the better). The purpose of this set of measures is to ensure that the acquisition of and interest in reading is not hampered by Standard-language deficiencies, and that reading and language-learning should reinforce each other; once reading is firmly acquired, however, there is no longer any point in linking it to the formal learning of language structure.

6. For all learners, use is made in writing only of those linguistic structures that have already been learned as at 3. and in most cases the content of the writing is restricted to topics treated as at 2. By this means, writing is closely linked to proficiency in speech, and one reinforces the other.

7. The various subject-areas of the total school curriculum enter into the selection of topics explained as at 1. so that aspects of these areas get re-worked in controlled speech, reading and writing in the same way as all other experiences.

The difference between what is outlined here and strictly foreign-language teaching procedures lies in what has been termed free talk and the way in which controlled talk, reading and writing are linked to it and to one another; the different parts of the program have to be planned together and be well integrated. In this way, the learner gets the kind of stimulating education that ought to be present in a first-language program, but at the same time, linked to this stimulation and arising out of it, there is concentration on the ordered and sequenced teaching of new language elements. The built-in resistance of the second-dialect learner to such teaching is countered by the carry-over of his free-talk interests into other activities, by the constant reinforcement passing from one activity to another, and by the encouraged possibility of newly learned language gradually infiltrating into free talk, becoming a part of it and becoming gradually augmented. This last mentioned possibility is in fact more than just a possibility since it has been shown, as already discussed, to be the inevitable way in which language learning proceeds in this situation, i.e., as a gradual mixture and replacement of items along the continuum. This mixture and replacement occasioned by new language learning, as explained already, does not mean that the learners lose their original vernacular. They retain their original vernacular for such occasions as it is needed in their home and peer-group environment, but at the same time they acquire an increasing ability to shift their formal speech into the Standard-language end of the continuum until they achieve some acceptable proficiency in Standard speech. On the way towards the achievement of such proficiency, many compromises are inevitable: some learners might persist in retaining certain of their original speech characteristics in the most nearly Standard language they learn to produce, others might achieve good native proficiency in reading and writing the Standard language but at the same time persist in their original non-Standard speech even on the most formal occasions, and so on. It does not seem that bidialectal education ought to expect more than this. Fishman and Lueders-Salmon (1972) have shown that German dialect speakers react to the necessity as well as the experience of learning High German in some of the characteristic ways that are now well known in the United States of America and the West Indian language situations. It would thus seem that the factors discussed here are to be found universally in many different bidialectal situations.

The principles and procedures sketched in the preceding paragraphs will not be found in uniform application in schools within the West Indies. In Jamaica, where the educational principles just discussed were first and still are being worked out, indications of the methodology will be noticed in Ministry of Education school syllabuses and guidelines for teachers where 'an integrated approach' to language teaching is spoken of; the 'integration' involves the components of the programme already outlined here. At the present time, an effort is being made in the Ministry's Curriculum Development Thrust to supply teachers with detailed guides and materials for teaching along the suggested lines. The ideas and procedures are also in process of being disseminated through others of the officially English-speaking West Indian territories; in Guyana, for example, much consideration has been given to the nature of the Guyanese language situation and the needs that exist in education. The discussion has proceded very much along the general lines followed in this chapter, and some of it is exampled in Tyndal (1965, 1972), Armstrong (1968), Wilson (1968), Cave (1970, 1971), Craig (1971), and Trotman (1973). In the last mentioned territory also, the production of classroom materials incorporating the relevant procedures is in progress.

In the Eastern Caribbean, independently of the Jamaica-based work, the School of Education of the University of The West Indies together with a UNESCO curriculum development program in that area has been working on the development of language-teaching materials with an English-as-a-second language approach. Preceding this development and continuing concurrently with it, there is in Trinidad an on-going survey of school-children's language (Carrington and Borely 1969); there has also been concluded a survey of teaching practices (Carrington, Borely, and Knight (1972), textbooks in use in schools (Knight, Carrington, and Borely 1972), and the home-language background of Trinidad children (Carrington, Borely, and Knight 1972a); the latter collections of information are considered as a preliminary to the development of teaching procedures in that territory.

No matter what stage of development has been reached at present in the development of bidialectal educational procedures in the relevant individual West Indian territories, however, it seems quite clear that, in the long run, the fact that such procedures are necessary and are at the same time inevitably different from both native and foreign-language teaching procedures will have to be faced; it seems important that when this happens, the principles and procedures discussed above should be available for more extensive trial throughout the region.

## Notes

First published in *International Journal of the Sociology of Language*, 8, 1976.

# Social dialects and education
Walt Wolfram and Ralph Fasold

The study of social dialects has particular relevance for many kinds of pedagogical problems involving language variation. Public education in our society serves the function of inculcating in children the values that are shared by the society in which they will be participating members. Included in these values are attitudes and beliefs about language and language varieties. Where the value system being promoted by the school matches that of the sector of society from which the children come, the value-socialization process of public education is served fairly well. In the area of language, the notion of what is correct in speech and what is not simply reinforces the values the children have already begun acquiring at home.[1] What the teacher says is correct English will in most details be not only what the child has already been told is correct, but will also be what he has heard adults using all his life.

When the value system of the educational institution differs from that of the community from which the children come, an obvious conflict arises. In the area of language, a child from a sector of society in which a nonstandard dialect is the real medium of community life will be told by his teacher that certain things in the language patterns he is used to are wrong. Even so, Labov (1966) was able to show that speakers of non-standard dialects share with the rest of the larger community the overt opinions that nonstandard speech is bad and pass these overtly conscious opinions on to their children. But the child will have heard Nonstandard English being used effectively by adults and older children all his life. The day-to-day proof that nonstandard language is, in fact, adequate for the needs of those closest to him simply overwhelms the occasional remarks he hears to the contrary. We see, then, that although the overt opinions about speech may match those of the dominant social class, on a covert level the nonstandard dialect is obviously preferred for actual usage.

The overwhelming majority of teachers of children from such communities, even those who have come from the same communities, feel that part of their duty is to upgrade (as they see it) the nonstandard dialect of their students. Few teachers are even exposed to the linguist's position on the inherent adequacy of nonstandard varieties and so they simply accept the prevalent idea among educated people that differences from 'correct' English represent deficiencies to be overcome. As he is taught to read and write, as his classroom recitations are corrected, as he is assigned to speech therapists for special language work, as his standardized test scores are misinterpreted, the child gradually is taught that the dialect he has always known only as an efficient tool of communication is considered a distortion of proper English.

In the course of their study of social variation in language, many sociolinguists have realized that what they were learning had potential for educational application. The lists of the publications of almost all of the linguists who have studied social variation include some written for educators. In addition, a few have worked directly with teachers in schools (see Shuy 1971). This involvement has led to the realization that language differences per se are only a small part of the problems faced by educators of economically impoverished children. Nevertheless, most sociolinguists are convinced that language differences are far from being a negligible part of the picture and that the application of the insights of their research is likely to have a beneficial effect. It is our intention to summarize these insights in this chapter.

## Teacher attitudes

Our experience in working with teachers has indicated that the most crucial contribution that the study of social dialects can make to education is in the area of teacher attitudes. A teacher who has been freed from the opinion that nonstandard dialect is simply distorted English will be a better teacher even without new materials and techniques specifically designed to deal with language variation. A teacher with his insight into language will be slower to correct grammatical and phonological manifestations that differ from standard dialects—he or she will spend less time on nonstandard pronunciations and grammar in oral reading and get on with the teaching of the reading skill itself. This teacher will not be so ready to conclude that a child has a speech pathology that requires the services of a speech clinician simply because his speech is not standard. Furthermore, he will be less likely to conclude low intelligence on the basis of Nonstandard English and will be skeptical of the results of standardized tests that contain segments presuming mastery of a standard dialect of English.

In a well-known experiment, Rosenthal and Jacobson (1968) were able to show that teacher attitudes toward students can have a profound effect on the students' performance. In their experiment, certain students were selected at random and their teachers were told that they had been found very gifted. At the end of the experiment, these particular children were actually performing better than their classmates. Presumably, the opposite belief about students on the part of a teacher could have a deleterious effect on the performance of a student of adequate intelligence. Therefore it is of considerable importance that teachers learn not to infer lack of intelligence from the use of nonstandard speech. Although we consider attitudinal change to be of central importance, it is an arduous task to realistically bring about such changes.

## Spoken standard English

In the remainder of this chapter, we shall examine the insights provided by social dialect study in the areas of teaching spoken Standard English, teaching reading, teaching comprehension, and evaluating the language aspects of standardized testing. Before we discuss the methodology of teaching spoken Standard English to speakers of nonstandard dialects, we need to outline the possible goals and the prospects for success, given a classroom environment.

## Possible goals

Exhausting the logical possibilities, there are four conceivable goals of teaching spoken English. Of these, one has been the historic goal of educators and has only been questioned recently, two are recently proposed and quite controversial, and the remaining goal is nonsense. Figure 1 displays the four goals in terms of the control of language an individual should have as a result of the spoken language curriculum.

|                |     | STANDARD ENGLISH | |
|                |     | Yes | No |
|----------------|-----|-----|----|
| NONSTANDARD    | No  | 1   | 2  |
| ENGLISH        | Yes | 3   | 4  |

Figure 1. Combinations of control over Standard and Nonstandard English which are conceivable as goals for an individual as a result of a spoken language curriculum.

The cell labeled 1 means the individual should control Standard English and should have given up Nonstandard English. Cell 2 means that Nonstandard English would be eradicated, but Standard English not explicitly taught. Cell 3 corresponds to the goal of teaching Standard

English while allowing the retention of the nonstandard dialect, and cell 4 indicates the retention of nonstandard dialect as a goal without the teaching of Standard English. Of the four, cell 2 can be dismissed as nonsense. To attempt to eradicate Nonstandard English without teaching Standard English in its place would entail the student's becoming mute as a result of the spoken language curriculum! As ridiculous as this sounds, it appears that some teachers, in trying to achieve the goal designated by cell 1, inadvertently come closer to the goal of cell 2, achieving the 'mute child' result. Certainly no teacher would intentionally aim at such a result, but by constantly correcting nonstandard speech without providing effective Standard English instruction, some teachers convince children that it is better to not respond in school at all rather than risk having every sentence corrected.

The cell 1 goal, called *eradicationism*, is the one historically accepted by educators. Indeed, it probably has not occurred to some educators that any other alternative is possible. The goal of eradicationism is to eliminate the negative concord, zero copula, and other nonstandard grammar and pronunciation features from the speech of students completely, replacing them with the Standard English equivalents. Much of the motivation for setting this goal is based on the conviction that Nonstandard English is a corruption of Standard English that leads to cognitive deficits and learning disabilities. The indefensibility of this view weakens the position of eradicationism as a goal. Another incentive for the eradicationist approach is based on the premise that Nonstandard English, although perhaps linguistically the equal of the standard dialects, still confers a social stigma on its speakers, and should therefore be eliminated in order to eliminate the stigma and allow the student full opportunity to enter the mainstream of society. Even this line of reasoning is questionable, as we shall see in our discussion of the goal indicated in cell 4. If it is valid, the line of reasoning based on social stigma leads more directly to the goal of cell 3. A further problem with the eradicationist approach is that the goal is usually pursued with methods of questionable effectiveness. The traditional methods of random correction of a child's oral recitations, the rote learning of grammar rules, and the use of written exercises cannot be expected to have much effect on a student's habitual use of the language. From the point of view of a linguist who has studied socially diagnostic language variation, the eradicationist approach has little to recommend it.[2]

*Bidialectalism*, the goal indicated by cell 3, means that Standard English is to be taught, but with no effort to eradicate the student's native nonstandard dialect. At the end of the spoken language curriculum, the student ideally would be able to use either Standard or Nonstandard English as the situation required. In classroom, job interview, or similar settings, Standard English would be selected from the individual's dialect repertoire, and Nonstandard English would be used in more normal situations. Unlike the eradicationist position, the bidialectalism position overtly rejects the notion that Nonstandard English is inherently inferior. Like the eradicationist position, it assumes that social stigmatization of Nonstandard English is both significant and inevitable. With bidialectalism as a goal usually goes the adoption and adaptation of some of the techniques of foreign language teaching as part of the methodology, but there is no reason why these techniques could not also be used in pursuit of the eradicationist goal. The majority of sociolinguists who have studied social dialects advocate the bidialectalist position.

The goal designated by cell 4 calls for the retention of Nonstandard English with no attempt to teach Standard English either as a replacement dialect or a second dialect. Advocates of this goal reject the notion that Nonstandard English is inherently inferior (as do advocates of bidialectalism), but they also reject the idea that language prejudice is significant and inevitable. This rejection of Standard English acquisition as a goal has been called to the attention of mainstream educators in two widely read articles by the linguist James Sledd (1969, 1972). In a scathing attack on bidialectalism and its proponents, Sledd questions the moral adequacy of assuming the inevitability of language prejudice and formulating educational goals so as to accommodate it. Rather than teach standard English to speakers of Nonstandard English, Sledd would devote attention only to an attack on the negative language attitudes of wielders of power in the mainstream of society. Some black scholars also have raised the question of the significance of nonstandard speech as a force in limiting opportunities for Blacks (R. Williams 1971; Wiggins 1972). They see racial prejudice on the part of the white society as the real problem and the language question as something of an attempt to dodge the central issue.

In connection with this position, it is sometimes advocated that a stigmatized dialect such as Vernacular Black English be taught in schools serving white Standard English-speaking students as a means of fostering understanding. Although this proposal has a certain appeal to some liberal whites, it seems to us to be completely unworkable. The parents of the white students involved would almost surely reject the idea as a subversive attempt to undermine the language of their children. Blacks who do not accept the validity of the concept 'Vernacular Black English' may see it as a racist attempt to teach whites that Nonstandard English is associated with blacks. On the other hand, blacks who do recognize Vernacular Black English might not accept the effort to teach it in white schools as valid if carried on by whites, and they would probably not consider it to be a project of sufficient priority to engage in it themselves.

One of the important considerations in teaching Standard English

# 190 Designing the language curriculum

must be the desires of the community. It would be a mistake to conclude that Nonstandard English-speaking communities do not want Standard English taught. According to recent research (Taylor 1973), most black parents profess to want their children to learn the standard dialect. Although the fourth goal, that of teaching the stigmatized dialect, is the most radical, it nonetheless deserves careful consideration along with the others. We have no information on whether or not this position is taken in connection with other Nonstandard English-speaking communities, but it would not be surprising to learn that it is. Wherever it is advocated, it is bound to be controversial.

There is no 'safe' position among these proposals. Advocates of eradicationism face the ire of all who accept the legitimacy of nonstandard dialects. To accept bidialectalism invites the criticism of traditional educators and language purists on the one hand and of the more outspoken members of minority communities and their allies on the other. Taking the position that Standard English should not be taught or that a nonstandard dialect should be taught means being resisted by all those who for one reason or another believe in the importance of Standard English in American society.

## Prospects for success

Aside from the question of what goals should be set as the aim of spoken Standard English programs on a priori grounds, it is useful to ask what degree of success can be expected if the teaching of Standard English as a spoken dialect is to be the goal. There seems to be reason for a fair amount of pessimism. It is possible to come to the conclusion that what the English teacher does in the classroom with regard to spoken Standard English is irrelevant. Speakers who start out speaking Nonstandard English but find that they need to learn Standard English will learn it, and those who do not will not, almost independently of what their English teachers do. The reason is that learning spoken language is unlike any other kind of learning. It cannot be taught only with the methods, materials, and motivational strategies used to teach other subjects. It is even open to serious question that one very necessary factor in learning new spoken skills, whether a new dialect or a whole new language, *can* be supplied in the classroom. It is crucial that there be a viable expectation and desire on the part of the learner to become a member of the group represented by the speakers of the new language, dialect, or style. If this factor is present, other methods and motivations may also contribute to successful learning of new spoken language skills. But if it is missing, nothing that goes on in the classroom can make up for its absence.

[ . . . . ]

## Methodology

If the group reference factor is present and the student is oriented toward learning Standard English, a well-designed methodological program developed particularly for spoken skills may be of significant help in guiding the student toward his goal. Techniques developed by linguists for teaching foreign languages to speakers of English or English to speakers of other languages, such as contrastive analysis, mimicry, and pattern practice, can be used with good effect, *if* the differences between second language and second dialect learning are taken into account. There are a number of programs available which purport to apply the methodology of second language teaching to teaching spoken Standard English as a second dialect that are so unimaginatively adapted that they are likely to produce no results other than profound boredom.

One of the best adaptations of these second language techniques has been made by Irwin Feigenbaum. His approach is described and illustrated in two articles (Feigenbaum 1969, 1970a) and applied in materials he has developed for use in public schools (1970b). The drill techniques are designed to overcome boredom in several ways (1970a). First, it is suggested that they be used for brief periods of time. Second, the pace should be quick with a minimum of explanation. Third, the sentences being drilled are given content with a certain amount of inherent interest. Finally, the sequential progression of the drills is programmed so that each activity is more difficult than the last—thus the student is constantly being challenged. The final drills in each sequence allow for a degree of free expression that begins to approach normal conversation.

A typical lesson designed by Feigenbaum has five types of drills.[3] The first is a *presentation* of less than half a minute. If the feature to be taught is the Standard English verbal *-s*, two sentences such as *He work hard* and *He works hard* are presented and it is quickly pointed out to the students how they differ and which one is standard and which is nonstandard (Feigenbaum prefers the terms *formal* and *informal* in classroom situations). The next activity is a *discrimination* drill. In this drill, the class hears pairs of sentences like the following:

He work hard.
He works hard.

He work hard.
He work hard.

He works hard.
He works hard.

They respond 'different' to examples like the first pair and 'same' to examples like the second and third pairs.

Next follows an *identification* drill. In this drill, the students hear only one sentence, which they must identify as standard or nonstandard (or formal or informal). Examples might include:

He work hard.
He works hard.
Paula likes leather coats.
She prefer movies.

Only one socially diagnostic feature—the one being taught—distinguishes standard and nonstandard sentences. The appropriate response to the first and fourth of the above sentences is 'informal' and to the second and third 'formal'.

Various types of *translation* rules are next. In these activities, the teacher gives either a standard or nonstandard sentence and the student is to respond with the corresponding sentence of the opposite type. This requires the students to demonstrate two skills. First, it must register with them whether the original sentence was standard or nonstandard. Then they must know what the corresponding sentence is in the other dialect and produce it. One of the unique aspects of Feigenbaum's program is translation from Standard to Nonstandard English as well as the reverse. Some examples of teacher stimuli and student responses follow:

| TEACHER STIMULUS | STUDENT RESPONSE |
| --- | --- |
| He work hard. | He works hard. |
| He works hard. | He work hard. |
| Paula likes leather coats. | Paula like leather coats. |
| She prefer movies. | She prefers movies. |

A variety of *response* drill activities conclude the lesson. In these exercises, the student is required to supply a certain amount of original content as well as the correct sentence in the appropriate dialect. A little imagination can lead to considerable variety, so the example given here is more an illustration than a pattern. In this drill, the instructor asks a question with either standard or nonstandard grammar. The student supplies his own answer, but it must be in the same dialect grammar in which the question was asked. For example, if the question is *Do your brother get good grades?* the answer might be *Yes, he do,* or *No, he don't; he get lousy grades,* or *In some subjects he do and in some he don't.* Regardless of the answer, if the question comes in nonstandard grammar, the answer must be in nonstandard grammar also. If the question is something like, *Does your English teacher give hard homework?* the answer may be *She certainly does!* or *No, she gives easy homework,* or any other sort of content the student feels is appropriate. But the answer must include the *-s* suffix because the question was asked in Standard English.

The approach taken by Feigenbaum, where both students and

teacher are required to use nonstandard grammar in the course of the drilling, is clearly designed to implement the bidialectal approach. Teachers frequently object to those parts of the exercise calling for the use of nonstandard grammar. But the use of nonstandard grammar is necessary to focus on the point of contrast between standard and nonstandard grammar. Some teachers complain that they have difficulty producing nonstandard structures. Others express the fear that they will teach or reinforce Nonstandard English by using it in the classroom exercises. But the lessons are designed to be used with speakers who already control a nonstandard dialect. The few times that they are required to use nonstandard sentences in the drills will have no effect on the grammar they have internalized already. Furthermore, wherever Nonstandard English is required, it is always in direct contrast with the equivalent standard construction, so that the difference between the two is foremost in the student's mind. In classes in which there are students who already speak Standard English, there is negligible danger that they will learn the nonstandard from the drills. First of all, it will always be clear that the goal is learning the standard sentences, not the nonstandard ones. Second, while it is assumed that at least some of the Nonstandard English speakers are motivated to learn Standard English, there will be no Standard English speakers who will be motivated to learn the nonstandard dialect, at least not from their schoolteacher. The possibility of Standard English speakers learning nonstandard patterns from the drills, then, seems to be rather minimal.

*Teaching reading*

The child who speaks a nonstandard dialect faces two problems when he is being taught to read, while the Standard English-speaking child has only one. The Standard English-speaking child primarily needs to learn the process and mechanics of reading: of deriving meaning from the printed page. The child who speaks a nonstandard variety must learn the reading process, but must also learn the language of the reading materials at the same time—and this is a language variety which matches his spoken language very poorly.[4] The match between spoken and written language is very important, because spoken language is primary and writing derived from it. Speaking is not an attempt to approximate written forms, but written forms are basically attempts to reflect speech. Therefore any mismatch between speech and writing, whether at the level of spelling, vocabulary, or grammar, reflects a failure of the writing system, not of spoken language.[5] In learning to read, a student is really learning to see his speech on the printed page. To the degree that his speech is not represented on the pages of the material being used to teach him to read, an obstacle is being raised for him.

This view of the relationship of spoken and written language is basically the only one the linguist has to contribute as a linguist. But there are a number of applicational strategies consistent with this principle. It is important to note that there is no unitary 'linguistic approach'—that mythical but marketable item that has become a token of prestige in language arts curricula. Rather, there are several alternatives which attempt to eliminate the possible effect that dialect differences may have in the acquisition of reading skills. As will be seen, there are no easy solutions. The advantages and disadvantages of each alternative we shall present must honestly be faced if we are going to arrive at a feasible solution. The fact that we have no infallible alternative should not, however, be taken to mean that all alternatives that attempt to deal with the discrepancy between the language of the primer and the indigenous language of the child are equal. As the different approaches are evaluated, it should be apparent that some can be more highly recommended than others.

Although there are idiosyncratic aspects of practically every proposed reading program, the various alternatives can be roughly divided into two main groups. Some call for different methods in teaching reading with extant materials and others call for the development of new types of reading materials.

If the linguistic diversity between the dialect of children who speak Nonstandard English and the dialect of the reading materials is going to be neutralized without altering basic materials, then two options are open; either the child's language patterns must be changed to conform to Standard English patterns prior to the teaching of reading, or some accommodation to the dialect in the traditional type of reader must be made. The feasibility of these two alternatives is discussed below.

## Teaching Standard English prior to reading

To neutralize the difference between the 'language of reading' and the language which the lower-class child brings to school with him, it has sometimes been suggested that the teaching of Standard English should precede the teaching of reading (McDavid 1969; Venezky 1970). Although this may appear to be similar to the simultaneous teaching of reading and Standard English that is often engaged in, it is essential not to confuse these procedures. When teachers correct children for dialect interference in reading as well as for the usual types of errors that occur in learning to read, the teaching of Standard English is usually accomplished in a haphazard and unsystematic way. Furthermore, legitimate dialect interference and reading problems arising from the incomplete mastery of the reading process are often not distinguished from each other.

The approach suggested here, however, first concentrates on the systematic teaching of Standard English before any reading is taught; when a child has adequately acquired Standard English, the teacher may proceed to the teaching of reading—the teaching of reading begins with the assumption that the source for dialect interference has been eliminated. This is not necessarily to say that the child's indigenous dialect will be eradicated, only that he will have capacity in Standard English as well as the vernacular.

Most school curricula call for the teaching of Standard English eventually, but the program described here inevitably means that Standard English will be taught at the initial stages of the child's experience, because the acquisition of reading is obviously one of the earliest priorities of formal education. One might further suggest that because Standard English will probably be taught anyway, it is most reasonable to teach it before the failure to learn it can inhibit reading development.

If we were simply dealing with linguistic considerations, teaching Standard English prior to reading would certainly be an attractive alternative, as well as a seemingly obvious procedure. We know that children are quite adept at language learning, so why not take advantage of this fact and teach them Standard English at an early age? Before we accept the potential advantages of this alternative, we must realistically consider the total sociolinguistic situation, for potential linguistic advantages cannot be treated in isolation from sociocultural facts.

Probably the most essential sociolinguistic point that militates against this alternative is the fact that teaching Standard English may not even be possible without the group reference orientation we have discussed earlier. Children want to speak like their peers, and the conflicts between school and indigenous value systems have repeatedly shown that school values will most often come out on the short end of a compromise.

Given the pessimistic but realistic predictions about the teaching of Standard English, it is therefore surprising that Venezky observes that the teaching of Standard English may only involve a delay of several months in the introduction of reading. He observes:

> There is no reason to believe that a delay of a few months in the introduction of reading will seriously impede any child's natural development. (1970: 342).

Kochman, who seriously questions the wisdom of teaching Standard English at all, bases part of his argument for not teaching it on what he calls the 'efficiency quotient' (1969: 87). By this he means the excessive time that must be spent in order to produce even a mediocre and restrictive performance in Standard English. He notes that with maximum cooperation, for example, it takes several months of drills simply to get a student to say *ask* where he formerly said *aks*. Kochman therefore concludes that 'the input in time and effort is prodigious and the results negligible' (1969: 87).

Even if we take a more optimistic view on the teaching of Standard English, we cannot assume that the first grade is the most conducive age for teaching it. Some sociologists and educators suggest that it is most reasonable to start teaching Standard English at an age when there is an increasing awareness of the social consequences of using certain nonstandard features of speech. According to Labov, the social perceptions of speech stratification start to match the adult norms around the ages of 14 to 15 (Labov 1964b: 91; but see also Rosenthal 1973). If the 5 to 6-year-old child perceives little social differentiation in speech, it may be argued that it is senseless to teach Standard English at the first-grade level, the level at which reading skills are expected to be developed. Rather, Standard English should be initiated at a secondary level, when students have acquired the notion of social appropriateness for different types of behavior more fully.

Before we could endorse teaching Standard English as a prerequisite for reading, we would have to have evidence that it can be extensively taught given the current sociolcultural facts, and that it is most effectively taught at the initial stages of education. At this point, the sociocultural facts that inhibit the widespread acquisition of Standard English even as a second dialect do not suggest this alternative as a reasonable solution.

## Dialect readings of extant materials

The other alternative that retains the traditional materials does not involve the teaching of Standard English in any form. Rather, it involves the acceptance of dialect renderings of Standard English reading materials. Goodman is probably the most explicit spokesman for this position when he states:

> No special materials need to be constructed but children must be permitted, actually encouraged, to read the way they speak. (1969: 27).

The child is given the standard types of reading materials and simply asked to read them aloud in a dialect-appropriate manner. In silent reading, this approach is irrelevant, but it must be remembered that oral reading is the primary basis for evaluating a child's reading skills in the incipient stages. If a child can read the passage in such a way that it systematically differs from Standard English where his indigenous dialect differs, he has successfully read the passage. For example, if a lower-class black child reads a standard sentence such as *Jane goes to Mary's house* as *Jane go to Mary house*, he is considered to have read it properly, because third-person singular -*s* and possessive -*s* suffixial absence are part of the lower-class black child's vernacular. It is held that by permitting the child to read the traditional materials in his own dialect, the teacher can focus on the essentials of the reading process and the child will not be confused about reading problems that may result from dialect interference and legitimate types of reading errors arising during the course of the acquisition of reading skills.

There are several assumptions implicit in accepting what Goodman suggests as the only practical alternative for the reading problem among children with nonstandard speech, and our evaluation of its relative merits is based on these assumptions. In the first place, it assumes that the Standard English contained in the beginning materials is comprehensible to the child. Claims about the comprehension of Standard English by Nonstandard-speaking children vary greatly, but we still lack definitive empirical evidence on this question. At this point, the most reasonable position seems to be that for the most part, the dialect speaker has a receptive competence in Standard English. (The converse, Standard English speakers comprehending lower-class dialects, may not necessarily be true to the same extent because of the sociopsychological factors which enter into the comprehension of the speech of a socially subordinate class by a superordinate one [see Wolff 1969].) This position seems to be most realistic for several reasons. For one, the majority of differences between the child's vernacular and Standard English appear to be on the surface rather than the underlying levels of language (Labov and Cohen 1967). One might expect that differences on the surface level would usually affect comprehension less than differences on the underlying levels of language. A more important reason for this position is found, for example, in the indirect evidence that we have from the lower-class child's ability to perform certain types of tasks based on the receptive competence of Standard English. In performing a sentence repetition test devised by Baratz, lower-class black children could comprehend Standard English sentences that focused on the areas of difference between the child's vernacular and Standard English sufficiently well to repeat them in the nonstandard dialect (Baratz 1969). That these children were able to give back a nonstandard equivalent was indicative of the basic comprehension of the content of the sentence.

This position on comprehension does not, however, preclude the possibility of some information loss when reading Standard English. The loss of information would not be as great, of course, as it would be if the readers were written in a foreign language. We would certainly not argue that a speaker of a nonstandard dialect is going to understand as little Standard English as a monolingual German speaker reading English. When some information loss does occur because of dialect differences, what should be done about features that might be unfamiliar

to the Nonstandard English speakers? Are these unfamiliar features
sufficiently infrequent to warrant their retention in the materials, inas-
much as any child can expect some unfamiliar constructions in reading
material; or will the unfamiliar constructions be sufficiently great to
impede the reading process? These are empirical questions, but ones
that must be faced squarely if no change in traditional reading materials
is advocated.

Another factor that must be considered in using extant materials
concerns the orthography, particularly if the phonics approach to reading is employed. It appears that the traditional orthography is not totally
inappropriate for the dialects of children who do not speak Standard
English (Fasold 1969). Hence, we do not consider this factor to be a
major disadvantage as long as the teacher knows the type of sound-
symbol relations appropriate for the dialect.

Our reference to the teacher's knowledge of the appropriate sound-
symbol relations brings out another assumption of this alternative;
namely, that the reading reacher is thoroughly familiar with the dialect
of the children. When Goodman says that the student should be encouraged to read the way he speaks, this assumes that the teacher knows
what particular dialect rendering of a given passage can be expected.
Otherwise, there is no way of distinguishing legitimate reading problems
arising from an incomplete mastery of the sound-symbol relations and
reading differences that are the result of dialect interference. For example,
if a lower-class black child reads the word *thought* as *fought*, the teacher
must know whether this is simply a problem of sound-symbol relations
due to the incomplete mastery of these relations or a legitimate dialect
rendering of *th*. In this case, the pronunciation cannot be attributed to
dialect interference because there is no known dialect rule which renders
*th* as *f* in word-initial position. But what if the student reads *Ruth* so that
it is identical with *roof*? In this case, it is a legitimate dialect pronunciation and should not be corrected. The type of discernment which
might correct the homophony of *thought* and *fought* but not the homophony of *Ruth* and *roof* assumes that the teacher knows the dialect rule
that realizes *th* as *f* at the middle or end of a word, but not at the
beginning. Some teachers may inductively arrive at such types of discernment because of consistence in the oral reading of nonstandard
dialect speakers, but if the alternative proposed by Goodman and others
is to be adopted on an extensive level, it will require the training of
teachers in the structural patterns of the dialect. (An acquaintance with
the structural patterns does not, of course, mean that the teacher will be
able to speak the dialect.)

Although this alternative has several potential disadvantages, it does
have one very practical advantage: it can be established much more
immediately than some of the other alternatives. For example, it can be

adopted while further experimentation with other alternatives which require more drastic curriculum reorganization is carried out. Indeed, the teacher who thoroughly acquaints himself with the description of the dialect features and is convinced of the legitimacy of the dialect as a highly developed language system is in a position to start initiating this alternative. Chapters Six and Seven were designed to provide this kind of information.

A seemingly more drastic alternative to the reading problem for speakers of nonstandard dialects involves the incorporation of new types of materials into the reading curriculum for lower-class children. Basically, there are two approaches that have been proposed—one involving the elimination of all features that might be unfamiliar to the Nonstandard-speaking child and one that involves the writing of new sets of materials designed specifically to represent the language and culture the child brings with him when he enters school.

*The neutralization of dialect differences.* One method of revising current materials for nonstandard dialect speakers is to simply eliminate features that might predictably be problematic for the nonstandard speaker because they are not an integral part of his linguistic system. This alternative essentially follows the suggestion of Shuy that grammatical choices in beginning material should not provide extraneous data. Shuy observes:

> In the case of beginning reading materials for nonstandard speakers, the text should help the child by avoiding grammatical forms which are not realized by him in his spoken language (third singular verb inflections, for example). (Shuy 1969: 125).

It should be noted that this alternative would *not* incorporate any non-standard features present in the dialect but absent in Standard English.[6] For example, the use of *be* to indicate distributive action in a sentence such as *He be here every day* would not be used, because this feature is unique to nonstandard speech. Accommodation would be made only by excluding features in Standard English that do not have isomorphic correspondences in the dialect. It capitalizes on the similarities of large portions of the grammar of these dialects so that the possibility of grammatical interference is eliminated. This alternative would only concentrate on grammatical differences, because differences in pronunciation would involve most of the words in the English language. It thus appears that this choice involves the neutralization of grammatical differences along with the acceptance of dialect pronunciations of reading materials, as was suggested in one of the previously discussed alternatives.

There are several assumptions which form the basis of this alternative, and it cannot be evaluated apart from these. For one, it assumes that there is a sufficient common core between the standard and nonstandard language system which allows for the practical implementation of these suggestions into our reading materials. The validity of this assumption is an empirical question, and on the basis of our research, we can answer that there are many similarities, at least between Standard English and the varieties of nonstandard dialects we have been discussing. The inventory of similarities is certainly greater than the inventory of of differences. But the fact remains that there are differences and so we must ask if they might be of the sort which would make it difficult to effectively incorporate this type of change into materials.

To examine this problem more closely, we can take one of the sample inventories of the prominent features of lower-class black dialect, and see what changes would have to be made in order to neutralize the grammatical differences between it and Standard English. For example, consider the sample inventory that Shuy delimits, which seems to be a fairly typical list:

| Written Expression | Linguistic Feature | Oral Expression |
|---|---|---|
| 1. John's house | possession | John house |
| 2. John runs | 3rd sing. pres. | John run |
| 3. ten cents | plurality | ten cent |
| 4. He jumped | past | He jump |
| 5. She is a cook | copula | She a cook |
| 6. He doesn't have any toys | negation | He ain't got no toys |
| | | He don't have no toys |
| | | He don't got no toys |
| 7. He asked if I came | past conditional question | He asked did I come |
| 8. Every day when I come he isn't here | negative + be | Every day when I come he don't be here |

(Shuy 1969: 128)

What would be involved if we were to eliminate the above types of constructions from extant reading materials at the beginning level of reading? For No. 1, possession, it would mean that we could only express possession via the preposition *of* or the verb *has*, or avoid possessive constructions altogether. For some items such as *John's hat* or *Bill's bike*, the use of *of* might be stylistcally unacceptable even though it might be grammatical (e.g., *the hat of John, the bike of Bill*). Using the construction *John has a hat* or *the hat which John has* every time we want to indicate possession might lead us into even more serious stylistic difficulties. Thus a sequence of sentences in discourse such as

John's new bike is blue. Mary's new bike is red. John's bike is bigger than Mary's.

might be restructured something like

John has a new blue bike. Mary has a new bike too and it is red. The bike John has is bigger than the one Mary has.

It seems that the only way one could eliminate such stylistic unacceptability would be to avoid the possessive construction. When we look at No. 2 on Shuy's list, we find that a problem with the use of third-person singular present tense -s occurs. The use of *has* in our above sentence is therefore unjustified if we are to hold to our stated principle. In fact, this difference eliminates virtually all stories in the present tense that call for the use of third-person singular forms, a rather restricting limitation to be placed on reading materials. As for No. 3, which has plurals that might not appear in the nonstandard vocabulary of the child, this would probably take even more ingenuity, if in fact, there is any way anyone could deal with this. The elimination of structures calling for copulas, as in No. 5, would certainly add a further restriction to a growing inventory of structures to be avoided, although one might maintain that copulas can be used as long as the full form (e.g., *He is big*) and not the contracted from (e.g., *He's big*) is used, based on the conclusion that the full form of the copula is an integral part of the dialect whereas the contracted form may not be. Item No. 6 involves the elimination of potential negative concord sentences so that sentences such as *He doesn't have any toys* would not be permitted. One might suggest that this may be remedied by using only a negative indefinite (instead of a negative auxiliary and indefinite) such as *You have no toys*, but this is not feasible because the rule that transfers the negativized auxiliary to the indefinite form (e.g., *You don't have any toys* to *You have no toys*) is not an integral part of the dialect. The embedded question in No. 7 could be handled fairly simply by making a direct question out of it, such as *He asked, 'Can I come?'* instead of *He asked if he could come*. If one wanted to avoid constructions where the dialect might potentially use *be*, discourses involving certain types of habituality would have to be avoided, a stringent limitation if the principle is to be followed faithfully.

The above exercise demonstrates several important points with respect to the accommodation of materials for at least lower-class blacks. First, it shows that the feasibility of neutralization varies from feature to feature. There are some that can be handled by minor adjustments in current materials; others, however, require the elimination of significant portions of narratives or the cumbersome use of certain circumlocutions. It should be noted that when there are a number of different features that must be avoided in a particular type of passage, the problem of restructuring a narrative with these in mind can become quite difficult. Even if the overall differences between the standard and nonstandard dialect are significantly less than the similarities, the clustering of differences may make this strategy virtually unusable for particular types of passages.

Materials developers would not necessarily have to be as rigorous in their avoidance strategy as we have described above. One might just avoid certain types of grammatical differences while disregarding others. For example, a decision might be made to avoid grammatical differences which involve lexical changes, while disregarding those which involve affixial forms. This would mean that the use of embedded questions would be avoided because they involve a change of word order and the use of 'question' *if* or *whether*. But the avoidance of constructions involving the third-person singular present-tense forms, certain plurals, or possessives would not be maintained because these only involve the addition of a suffixial -*s* in Standard English. This procedure would reduce some of the problems caused by trying to eliminate frequently occurring inflectional forms.

There is one further aspect of the alternative discussed here that should be explicated because it may not be obvious from the presentation thus far; namely, the implicit assumption that a 'dialect-free' basal reader is a legitimate end-product of this method. Venezky observes:

> Reading materials for beginning reading should, in content, vocabulary and syntax, be as dialect free (and culture free) as possible. Given the inanity of present day materials, this should not be overly difficult to achieve. (1970:343)

Although Venezky assumes that the production of dialect-free materials is a reasonable and achievable goal, the pervasiveness of dialect pattern may be considerably more extensive than he anticipates. He does not define what he means by *dialect-free*, but he presumably is referring to the fact that features that might differentiate dialects can be eliminated. That is, readers can be made 'neutral' with respect to dialect. This term should not be confused with *dialect-fair*, which does not refer to neutrality, but to the adaptation of materials so that they are not biased against speakers of a given dialect. As Venezky himself admits, these terms are, in reality, reflections of the more inclusive concepts, *culture-free* and *culture-fair*. The former is highly suspect as an anthropologically valid concept because of the all-pervasive effect of cultural patterns on behavior (both linguistic and nonlinguistic), whereas the latter is an essential tenet of cultural relativism. With this in mind, we may ask if the effort to accommodate different dialects and cultures in terms of one set of materials is a naive attempt to achieve an unreal goal. At any rate, one must take these notions considerably more seriously than Venezky suggests.

Although we have described several apparent disadvantages of this alternative, we must not conclude our discussion before pointing out some potential advantages. For one, a modification of this method may eliminate some of the most salient features of Standard English that might be unfamiliar to the nonstandard-speaking child who comes to the schoolroom. Also, it would not incorporate socially stigmatized features of language, eliminating the controversy that inevitably surrounds the inclusion of nonstandard patterns in reading materials. The changes this alternative would require in materials could, in fact, be incorporated without necessarily being noticed by teachers who are using such materials.

*Dialect Readers.* The final alternative dealing with linguistic aspects of the reading problem involves the use of readers that are written in the vernacular of the children. That is, every effort is made in the beginning materials to represent the cultural and linguistic content indigenous to the child. As a brief illustration of how such materials might differ from the conventional materials, we may compare two versions of the same passage, one in Standard English and one in the dialect of the children.

*Standard English Version*
'Look down here,' said Suzy.
'I can see a girl in here.
That girl looks like me.
Come here and look, David!
Can you see that girl?' . . .

*Vernacular Black English Version*
Susan say, 'Hey, you-all, look down here!'
'I can see a girl in here.
That girl, she look like me.
Come here and look, David!
Could you see the girl?' . . .

(Wolfram and Fasold 1969: 147)

The second passage is a deliberate attempt to incorporate the features of the children's dialect into the basal readers. The absence of third-person singular *-s* (e.g., *Susan say, she look*), left dislocation (e.g., *That girl, she . . .*), *could* for *can*, and *you-all* are direct efforts to accurately represent the indigenous dialect of the child. Although it has sometimes been misunderstood by opponents of this alternative, the proposal of dialect readers does not advocate an eventual dualist reading system in

American society. It is only proposed as an initial step in the adequate acquisition of reading skills. Once reading fluency has been attained in the dialect readers and the child is sufficiently confident in his ability to read, a transition from dialect to Standard English readers is made. Stewart has illustrated the several stages of transition:

Stage 1
*Charles and Michael, they out playing.*
Grammatically, sentences at this stage will be pure non-standard Negro dialect. The vocabulary, also, will be controlled so that no words which are unfamiliar to the Negro dialect-speaking child will appear. Thus, all linguistic apsects of texts will be familiar to the beginning reader, and his full attention can be focused on learning to read the vocabulary. At this stage, no attempt should be made to teach standard-English pronounciations of the words, since the sentence in which they appear is not standard English.

Stage 2
*Charles and Michael, they are out playing*
At this stage, the most important grammatical features of standard English are introduced. In the example, there is one such feature— the copula. Apart from that, the vocabulary is held constant. Oral-language drills could profitably be used to teach person accord of the copula (*am, is, are*), and some standard-English pronunciations of the basic vocabulary might be taught.

Stage 3
*Charles and Michael are out playing.*
Grammatically, the sentences at this stage are brought into full conformity with standard English by making the remaining grammatical and stylistic adjustments. In the example, the 'double subject' of the nonstandard form is eliminated. Oral-language drills could be used to teach this and additional standard-English pronunciations of the basic vocabulary could be taught.　　　　　　　(Stewart 1969: 185)

The alternative that advocates the use of dialect readers seems to be based on three assumptions: 1. that there is sufficient mismatch between the child's system and the Standard English textbook to warrant distinct materials, 2. the psychological benefit from reading success will be stronger in the dialect than it might be if Standard English materials were used, and 3. the success of vernacular teaching in bilingual situations recommends a similar principle for bidialectal situations.

　　In order to evaluate the potential success of such an alternative, each of these assumptions must be discussed in more detail. Whether or not there is sufficient mismatch between even the most distinctive non-standard dialects and the language reading materials to warrant the use of dialect readers is a thorny question. We acknowledge that there are even differences between the spoken language of the middle-class child and the written language of the reading materials, but it is clear that the lower-class child can be expected to have a considerably greater divergence than the middle-class child. We concur with Goodman that

> the more divergence there is between the dialect of the learner and the dialect of learning, the more difficult will be the task of learning to read. (1969: 15).

But while such divergence exists, Fishman, for one, doubts whether the degree of difference is great enough to be a major problem. He cites examples of widespread literacy in countries where standard materials are used for speakers who speak dialects that are probably more linguistically divergent from the language of the readers than Standard English is from any American nonstandard dialect, and asks,

> if the distance or difference between the vernacular and the school variety is truly so central in causing reading difficulties, then how do we explain the widespread literacy not only in the same population [among impoverished pre-War *shtetl* Jews], but also among rural Japanese and Germans and Frenchmen and Swedes and Swiss-Germans and many others during the past quarter century and more?
> (1969: 1109)

Studies such as Labov and Robins's (1965), dealing with the relation of peer-group involvement and reading failure for adolescent males in Harlem, point to a value conflict more than a linguistic conflict as the basis of reading difficulty. But it is certainly not the case that linguistic conflict plays no role whatsoever. Until empirical evidence determines otherwise, it seems reasonable to assume that language divergence is of some significance.

Before leaving our discussion of oral and written language mismatch, we must submit a word of caution about the style of dialect readers. To what extent should the beginning materials reflect the 'pure nonstandard dialect' as opposed to the way in which children actually speak? In this regard, it is instructive to compare two passages, entitled 'Dumb Boy' and 'See a Girl,' included in Wolfram and Fasold (1969: 145ff.). 'Dumb Boy' was simply transcribed from a dialogue as it was actually recorded and 'See a Girl' was an attempt at 'pure' dialect. In the former case, there is considerable variation between forms, and as Labov (1969) has observed, some of this variation cannot simply be dismissed as importation from a superposed dialect; rather, it is an inherent part of the indigenous dialect. Some of the beginning dialect materials which start with pure dialect may, in effect, be creating a new type of mismatch between written and spoken language. That is, they have made the dialect to be more divergent from Standard English in written form than it actually is in spoken form. For example, the dialect reader entitled 'I Be Scared', by Davis, Gladney, and Leaverton (1969), overuses the habitual use of *be* in terms of the types of constructions in which it occurs and the relative frequency with which it occurs. Mismatch of this type must be minimized just as much as we minimize the difference between the mismatch of oral and written language for middle-class children learning to read.

The next assumption we must consider deals with the psychological reinforcement that such an approach might give to the child. Baratz observes that one of the prime advantages of this program is

> the powerful ego-supports of giving credence to the child's language system and therefore to himself, and giving him the opportunity to experience success in school.                          (1969: 114)

Ideally, we must concur that a program involving language familiar to the child (and, of course, an appropriate cultural setting, which must be its concomitant) will potentially hold a great opportunity for success. But if we look more closely at current attitudes toward reading materials as expressed by the community leaders and parents, we are faced with a sociopsychological fact that may force us to question these psychological advantages.

For a number of reasons, the notion of giving children nonstandard reading materials has provoked considerable controversy in communities for whom these materials have been intended. In fact, one recent attempt to experiment (one should note that this was only experimental, not curriculum revision) with dialect primers for speakers of Vernacular Black English was canceled before it ever had an opportunity to be tried. Commenting on the reasons for this cancellation, columnist William Raspberry of the *Washington Post* reported:

> Objections were made on a number of counts: Some found the text and illustrations 'uninspiring' or downright offensive; others concluded that white people were trying to use black children for their dubious experiments . . . But most of the parents, knowing that society equates facility in standard English with intelligence, do not want to risk confirming their children in 'undesirable' speech patterns —a risk that advocates insist is virtually nonexistent.
>
> (March 4, 1970: column 1)

At the heart of the rejection of dialect materials by the community (i.e., educators in lower-class schools, as well as parents and community leaders) seems to be the general attitude toward nonstandard dialects as a medium of education. The codification of a nonstandard language system may be viewed as a threat to social mobility in our society. For those who are attempting to attain middle-class status (within either the black community itself or the broader society), it may be seen as a program that implicitly attempts to 'keep the black man where he is'. For middle-class leaders in the black community, some of the negative reactions may be fostered by embarrassment or linguistic insecurity. Or, it may be viewed as a new type of paternalism toward the black community.

One fact that seems basic to the negative reactions towards the use of dialect in reading is the assumption that different materials for different social or ethnic groups implies the inherent incapability of these groups to learn using the traditional methods (apparently a by-product of the American 'melting-pot' myth). Difference is interpreted as inferiority.

Whether the reasons for rejecting dialect readers are real or imagined, the fact remains that the sociopolitical controversy over such a program and the community's negative reactions to it may seriously impede what otherwise might be an 'ego-supportive' activity. The attitudes of teachers, parents, and community leaders projected to children may be sufficiently strong to affect the children's motivation.

Finally, it is assumed on the basis of vernacular learning throughout the world that such a program can be expected to be successful. In fact, the UNESCO report on the use of vernacular languages in education specifically recommended that every pupil should begin formal education in his mother tongue (1953). For studies that compare beginning reading in the mother vis-à-vis the national language, the most predominant conclusion is that

> the youngsters of linguistic minorities learn to read with greater comprehension in the national language when they first learn to read in their mother tongue than when they receive all their reading instruction in the national language. (Modiano 1968: 9)

Nevertheless, there are still scholars who have reservations about vernacular reading for one reason or another. Bull (1955), for example, cites the vast expense (both in terms of financial considerations and curricula development) that this method may involve. Venezky (1970) cites many extralinguistic factors which bias experiments comparing vernacular and national language reading. He thus concludes that

> the native literacy approach, although possessing obvious cultural advantages over the standard language approach, has yet to be proven scholastically superior. (1970: 338)

A more relevant consideration in terms of the vernacular reading situation is the validity of using this procedure for different dialects as well as languages. A study by Österberg (1964) suggests that this alternative may be just as valid for different dialects as for different languages.

Other things being equal, we would expect that the reported success of teaching reading initially in the vernacular in other situations would recommend its usage for nonstandard-speaking children. But we cannot ignore the fact that sociopsychological factors we have discussed earlier may be sufficient to impede the acquisition of reading skills. We should note in this regard, however, that in a number of bilingual situations in which reading was initially taught in the vernacular, attitudes towards the indigenous language vis-à-vis the national language are quite comparable to the attitudes toward nonstandard dialects. That is, the vernacular is overtly socially stigmatized both by the dominant class and by those who actually use the stigmatized forms. Despite these attitudes, vernacular reading materials have been reported to be successful as a bridge to literacy in the national language.

Although none of these alternatives is completely satisfactory, they do suggest the directions in which solutions to the linguistic aspects of reading problems can be found. Some combination, modification, or adaptation of one or more of them would almost certainly make a contribution to the improvement of the quality of reading instruction for the speakers of nonstandard dialects.

## Teaching writing

With regard to writing, it may be important to take a hard look at just what kinds of writing are likely to be needed by a given group of nonstandard dialect-speaking children. Perhaps it would be more realistic to focus on writing personal and business letters and on answering questions on various forms than developing the ability to write a literary critique of a short story, novel, or poem. In some of these styles, personal letters, for example, it may be unnecessary to insist that every detail of Standard English grammar be observed. If a personal letter is to be written to a peer, there would seem to be little point in writing it in a 'foreign' standard dialect. However, in business letters, in filling in forms, and in other official kinds of writing, only Standard English grammar is considered appropriate and the ability to use it is a justifiable goal for an English teacher to set for all her students. In the process, it would be useful for the teacher to be able to distinguish three categories of errors. 1. There are problems in organization and logical development of arguments and similar difficulties. This kind of problem is not related to dialect differences. 2. There also are spelling and grammatical errors based on interference from a nonstandard dialect. We reviewed a set of written compositions by black inner-city students admitted to a major university, and found that over 40 per cent of the errors found could have been attributed to dialect interference. 3. Finally, there are errors in spelling, punctuation, and grammar which are not traceable to dialect interference.

A variety of apparent errors in the written work of Nonstandard English-speaking people are not errors in the strictest sense at all. They are simply the reflection in writing of the differences in grammar, pronunciation, and verbal expression between the nonstandard dialect and the standard one by which the writing is being judged. As we have pointed out, writing is a reflection of speech, so that if a student's writing contains features of his nonstandard dialect, it simply proves that his writing is fulfilling its basic function very well. In the area of grammar, when one of the university freshmen mentioned above wrote "Keith attitude' where Standard English would call for 'Keith's attitude', he was merely reflecting the rules of his nonstandard grammar. According to the rules of the nonstandard dialect in question, possessive *'s* may be used, but does not have to be. When another of these students spelled 'closest' as 'closes', he revealed that his pronunciation rules allow final consonant cluster simplification. Other cases arise in which a writer uses an expression that is current in his speech community but perhaps is unknown to the teacher. When one of the university freshmen wrote 'Keith had negative changes about DeVries', he was using an expression common among some black people. A teacher unfamiliar with the expression 'to have changes' might well treat this expression as an error.

Other spelling, grammar, and style errors occur which cannot be traced to dialect interference and should be considered genuine errors. In the same set of compositions discussed above, the misspellings 'laied' for 'laid' and 'tring' for 'trying' were observed. There is no pronunciation feature of the nonstandard dialect involved that would account for these spellings. In grammar, the use of the clause 'in which you live in' is not called for by the grammar of any nonstandard dialect. An example of what might be called a style problem is the expression 'in results of this', presumably for 'as a result of this'. All of these usages, along with mistakes in capitalization and punctuation, are appropriately treated as errors unrelated to dialect conflict.

This division into dialect and general errors has implications for teaching writing. In a real sense, the dialect-related 'errors' are not errors at all, but are correct usages based on a different grammar rule system. Because this is the case, their correction is perhaps not as urgent as the corrections of mistakes that are not founded on *any* rule system. This may mean that several writing exercises would be allowed to go by with no mention being made of the dialect-related errors. In some styles of writing—personal letters perhaps—elimination of dialect interference might not ever be appropriate.

To illustrate from a sample composition how a teacher might classify dialect features and genuine errors, let us take an example composition written by a rural sixth-grade student in south central Pennsylvania. The assignment was to write a short story from the point of view of any animal

the student wished. One student submitted this composition about a
cow. In the composition, we have attempted to indicate places at which a
teacher might mark corrections. Because we have never been elementary
school teachers, it may be that we have marked too many places or too
few, but we believe it is realistic enough to illustrate the point. The errors
marked with (a) numbers are general errors not related to the student's
dialect. The ones marked with (b) numbers are dialect-related.

> Cow
> Well (1a) at first I will (2a) Iterduce myself a little bit. I am (3a) rosy
> the cow (4a) My (1b) favert dish is cow feed. Well (5a) Well, here I
> am—OUCH! Oh! oh, ah, ah, ah, there (6a) sorry for the disturbance
> (7a) I just bit a (2b) jager. Well (8a) here I am eating grass. Cow feed
> (3b) don't have jagers (9a) (10a) thats (11a) wy I like (12a) I (13a)
> Here comes the farmer with the chop wagon (14a) I've got to go.
> Oh no (15a) haylage again (16a) it has jagers (17a) to (18a) I wish he'd
> bring corn. May the corn got (4b) all. I hate jagers. . . . OUCH! (19a)
> see (20a) wath I mean (21a) (22a) bossy just got a jager. Oh (23a) here
> come the boy. . . . Hey! Hey! Get in! HEY! good-by.
> Well you finally got here (24a) they just put the milker on me. It's a
> bother. Well (25a) good-by. See you next time.

It appears that the dialect-interference occurrences are a small minority,
and that the great majority of the general errors are examples of a general
punctuation problem (1a, 4a, 5a, 6a, 7a, 8a, 9a, 13a, 14a, 15a, 16a, 18a,
21a, 23a, 24a, 25a). Another very pervasive general problem is with
capitalization (2a, 3a, 5a, 16a, 19a, 22a, 24a). There are several spelling
errors not related to dialect (2a, 11a, 17a, 20a). There is an error involving the apostrophe in *that*'s (10a) and the student seems to have temporarily lost his train of thought and to have written *I* where he intended *it*
(12a). Once this student has mastered capitalization and punctuation,
the only specific local flaws will be the four spelling errors, the apostrophe
problem, the carelessness at 12a, and the dialect interferences. The
teacher also may wish to work with organization and transition as well,
but the composition impresses us as having considerable potential,
considering the age of the student.

The first of the dialect errors occurs at 1b, where the spelling *favert*
is doubtless far more accurate a representation of the writer's pronunciation than *favourite* would be. The word *jager* (perhaps a better spelling
would be *jagger*) is a common term in the area in which this boy lives for
thorns and other objects capable of causing scratches. It is not the sort
of term one expects to be used in writing, but it is again an accurate
reflection of the spoken language. At two places (3b and 5b) the student's
writing reflects the fact that the third-person singular present tense
suffix -*s* is not required by the grammar of his dialect in every situation

in which the standard dialect requires it. At 4b, he uses the expression *got all* (was used up), a common expression in this region borrowed from Pennsylvania Dutch.

A teacher aware of the nature of dialect interference might well spend his efforts on capitalization, punctuation, spelling, and organization and development problems and ignore the dialect errors until much later. The composition, with improvement in the general areas and in organization, but with the dialect interference allowed to pass, might look like this.

> Cow
> Well, at first I will introduce myself a little bit. I am Rosy the cow. My favert dish is cow feed. Well, well, here I am—OUCH! Oh! oh, ah, ah, ah, there, sorry for the disturbance. I just bit a jagger. Well, here I am eating grass. Cow feed don't have jaggers, that's why I like it.
> Here comes the farmer with the chop wagon. I've got to go.
> Oh no, haylage again! It has jaggers, too. I wish he'd bring corn. Maybe the corn got all. I hate jaggers—OUCH! See what I mean? Bossy just got a jagger. Oh, here come the boy. He's yelling, 'Hey! HEY! Get in! HEY!'
> Well, we finally got here. They just put the milker on me. It's a bother. Well, that's all for now.

If the student showed this degree of improvement (we do not mean to suggest that the composition could not be further improved, even aside from the dialect items), he might well be worthy of praise and an A grade. It would then be time to teach him the necessity of using Standard English in written work. The two basic assumptions stressed in our discussion of both reading and writing—respect for linguistic integrity of nonstandard dialects and a realization of the primacy of speech over writing—put a new and helpful perspective on the teaching of both these language arts.

## Notes

First published in *The Study of Social Dialects in American English*, Prentice-Hall, 1974.

1. Rosenthal (1973) has shown that many preschool children have remarkably consistent notions on what is 'correct' and 'not correct' in language. Many also are able to make accurate judgments about the ethnicity of a speaker from speech alone.
2. There is a possible position, which we call 'enlightened eradicationism', that is more defensible. Under this position, the bidialectal goal

(cell 3) is pursued, but with the idea that eradication is the likely result if the curriculum is successful at all. The reason given for this is that the maintenance of two dialects is not possible because there are not enough linguistic distinctions between them. The attitudes, motivation, and methods of enlightened eradicationism, however, are those of bidialectism, not eradicationism as we have described it.

3. This description is a summary of Feigenbaum 1970a: 92–99. Readers interested in developing lessons of this type should consult this source.

4. It has been pointed out (e.g., Weber 1969: 38) that the language of the typical reading text does not match the speech of the Standard English-speaking child very well either. But the degree of difference is greater if the student does not control spoken Standard English.

5. Some qualification of this statement is necessary, because written language probably represents a level of formality never used in spoken language in most cases. However, the basic relationship between speech and writing is the one we have described.

6. In the article by Shuy in which this procedure is suggested, this is only one of several types of changes that Shuy recommends for materials to be used by nonstandard dialect speakers.

# Bibliography

**Aarons, B.** and **W. A. Stewart** (eds), 'Linguistic-cultural differences and American education', *The Flordia FL Reporter*, Anthology issue.

**Abrahams, R. D.** (1970), 'The advantages of black English', Southern Conference of Language Learning, Florida 1970.

**Abrahams, R. D.** and **G. Gay**, 'Black culture in the classroom', in R. D. Abrahams and R. C. Troike (eds), *Language and Cultural Diversity in American Education* Englewood Cliffs, N. J.: Prentice-Hall.

**Alatis, J. W.** (ed), Twentieth Annual Round Table Meeting, Number 22, Georgetown University School of Linguistics.

**Alatis, James** (ed) (1970). Bilingualism and Language Contact: Anthropological, Linguistic, Psychological and Sociological Aspects. Monograph Series on Languages and Linguistics 23. Washington, D.C.: Georgetown University Press.

**Alford, N. D.** (1970). Research Report on some Aspects of the Language Development of Pre-School Children. Brisbane.

**Allen, Jones J.** (1968, 1969). English language teaching in a social/cultural dialect situation. English Language Teaching 22.199–204; 24.18–23.

**Alleyne, M. C.** (1961). 'Communication and politics in Jamaica', *Caribbean Studies* 3.

(1963). 'Language and society in St. Lucia', *Caribbean Studies* 1(1).

**Allsopp, S. R. R.** (1949–53). 'The language we speak', *Kyk-over-all*, Vols. 2, 3, 5 Guyana.

(1958a), 'The English language in British Guiana', *English Language Teaching* 12(2).

(1958b), 'Pronominal forms in the dialect of English used in Georgetown (British Guiana) and its environs by people engaged in non-clerical occupations', M.A. thesis. University of London.

(1962), 'Expression of state and action in the dialect of English used in the Georgetown area of British Guiana', Ph.D. dissertation. University of London.

(1965), 'British Honduras—The linguistic dilemma', *Caribbean Quarterly* 11(3 and 4).

(1972a), 'Some suprasegmental features of Caribbean English'.

(1972b), 'The problem of acceptability in Caribbean creolized English', in: *Creole Languages and Educational Development: Papers from the Conference Sponsored by UNESCO and UWI, July 1972*, ed. by D. R. Craig. To be published London, New Beacon Publications.

**ALSED** Newsletters, The Division of Structures, Content, Methods & Techniques of Education, UNESCO, 7 place de Fontenoy, F-75700 Paris.

**Armstrong, B.** (1968). 'The teaching of English in Guiana', *The Guiana Teacher*, 2(7).

**Ashton-Warner, Sylvia** (1963). Teacher. New York.

**Bailey, B. L.** (1953). 'Creole languages of the Caribbean area', M.A. thesis. Columbia University.
(1962), *A Language Guide to Jamaica*. New York, Research Institute for the study of Man.
(1963), 'Teaching of English noun-verb concord in primary schools in Jamaica', *Caribbean Quarterly*, 9(4).
(1964), 'Some problems in the language teaching situation in Jamaica', in: *Social Dialects and Language Learning*, by Roger W. Shuy. Champaign, Illinois, National Council of Teachers of English.
(1966), *Jamaican Creole Syntax: A Transformational Approach*. Cambridge University Press.
(1971), 'Jamaican creole: can dialect boundaries be defined?', in: Hymes (ed).

**Bailey, C. J. N.** (1969–70). 'Studies in three-dimentional language theory I–IV', *Working Papers in Linguistics*, University of Hawaii.
(1970), 'Using data variation, to confirm rather than undermine, the validity of abstract syntactic structures', *Working Papers in Linguistics*. University of Hawaii.

**Bamgbose, A.** (1971). The English Language in Nigeria. In John Spencer, The English Language in West Africa. London: Longman.

**Baratz, Joan C.** 'A Bidialectal Task for Determining Language Proficiency in Economically Disadvantaged Negro Children'. *Child Development 40* (1969): 889–902.

**Baratz, J. C.** (1969). 'Teaching Reading in an urban negro school system', in: Baratz and Shuy (eds).

**Baratz, J.** and **R. W. Shuy** (eds) (1969). *Teaching Black Children to Read*, Washington, D.C., Center for Applied Linguistics.

**Barik, H. C.** and **M. Swain** (1974). English-French bilingual education in the early grades: The Elgin Study. *The Modern Language Journal*, 58, 392–403.

**Barik, H. C.** and **M. Swain** (1975a). A Canadian experiment in bilingual education at the grade eight and nine levels: The Peel Study. *Foreign Language Annals.*

**Barik, H. C.** and **M. Swain** (1975b). Three-year evaluation of a large-scale early grade French immersion program: The Ottawa Study. *Language Learning*, 25.

**Barik, H. C.** and **M. Swain** (1976). Primary grade French immersion in a unilingual English Canadian setting: The Toronto study through grade two. *Canadian Journal of Education.*

**Bazell, C. E.** et al (1966). In Memory of J. R. Firth. London.

**Bennett, L.** (1942). 'Jamaica dialect verse: comp. George R. Bowen', *The Herald*, Kingston.

(1943), *Jamaica Humour in Dialect*, Kingston, Gleaner Jamaica Press Association.

(1950), *Anancy Stories and Dialect Verse.* Kingston, Jamaica, Pioneer Press.

**Benton, Richard** (1964). Research into the English Language Difficulties of Maori School Children, 1963–64. Wellington: Maori Education Foundation.

**Bernstein, Basil**. 'A Socio-linguistic Approach to Sociolization: With Some References to Educability'. In *Language and Poverty: Perspectives on a Theme*, edited by Frederick Williams, pp. 25–61. Chicago: Markham Publishing Co., 1970.

**Berry, J.** (1972). 'Some Observations on residual tone in West Indian English', in: Craig (ed). To be published.

**Bickerton, D.** (1971). 'Guyanese Speech'. Manuscript. University of Guyana.

(1971a), 'Inherent variability and variable rules', *Foundations of Language 7.*

(1972), 'The structure of polyectal grammars', in: Shuy (ed), 1973.

(1973), 'On the nature of a creole continuum', *Language* 49 (3).

**Blom, Jan-Petter** and **John Gumperz** (1972). 'Social Meaning and Linguistic Structure: Code-Switching in Norway'. In: *Directions in Sociolinguistics*, edited by John Gumperz and Dell Hymes. Holt, Rinehart and Winston.

**Blom, J. P.** and **J. J. Gumperz**. 'Some Social Determinants of Verbal Behaviour'. *Directions in Sociolinguistics*, edited by J. J. Gumperz and D. Hymes. New York: Holt, Rinehart and Winston, 1972.

**Bolinger, D.** 'Let's change our base of operations', *Modern Language Journal*, March 1971.

**Bowers, J.** (1968). 'Language Problems and Literacy', in J. A. Fishman, et al. pp. 381–401.

**Bronkhurst, H. V. P.** (1888). *Among the Hindus and Creole of British Guiana*, London, T. Woolmar.

**Brooks, C. K.** (1964). 'Some approaches to teaching English as a second Language', in: Stewart (ed).

**Brooks, Sammie**. 'A Study of the Rhetorical Styles of Bobby Seale, Chairman of the Black Panther Party for Self-Defense'. Term paper, Rhetoric 152, University of California, Berkeley, 1971.

**Brosnahan, L. F.** (1963). Some historical cases of language imposition. In John Spencer, *Language in Africa*. Cambridge.

**Bruck, M., M. S. Rabinovitch** and **M. Oates** (1975). The effects of French immersion programs on children with language disabilities— a preliminary report. *Working Papers on Bilingualism*, 5, 47–86.

**Bruck, M., G. R. Tucker** and **J. Jakimik** (1973). Are French immersion programs suitable for working class children? A follow-up investigation. McGill University, Psychology Dept., (mimeo).

**Bruner, J. R.** and **N. H. Mackworth** (1970). How adults and children search and recognize pictures. *Human Development*, 13, 149–177.

**Bujra, J.** (1972). 'Pumwani: language usage in an urban muslim community.' In: *Language in Kenya*, ed. by W. H. Whiteley. Oxford University Press.

**Bull, W. E.** 'The use of vernacular languages in education' in D. H. Hymes *Language in Culture & Society*, London & New York: Harper & Row.

**Bull, W. E.** (1955). 'Review of: The use of vernacular languages in Education', IJAL 21:288–94.

**Burstall, C.** (1968). *French From Eight: A National Experiment*. Slough: NFER.

**Burstall, C.** (1970). *French in the Primary School: Attitudes and Achievement*. Slough: NFER.

**Burstall, C., M. Jamieson, S. Cohen** and **M. Hargreaves** (1974). *Primary French in the Balance*. Slough: NFER.

**Burstall, C.** 'Factors affecting foreign-language learning: a consideration of some recent research findings', in *Language Teaching and Linguistics: Abstracts*, 1975.

**Carrington, L. D.** (1967). 'St. Lucia: A descriptive analysis of its phonology and morphosyntax', Ph.D. dissertation. Mona, University of the West Indies.

(1968), 'English language learning problems in the Caribbean', *Trinidad and Tobago Modern Language Review* No. 1.

(1969), 'Deviations from standard English in the speech of primary school children in St. Lucia and Dominica', *IRAL*, Vol. VIII/3.

(1970), 'English language teaching in the Commonwealth Caribbean', *Commonwealth Education Liaison Committee Newsletter* 2(10).

**Carrington, L. D.** 'Determining language education policy in Caribbean sociolinguistic complexes', *Linguistics*, 175, (July 1, 1976).

**Carrington, L. D., C. Borely** and **E. H. Knight** (1972). *Away Robin Run: A Critical Description of the teaching of the Language Arts in the Primary Schools of Trinidad and Tobago.* St. Augustine, Trinidad, Institute of Education.

(1972a), *Linguistic exposure of Trinidad children,* St. Augustine, Trinidad, Institute of Education.

**Carroll, J. B.** (1960). 'Language development in children', in: Saporta (ed), 1961.

**Carroll, John B.** (1960). 'The prediction of success in intensive foreign language training', Cambridge, Mass., Graduate School of Education, Harvard University (mimeo).

(1965), 'The prediction of success in intensive foreign language training. In Robert Glazer (ed), *Training research and education.* New York, Wiley.

(1966), 'The contributions of psychological theory and educational research to the teaching of foreign languages'. In Albert Valdman (ed), *Trends in language teaching.* New York. McGraw-Hill Company.

**Carter, T. P.** (1970). *Mexican Americans in school: A history of educational neglect.* N.Y., College Entrance Examination Board.

**Carton, Aaron S.** (1966). *The method of interference in foreign language study.* The Research Foundation of the City of New York.

**Cassidy, F. G.** (1961). *Jamaica Talk: Three Hundred Years of the English Language in Jamaica.* London, Macmillan.

**Cassidy, F. G.** and **R. B. LePage** (1967). *Dictionary of Jamaica English.* Cambridge University Press.

(1972), 'Jamaican creole and Twi: some comparisons', in: Craig (ed), to be published.

**Cassidy, Frederick G.** (1971). 'Tracing the pidgin element in Jamaican creole' in Dell Hymes (ed), Pidginization and Creolization of Languages, Cambridge.

**Cave, George N.** (1970). 'Some sociolinguistic factors in the production of standard language in Guyana and implications for the language teacher. *Language Learning* 20.249–263.

**Cave, G. N.** (1970). 'Sociolinguistic factors in Guyana language'. *Language Learning* 20 (2).

(1971), *Primary School Language in Guyana,* Georgetown, Guyana Teachers' Association.

(1972), 'Measuring linguistic maturity: the case of the noun stream', in: Craig (ed), to be published.

**Cazden, C. B., V. P. John** and **D. Hymes** (eds) (1972). *Functions of Language in the Classroom,* New York, Columbia University, Teachers College Press.

**Cazden C.** 'Approaches to social dialects in early childhood education', in: R.W. Shuy (ed)*Sociolinguistics: a Cross-Disciplinary Perspective,*

Washington, D.C.: Center for Applied Linguistics.

**Cazden, C.** *Child Language and Education.* New York: Holt, Rinehart and Winston.

**Chomsky, Noam.** (1965). *Aspects of the theory of syntax.* Cambridge, Mass.: M.I.T. Press.

**Christian, Jane** and **Chester, Christian** (1966). Spanish language and culture in the Southwest. In: Joshua Fishman, et al., Language Loyalty in the United States. The Hague: Mouton Press.

**Christie, P.** (1969). 'A sociolinguistic study of some Dominican creole speakers', Ph.D. dissertation. University of York.

**Clyne, Michael G.** (1967). *Transference and triggering.* The Hague: Martinus Nijhoff.

**Cohen, A. D.** *A Sociolinguistic Approach to Bilingual Education*, Stanford University Committee on Linguistics.

**Cohen, A. D.** 'Successful immersion education in North America', in: *Working Papers on Bilingualism*, 5, (1975): Ontario Institute for *Studies in Education*.

**Cohen, A.** and **M. Swain** 'Bilingual education: the 'immersion'' model in the North American context', *TESOL Quarterly*, 10, 1, 1976.

**Cohen, A. D.** and **L. M. Laosa** (1975). Approaches to second language instruction: A research model. Paper presented at the Annual Meeting of the American Educational Research Association, Washington, D.C., March 31—April 3, 1975.

**Cohen, A. D.** and **S. M. Lebach** (1974). A language experiment in California: Student, teacher, parent and community reactions after three years. *Workpapers in Teaching English as a Second Language*, Volume 8, Univ. of California, Los Angeles, 33–46.

**Cohen, D.** (1974). The Culver City Spanish immersion program: The first two years. *The Modern Language Journal*, 58, 95–103.

**Cohen, D.** (1975). Progress report on the Culver City Spanish immersion program: the third and fourth years. *Working Papers in English as a Second Language*, Vol. 9, University of California at Los Angeles, 47–65.

**Collymore, Frank** (ed) (1952 onwards). *Bim.* Barbados, Advocate Press.

**Cook-Gumperz, J.** *Social control and socialization: a study of class differences in the language of maternal control*, London: Routledge & Kegan Paul.

**Cooper, Robert L.** (1970). 'What do we learn when we learn a language?', *TESOL Quarterly*, 4, 303–14.

**Coulter, Kenneth** (1968). Linguistic Error-Analysis of the Spoken English of Two Native Russians. Thesis, University of Washington.

**Coulthard, R. M.** and **W. P. Robinson**. 'The Structure of the Nominal

Group and the Elaboratedness of Code'. *Language and Speech II*, (1968): 234–50.

**Corder, S. P.** (1967). 'The significance of learner's errors'. IRAL 5.161–169.

**Corder, S. P.** (1971). 'Idiosyncratic dialects and error analysis'. IRAL 9.147–159.

**Cowan, P.** 'The Link between Cognitive Structure and Social Structure in Two-Child Verbal Interaction'. Symposium presented at the Society for Research on Child Development meeting, 1967.

**Craig, D. R.** (1964). 'The written English of some 14-year-old Jamaican and English children' in: *Faculty of Education*. U.W.I.

(1966a), 'Some developments in language teaching in the West Indies', *Caribbean Quarterly*, 12(1).

(1966b), 'Teaching English to Jamaican creole speakers: A model of a multi-dialect situation', *Language Learning* 16(1–2).

(1967), 'Some early indications of learning a second dialect', *Language Learning* 17(3 and 4).

(1969), *An Experiment in Teaching English*. Caribbean University Press and London, Ginn and Co., Ltd.

(1971), 'English in Secondary Education in a former British Colony: a case study of Guyana', *Caribbean Studies* 10(4).

(1971a), 'Education and creole English in the West Indies: some sociolinguistic factors', in: Hymes (ed), 1971.

(1971b), 'The Use of language by 7-year-old Jamaican children living in contrasting socio-economic environments. Unpublished Ph.D. thesis. University of London.

(1972), 'Intralingual differences, communication and language theory', in: Craig (ed), forthcoming.

(1973), 'Social class, language and communication in Jamaican children', in: *Education in the Commonwealth 6*. London, Commonwealth Secretariat. (Forthcoming). *Creole languages and Educational Development: Papers from the Conference Sponsored by UNESCO and the UWI, July 1972*. London, New Beacon Publications.

**Craig, Dennis** n.d. 'Linguistic and sociolinguistic problems in relation to language education and policy in the English-speaking Caribbean.

**Craig, R. D.** 'Bidialectal education: creole and standard in the West Indies', *Linguistics*, 175, July 1, (1976).

**Criper, C.** and **P. Ladefoged** (1971). 'Linguistic complexity in Uganda' in: *Language use and social change*, (ed) by W. H. Whiteley, 145–59. Oxford University Press.

**Crow, L. D.** et al (1966). *Educating the Culturally Disadvantaged Child*. New York, David McKay Co.

**Cruikshank, J. G.** (1911). 'Negro English with reference particularly to Barbados', *Timehri*, 3rd series, 1(183).

(1916), *'Black Talk'. N Being notes on negro dialect in British Guiana with (inevitably) a chapter on the vernacular of Barbados*. Guiana, The Argosy Press.

**Cuffie, D.** (1964). 'Problems in the teaching of English in the island of Trinidad from 1797 to the present day'. M.A. Thesis. University of London, Institute of Education.

**Dale, R. R.** (1969). *Mixed or Single-Sex School? Vol. 1: A Research study in pupil-teacher relationships*. London: Routledge & Kegan Paul.

**Dale, R. R.** (1971). *Mixed or Single-Sex School? Vol. 2: Some social aspects*. London: Routledge and Kegan Paul.

**Dale, R. R.** (1974). *Mixed or Single-Sex School? Vol. 3: Attainment, attitudes and overview*. London: Routledge and Kegan Paul.

**Darnell, Regna.** (1971). 'The bilingual speech community: A Cree example. In Regna Darnell, Linguistic Diversity in Canadian Society. Edmonton.

**Davis, Olga, Mildred Gladney** and **Lloyd Leaverton** (1968). *Psycholinguistics Reading Series*. Chicago: Board of Education.

**DeCamp, D.** (1961). 'Social and geographical factors in Jamaican dialects! In: Creole language studies, II, (ed) by R. B. Le Page. Macmillan.

**DeCamp, D.** (1968). 'Toward a generative analysis of a post-creole speech continuum. Conference on Pidginization and Creolization of Languages, Jamaica. (To appear).

**DeCamp, D.** (1968). The field of Creole language studies. Studia Anglica Posnaniensia 1.30–51.

**DeCamp, D.** (1971). 'Toward a generative analysis of a post creole speech continuum', in: Hymes (ed), 1971.
(1972), 'Standard English books and creole speaking children', in: Craig (ed), forthcoming.

**Diebold, R.** 'Incipient Bilingualism'. *Language*, 1961, 37, 97–112.

**Dubin, F.** 'The sociolinguistic dimension of dormitory English'. ERIC 038637.

**Dulay, H. C.** and **M. K. Burt** (1974). Errors and strategies in child second language acquisition. *TESOL Quarterly*, 8, 129–136.

**Edwards, W.** (1972). 'Have' and 'be' in Guyanese creole', in: Craig (ed), forthcoming.

**Engle, P. L.** (1975). *The use of vernacular languages in education: Language medium in early schools for minority language groups*. Papers in Applied Linguistics, Bilingual Education Series No. 3. Arlington, Va., Center for Applied Linguistics.

**Elias-Oliveres, L.** 'Language use in a Chicano community: a sociolinguistic approach', *Working Papers in Sociolinguistics*, No. 30,

February 1976. (Southwest Educational Development Laboratory, 211 East Seventh St., Austin, Texas 78701).

**Ervin-Tripp, S.** 'Interaction of Language, Topic, and Listener', In: J. Gumperz and D. Hymes (eds), *Ethnography of Communication*. American Anthropologist, 1964, 66, no. 2, 86–102.

**Ervin-Tripp, S.** 'An Issei Learns English'. *Journal of Social Issues.* 1967, 23, 78–90.

**Ervin-Tripp, S.** (1970). 'Structure and process on language acquisition'. In: James E. Alatis (ed), *21st Annual Round Table*. Washington, Georgetown University Press.

**Ervin-Tripp, S.** 'Is second language learning like the first?', *TESOL Quarterly*, Vol. 8 no. 4 1974.

**Ervin-Tripp, S.** 'Children's sociolinguistic competence and dialect diversity', in A. S. Dil (ed). *Language Acquistion and Communicative Choice*, Stanford, California: Stanford University Press.

**Faculty of Education, University of the West Indies** (1965). 'Language teaching, linguistics and the teaching of English in a multilingual society', *Report of the Conference at University of the West Indies, April*, 1964.

**Fasold, R. W.** (1968). 'Isn't English the first language too?', *NCTE Annual Conference, Wisconsin* 1968.

(1969), 'Orthography in reading materials for black English speaking children', in: Baratz and Shuy (eds), 1969.

**Fasold, Ralph W.** (1969a). 'Tense and the form *be* in Black English', *Language*, 45:763–76.

(1969), 'Orthography in Reading Materials for Black English Speaking Children', in *Teaching Black Children to Read*, (ed). Joan C. Baratz and Roger W. Shuy. Washington, D.C.: Center for Applied Linguistics.

(1970), 'Two Models of Socially Significant Linguistic Variation', *Language*, 46:551–63.

(1971), 'What Can an English Teacher Do about Nonstandard Dialect?', in *Studies in English to Speakers of Other Languages and Standard English to Speakers of Non-Standard Dialect*, Special Anthology Issue and Monograph 14 of *The English Record*, (ed) Rudolfo Jacobson.

(1972), *Tense Marking in Black English: A Linguistic and Social Analysis*. Washington, D.C.: Center for Applied Linguistics.

**Fasold, R. W.** and **R. W. Shuy** (eds) (1970). *Teaching Standard English in the Inner City*. Washinton, D.C.: Center for Applied Linguistics.

**Fawcett, Nancy Fox** (1969). Teaching Bidialectalism in a Second Language: A Strategy for Developing Native English Proficiency in Navajo Students. Thesis, University of California, Los Angeles.

222    Bibliography

**Feigenbaum, Irwin** (1969). 'Using Foreign Language Methodology to Teach Standard English: Evaluation and Adaptation', in *Linguistic-Cultural Differences and American Education*, Special Anthology Issue of *the Florida FL Reporter*, (ed) Alfred A. Aarons, Barbara Y. Gordon, and William A. Stewart.

(1970a), 'The Use of Nonstandard English in Teaching Standard: Contrast and Comparison', in *Teaching Standard English in the Inner City*, (ed) Ralph W. Fasold and Roger W. Shuy, Washington, D.C.: Center for Applied Linguistics.

**Ferguson, C.** 'Diglossia'. *Word*, 1959, 15, 34–41.

**Ferguson, C. A.** (1964). Diglossia. *Word*, 15, 325–340.

**Ferguson, C.** (1966). 'Sociolinguistically oriented language surveys. Linguistic Reporter, 8/4.1–3.

(1966), National Sociolinguistic profile formulas. In: Sociolinguistics, ed. by W. Bright. 309–15. The Hague, Mouton.

**Ferguson, Charles A.** (1971). *Language Structure and Language Use*. Stanford: Stanford University Press.

**Ferguson, Charles A.** (1971). Absence of copula and the notion of simplicity: a study of normal speech, baby talk, foreigner talk and pidgin. In Charles A. Ferguson, *Language Structure and Language Use*. Stanford: Stanford University Press.

**Figueroa, J.** (1962). 'Language Teaching: Part of a general and professional problem', *English Language Teaching* 16(3).

(1966), 'Notes on the teaching of English in the West Indies', *New World Quarterly* 2(4).

(1972), 'Some Notes, together with samples of language occurring in the creole context', in: Craig (ed), forthcoming.

**Fischer, J. L.** 'Social Influences in the Choice of a Linguistic Variant', *Word* 14 (1958): 47–56.

**Fishman, J. A.** 'Language Maintenance and Language Shift as Fields of Inquiry'. *Linguistics* (1964), 9, 32–70.

**Fishman, J. A.** 'Who Speaks What Language to Whom and When?'. *Linguistics*, (1965), 2, 67–88.

**Fishman, Joshua**, et al (1966). Language Loyalty in the United States. The Hague: Mouton.

**Fishman, Joshua** (1967). Bilingualism with and without diglossia; diglossia with and without bilingualism. *Journal of Social Issues* 23.29–38.

**Fishman, Joshua** (ed) (1968). Readings in the Sociology of Language. The Hague: Mouton.

**Fishman, Joshua A.** 'Sociolinguistic Perspectives on the Study of Bilingualism'. *Linguistics*, (1968).

**Fishman, J. A.** (1968). Bilingualism in the barrio, vol. 1. Washington, D.C., Department of Health, Education and Welfare.

(1971), Sociolinguistics: a brief introduction. Newbury House.

**Fishman, Joshua A.** (1969). 'Literacy and the Language Barrier', Book Review of *Intellegence and Cultural Environment*, by Phillip E. Vernon, and *Teaching Black Children to Read*, ed. Joan C. Baratz and Roger W. Shuy. *Science* 165:1108–1109.

(1969b), 'Bilingual Attitudes and Behaviours', *Language Sciences* No. 5:5–11.

**Fishman, J. A.** 'The politics of bilingual education', in *Monograph Series on Languages and Linguistics*, No. 23, 1970 Georgetown University Round Table on Languages and Linguistics, Washington, D.C.

**Fishman, J. A.** Ch.'s 9, 15 of A. S. Dil (ed) Language in *Sociocultural Change*, Stanford, California: Stanford University Press.

**Fishman, J. A.** 'The sociology of bilingual education', *Etudes de Linguistique Appliquée*, 1974.

**Fishman, J. A.** (ed). *Bilingualism in the Barrio* Bloomington: Research Center for the Language Sciences, Indiana University.

**Fishman, Joshua, Robert L. Cooper** and **Roxana Ma** et al (1968). Bilingualism in the Barrio. New York: Yeshiva University.

**Fishman, Joshua, Charles Ferguson** and **Jyotirindra Das Cupta** (1968). Language Problems of Developing Nations. New York.

**Fishman, Joshua A., Robert L. Cooper** and **Roxana Ma** (1971). *Bilingualism in the Barrio, Language Science Monograph*, Vol. 7. Bloomington, Ind., Indiana University Publications.

**Fishman, J. A.** and **E. Lueders-Salmon** (1972). 'What has the sociology of language to say to the teacher? On teaching the standard variety to speakers of dialectal or sociolectal varieties', in: Cazden, John, and Hymes (eds), 1972.

**Fishman, J. A.** and **J. Lovas**. 'Bilingual education in a sociolinguistic perspective', in *The Language Education of Minority Children* edited by B. Spolsky Rowley, Massachusetts: Newbury House.

**Fishman, J. A.** and **E. Luders**. 'What has the sociology of language to say to the teacher?' in A. S. Dil (ed) *Language in Sociocultural Change* Stanford, California: Stanford University Press; also in C. Cazden, V. John, D. H. Hymes (eds) *Functions of Language in the Classroom* London and New York: Teachers College Press, Columbia University.

**Francis, John** (1971). New modalities for foreign language instruction. Unpublished paper, Center for Applied Linguistics.

**Francis, W. Nelson** (1958). *The Structure of American English*. New York: The Ronald Press.

**Fries, C. C.** (1922). *The Structure of English*. London, Longmans, Green, and Co.

(1940), 'American English grammar', *English Monograph 10* Champaign, Illinois, NCTE.

**Fries, Charles C.** (1940). *American English Grammar: the Grammatical*

*Structure of Present-Day American English with Especial Reference to Social Differences or Class Dialects.* New York: Appleton-Century-Crofts.

**Frender, R.** and **W. E. Lambert**. 'Speech style and scholastic success', in *Mongraph Series on Languages and Linguistics*, No. 25, 1972 Georgetown University Round Table on Languages and Linguistics, Washington, D.C.

**Gaarder, A. B.** 'The first seventy-six bilingual education projects *Monograph Series on Languages and Linguistics*, 23, 1970 Georgetown University Round Table on Languages and Linguistics, Washington, D.C.

**Gaidoz, H.** (1881). 'Bibliographic Creole', *Revue Critique d'Histoire et de litterature*, 13(35 and 45).

**Gardner, Robert C.** and **Wallace E. Lambert** (1959). Motivational variables in second language acquisition. *Canadian Journal of Psychology*, 13, 4, 266–272.

**Gay, G.** and **R. D Abrahams**. 'Black Culture in the Classroom', in *Language and cultural diversity in American education*. Edited by R. D. Abrahams and R. C. Troike, Englewood Cliffs, N.J.: Prentice-Hall.

**Geoghegan, W.** 'The Use of Marking Rules in Semantic Systems', Language Behaviour Laboratory Working Paper No. 26. Berkeley: University of California, 1969.

**Gilbert, Glenn** (ed) (1971). The German Language in America—A Symposium. Austin: University of Texas.

**Ginsburg, H.** *The Myth of the Deprived Child.* Englewood Cliffs, N.J.: Prentice-Hall.

**Gleason, H. A., Jr.** (1961). *An Introduction to Descriptive Linguistics.* Revised ed. New York: Holt, Rinehart and Winston.

**Gonzales, G.** and **E. Lezama**. 'The dual language model: a practical approach to bilingual education', *TESOL Quarterly* Vol. 8 No. 4, 1974.

**Goodman, Kenneth S.** (1969). 'Dialect Barriers to Reading Comprehension', in *Teaching Black Children to Read*. ed. Joan C. Baratz and Roger W. Shuy. Washington, D.C.: Center for Applied Linguistics.

**Gorman, T. P.** Ch.'s 14 (esp. p. 434 ff.), 16 of W. H. Whiteley (ed.) *Language in Kenya*, London: Oxford University Press.

**Gorman, T. P.** Ch. 1 of Gorman (ed) *Language in Education in Eastern Africa*. Nairobi: Oxford University Press.

**Granda, German de** (1968). *Transculturacion Interferencia Linguistica en el Puerto Rico Contemporáneo.* Bogota: Instituto Caro y Cuervo.

**Grant, D. R. B.** (1964). 'A study of some common language and spelling errors of elementary school children in Jamaica', in: Faculty of Education 1965.

**Gray, C.** (1963). 'Teaching English in the West Indies', *Caribbean Quarterly*, 9(1 and 2).

**Greenlee, Mel.** 'Rules for Code-Switching: A Pilot Study of Natural Conversation in Bilingual Children'. Term paper, Rhetoric 260, University of California, Berkeley, 1971.

**Grimshaw, Allen D.** (1971). Some social forces and some social functions of pidgin and creole languages. In Dell Hymes (ed.), *Pidginization and Creolization of Languages*. Cambridge.

**Gudschinsky, S.** 'Literacy in the Mother Tongue and Second Language Learning', in *Conference on Child Language* Chicago, November, 1971: *Les Presses de l Universite Laval, Quebec*.

**Gumperz, J. J.** (1964). Linguistic and social interaction in two communities. In: *The ethnography of communication*. ed. by J. J. Gumperz and D. Hymes. American Anthropologist, 66/6, pt. 2.137–53.

**Gumperz, J.** 'Linguistic Repertoires, Grammars and Second Language Instruction', Georgetown *Monograph Series*, No. 18, 1965, 81–90.

**Gumperz, J.** 'The Linguistic Markers of Bilingualism', *Journal of Social Issues*; 1967, 23, No. 2, 48–57.

**Gumperz, J. J.** 'On the Linguistic Markers of Bilingual Communication' In *Problems of Bilingualism*, edited by J. Macnamara, pp. 48–57, *Journal of Social Issues* 23 (1967): pt. 2, pp. 48–57.

**Gumperz, J. J.** and **Edward Hernandez**. 'Bilingualism, Bidialectalism, and Classroom Interaction'. In *Language in the Classroom*, edited by C. Cazden. New York: Teacher's Press, in press.

**Gumperz, J. J.** *Language in Social Groups*. Essays selected and introduced by A. S. Dil, Stanford, California: Stanford University Press.

**Gumperz, John** and **Dell Hymes** (1964). The ethnography of communication. American Anthropologist 66 pt. 2.

**Hall, R.** (1966). *Pidgin and Creole Languages*, Ithaca, N.Y., Cornell University Press.

**Halliday, M. A. K.** (1968). The users and uses of language. In Joshua Fishman, *Readings in the Sociology of Language*. The Hague: Mouton.

**Halliday, M. A. K.** et al (1964). The Linguistic Sciences and Language Teaching.

**Hasselmo, Nils.** (1961). *American Swedish: a study of bilingualism*. Diss., Harvard.

**Hatfield, William N.** (1965). 'The effect of supplemental training on the achievement in ninth grade French of students weak in sound discrimination and sound-symbol association skills'. Unpublished doctoral dissertation, The Ohio State University.

**Haugen, E.** 'The stigmata of bilingualism' in A. S. Dil (ed) *The Ecology of Language*, Stanford California: Stanford University Press.

**Haugen, Einar.** (1953). The Norwegian Language in America: a study in bilingual behaviour. 2 vols. Philadelphia. University of Pennsylvania Press. (Second printing revised 1969 1 vol. Bloomington Ind.: Indiana University Press.)

(1954) Review of Weinreich 1953. Languages in Contact. *Language* 30. 380–388.

(to appear). Bilingualism language contact and immigrant languages in the United States. A Research Report 1956–70. *Current Trends in Linguistics* ed. T. Sebeok vol. 10.

**Haugen, E.** 'Problems of Bilingual Description' *Georgetown Monograph Series* No. 7 1954 9–19.

**Haugen, E.** 'Language Contact' *Proceedings of the VIII International Congress of Linguistics*, Oslo, 1957, pp. 771–784.

**Haugen, Einar.** (1958). *Languages in Contact*. Oslo: University Press.

**Hayden, Robert G.** (1966). Some community dynamics of language maintenance. In Joshua Fishman, et al., Language Loyalty in the United States. The Hague: Mouton.

**Henrie, S. N.** 'Study of Verb Phrases Used by Five Year Old Nonstandard Negro English Speaking Children'. Ph.D. dissertation, University of California, Berkeley, 1969.

**Hernández-Chávez, Eduadro.** (1975). Introduction. *El Lenguage de los Chicanos*. Washington, D.C.: Center for Applied Linguistics.

**Hoffman, Gerard.** (1968). Puerto Ricans in New York: a language-related ethnographic summary. In Joshua Fishman, et al., Bilingualism in the Barrio. New York: Yeshiva University.

**Houston, Susan.** 'A Sociolinguistic Consideration of the Black English of Children in Northern Florida'. *Language* 45. (1969): 599–607.

**Houston, Susan.** 'Syntactic Complexity and Information Transmission in First Graders'. *Child Development*, in press.

**Hughes, A.** (1966). 'Non-standard English of Grenada', *Caribbean Quarterly* 12(4).

**Hughes, Everett C.** (1970). The linguistic division of labor in industrial and urban societies. In James Alatis (ed), Bilingualism and Language Contact: Anthropological, Linguistic, Psychological and Sociological Aspects. Monograph Series on Languages and Linguistics 23. Washington, D.C.: Georgetown University Press.

**Hunt, Chester.** (1966). Language choice in multilingual society. Sociological Enquiry 36 no. 2.

**Hymes, D. H.** 'On communicative competence', in J. B. Pride and J. Holmes (eds) *Sociolinguistics* Penguin.

**Hymes, D. H.** (ed) (1971). *Pidginization and Creolization of Language*, Cambridge University Press.

**Hymes, Dell.** (1971). 'On communicative Competence'. In *Language Acquisition: Models and Methods*, edited by R. Huxley and E. Ingram. New York: Academic Press.

(1972a), Introduction. In *Functions of Language in the Classroom*, edited by C. Cazden, V. John and D. Hymes. New York: Teachers College Press.

(1972b), 'Models of the Interaction of Language and Social Life'. In *Directions in Sociolinguistics*, edited by John Gumperz and Dell Hymes, Holt, Rinehart and Winston.

**Innis, L. O.** (1910). *Trinidad and Trinidadians*. Trinidad, Mirror Printing Works.

(1923), Creole Folklore and Popular Superstitions in Trinidad. Trinidad, Yuilles Printerie.

**James, Carl.** (1970). Foreign language learning by dialect expansion.

**Johnson, R.** 'Language usage in the homes of Polish Immigrants in Western Australia', *Lingua* 18.

**Jones, J. A.** (1966). 'English in the West Indies', *English Language Teaching* 20(2).

**Kachru, Braj.** (1965). The Indianness in Indian English. Word 21. 391–410.

**Kachru, Braj.** (1966). Indian English: a study in contextualization. In Bazell, C. E., et al. In memory of J. R. Firth. London.

**Kachru, Braj.** (1969). English in South Asia. In Thomas Sebeok (ed.), Linguistics in South Asia: Current Trends in Linguistics 5. The Hague: Mouton.

**Kandel Subcommittee** (1946). *Report of the Secondary Education Continuation Committee*. Jamaica, Government Printery.

**Kernan, Claudia M.** 'Language Behavior in a Black Urban Community'. Monographs of the Language-Behavior Laboratory, no. 2. Berkeley: University of California, 1969.

**Khubchandani, L. M.** 'Language ideology and language development: an appraisal of Indian education policy'. *Linguistics* 193, June 2, 1977.

**Kirk-Greene, A.** (1971). The influence of West African languages on English. In John Spencer, *The English Language in West Africa*. London: Longman.

**Kjolseth, R.** 'Bilingual Education Programs in the United States: for Assimilation or Pluralism?' *The Language Education of Minority*

# 228   Bibliography

*Children*. Edited by B. Spolsky Rowley, Massachusetts: Newbury House.

**Kjolseth, R.** 'Bilingual education: for what and for whom?' *Language in Society* vol. 6 No. 2, August 1977.

**Kloss, Heinz** (1966). German-American language maintenance efforts. In Joshua Fishman, et al. Language Loyalty in the United States. The Hague: Mouton.

**Knight, H. E., L. D. Carrington,** and **C. B. Borely** (1972), *Preliminary Comments on Language Arts Textbooks in Use in the Primary Schools of Trinidad and Tobago*, U.W.I., Institute of Education.

**Kochman, T.** (1969). 'Social factors in the consideration of teaching standard English', in Aarons and Stewart (eds), 1969.

**Kochman, Thomas** (1969a). 'Rapping in the Black Ghetto', *Trans-action* 6 (February): 26–34.

(1969), 'Social Factors in the Consideration of Teaching Standard English', in *Linguistic-Cultural Differences and American Education*, Special Anthology Issue of *The Florida FL Reporter*, ed. Alfred A. Aarons Barbara Y. Gordon, and William A. Stewart.

**Kochman, T.** 'Black American speech events and a language program for the classroom', in C. Cazden, V. John and D. H. Hymes (eds) *Functions of Language in the Classroom* New York and London: Teachers College Press, Columbia University.

**Kriedler, Charles.** 'A Study of the Influence of English on the Spanish of Puerto Ricans in Jersey City, New Jersey'. Ann Arbor, University Microfilms, 1967 (Univerity of Michigan Ph.D. dissertation, 1957).

**Labov, W.** 'The Linguistic Variable as a Structural Unit'. Presented at a meeting of the Washington Linguistics Club, October, 1964b.

**Labov, W.** 'On the Mechanism of Linguistic Change'. *Georgetown Monograph Series*, No. 18, 1965a, 91–113.

**Labov, W.** (1964). 'Stages in the acquisition of standard English', in: *Social Dialects and Language Learning*, ed. by Shuy, Champaign, Illinois, NCTE.

(1966), *The Social Stratification of English in New York City*. Washington, D.C., Center for Applied Linguistics.

(1969), *The Logic of Non-Standard English, Twentieth Annual Round Table Meeting*. No. 22, ed. by J. E. Alatis, Georgetown University School of Languages and Linguistics.

(1971), 8 'The notion of "system" ', in: *Creole Languages*, ed. by Hymes.

**Labov, William** (1966). The effect of social mobility on linguistic behavior. Sociological Enquiry (Spring).

**Labov, William** (1969). 'Contraction, Deletion, and InherantVaria-bility of the English Copula', *Language* 45:715–62.

**Labov, W.** 'The logic of non-standard English', in J. E. Alatis (ed) *Monograph Series on Languages and Linguistics*, No. 22, 1969. Georgetown University Round Table on Languages and Linguistics, Washington, D.C. Also in F. Williams (ed) *Language and Poverty*: (abridged) in P. P. Giglioli (ed) *Language & Social Context* (Penguin): in R. D. Abrahams and R. C. Troike (eds) *Language & Cultural Diversity in American Education*; in J. A. Fishman (ed) *Advances in the Sociology of Language*, Vol. 2 (Mouton); in j.S. De Stefano (ed) *Language, Society and Education* (C. A. Jones Publishing Co.); and in N. Keddie (ed) *Tinker Tailor: the Myth of Cultural Deprivation* (Penguin).

**Labov, William** (1970a). *The Study of Nonstandard English*. Illinois: National Council of Teachers of English.

(1970b), 'The Study of Language in its Social Context'. Studium Generale 23. 30–87.

**Labov, William** (1970). The notion of system in Creoleglanguages. In Dell Hymes (ed), *Pidginization and Creolization of Languages*. Cambridge.

**Labov, W., P. Cohen** and **C. Robins**. *A Preliminary Study of the Structure of English Used by Negro and Puerto Rican Speakers in New York City*. Cooperative Research Project No. 3091, Columbia University, New York, 1965b.

**Labov, W.** and **P. Cohen** (1967). 'Systematic relation of standard and non-standard rules in the grammar of negro speakers', *Project Litacy Report*, 8. Ithaca, New York, Cornell University.

**Labov, W., P. Cohen, C. Robins** and **J. Lewis**. *A Study of the Non-Standard English of Negro and Puerto Rican Speakers in New York City*. Final Report, OE-6-10-059. Columbia University, New York City, 1968.

**Labov, William** and **Clarence Robins** (1966). 'A Note on the Relation of Reading Failure to Peer-Group Status in Urban Ghettos', in *Linguistic-Cultural Differences and American Education*, Special Anthology Issue of *The Florida FL Reporter*, ed. Alfred A. Aarons, Barbara Y. Gordon, and William A. Stewart.

**Lambert, E.** (1974). A Canadian experiment in the development of bilingual competence. *The Canadia Modern Language Review*, 31, 108–116.

**Lambert, W.** 'A Social Psychology of Bilingualism', In *Problems of Bilingualism*, edited by J. Macnamara, *Journal of Social Issues* 23 (1967): pt. 2, pp. 91–109.

**Lambert, W. E.** and **R. C. Gardner**. *Attitudes and Motivations in Second Language Learning*, Rowley, Massachusetts: Newbury House.

**Lambert, W. E.** and **G. R. Tucker**. 'The Home/School Language

Switch Program in the St. Lambert Elementary School', in *Conference on Child Language* Chicago, November, 1971. Les Presses de l'Universite Laval, Quebec.

**Lambert, W. E.** and **G. R. Tucker**. *Bilingual Education of Children*, Rowley, Massachusetts: Newbury House.

**Latrobe, C. J.** (1837–38), Reports on negro education, to Lord Glenelg, Secretary of State for Education and for War. Government of Great Britain.

**Laver, John** (1968). Assimilation in educated Nigerian English. English Language Teaching 22.156–160.

**Lawton, D. L.** (1963). 'Suprasegmental phenomena in Jamaica creole'. Ph.D. dissertation. Michigan State University.

(1965), 'Some problems of teaching a creolized language to Peace Corps Members', *Language Learning* 14.

(1971), 'Tone and Jamaican Creole', Paper read at the Annual Conference on Caribbean Linguistics, May 17–21, Mona. Mimeo. U.W.I.

**Leachman, D.** and **Robert A. Hall** (1955). American Indian pidgin English: attestations and grammatical peculiarities. American Speech 30.163–171.

**Leibowitz, Arnold H.** (1970). Educational policy and political acceptance: the imposition of English as the language of instruction in American schools. Washington: ERIC.

**Lemaire, Herve B.** (1966). The French language in New England. In Joshua Fishman, et al. Language Loyalty in the United States. The Hague: Mouton.

**Leopold, Werner F.** (1939–49). *Speech development of a bilingual child.* 4 vols. Evanston, III.: Northwestern University.

**LePage, R. B.** (1952). 'A survey of dialects in the British Caribbean', *Caribbean Quarterly*, 2(3).

(1955), 'The Language problem in the British Caribbean', *Caribbean Quarterly* 4(1).

(1957), 'General Outlines of English Creole Dialects', *Orbis* 6.

**LePage, R. B.** (ed) (1961). *Proceedings of the Conference on Creole Language Studies*, 1961. London, Macmillan.

(1972), 'The concept of competence in a creole English situation', in Craig, (ed), forthcoming.

**LePage, R.,** and **David, Decamp** (1960). *Jamaican Creole: An Historical Introduction to Jamaican Creole by R. B. LePage and Four Jamaican Creole Texts, by David DeCamp.* London, Macmillan.

**LePage, R.** (1968). Problems to be faced in the use of English as the medium of education in four West Indian territories. In Joshua Fishman, et al., Bilingualism in the Barrio. New York: Yeshiva University.

**LePage, R.** (1968). Problems of description in multilingual communities. Transactions of the Philological Society.

**LePage, R. B.** 'Sociolinguistics and the problem of competence', in *Language Teaching and Linguistics: Abstracts*, 1975.

**Lester, N.** 'Bilingual education in the United States, the Pacific and Southeast Asia', *Topics in Culture Learning* Vol. 2, 1974.

**Lieberson, S.** (ed) (1966). 'Explorations in sociolinguistics', *Social Enquiry* 36.

**Light, R. L.** 'On language arts and minority group children', in *Language and cultural diversity in American education.* Edited by R. D. Abrahams and R. C. Troike, Englewood Cliffs, N. J.: Prentice-Hall.

**Litteral, R.** 'A proposal for the use of pidgin in Papua New Guinea's education system', *Kivung*, Special Publication No. 1, May, 1975, *Tok Pisini go we?*

**Litteral, R.** 'The use of Pidgin in education', in *Kivung*, Special Publication No. 1, May, 1975, *Tok Pisin i go we?*

**Llamzon, T.** (1969). Standard Filipino English. Manila.

**Lazano, Anthony** (1974). 'Grammatical Notes on Chicano Spanish'. *La Revista Bilingue* 1. (May-August), 147–151.

**Ma, Roxana** and **Eleanor Herasimchuk** (1968). Linguistic dimensions of a bilingual neighbourhood. In Joshua Fishman, et al., Bilingualism in the Barrio. New York: Yeshiva University.

**Mackey, W. F.** 'A typology for bilingual education', *Foreign Language Annals*, 3 4.

**Mackey, W. F.** *Bilingual Education in a Binational School.* Rowley, Massachusetts: Newbury House.

**Mackey, W. F.** 'The Description of Bilingualism'. *Canadian Journal of Linguistics*, 1962, 7, 51–85.

**Mackey, W. F.** 'The Measurement of Bilingual Behavior'. *Canadian Psychologist*, 1966, 7, 75–92.

**Mackey, W. F.** (1967). *Bilingualism as a world problem.* E. R. Adair Memorial Lectures, Harvest House, Canada. (Also in French: Le bilinguisme: phénomène mondial).

**Macnamara, John** (1971). The cognitive strategies of language learning. Unpublished papers of Conference on Child Language, Chicago, November 22–24, 1971.

(1972), The cognitive basis of language learning in infants. *Psychological Review*, 79, No. 1.

**Martinet, A.** *Economie des changements phonétiques.* Berne, 1965.

**Mafeni, Bernard** (1971). Nigerian pidgin. In John Spencer, The English Language in West Africa. London: Longman.

**McDavid, Raven I.** (1969). 'Dialectology and the Teaching of

Reading', in *Teaching Black Children to Read*, ed. Joan C. Baratz and Roger W. Shuy. Washington, D.C.: Center for Applied Linguistics.

**McKay, June Rumery**. 'A Partial Analysis of a Variety of Non-standard Negro English'. Ph.D. dissertation, University of California, Berkeley, 1969.

**Mintz, Sidney** (1971). The Socio-historical background to pidginization and creolization. In Dell Hymes (ed), *Pidginization and Creolization of Languages*. Cambridge.

**Modiano, Nancy** (1968). 'National or Mother Tongue in Beginning Reading: A Comparative Study'. Unbuplished manuscript.

**Mosher, F. A.** and **K. R. Hornsby** (1966). On asking questions. In J. S. Bruner, R. Olver, L. P. Greenfield et al. *Studies in Cognitive Growth*. New York, Wiley. pp. 86–102.

**Mueller, Theodore** (1971). The development of curriculum materials for individualized foreign language instruction. In Howard B. Altman and Robert L. Politzer (eds), *Conference on individualizing foreign language instruction*. Final report (unpuplished).

**Neale, B.** (1971). Language use among the Asian communities. In: Language in Kenya. ed. by W. H. Whiteley. Oxford University Press.

**Nemser, W.** (1971). Approximative systems of foreign language learners. *International Review of Applied Linguistics* 9.115–124.

**Nisbet, J. D.** and **J. Welsh** (1972). 'A local evaluation of primary school French', *Journal of Curriculum Studies*, 4, 2, 169–165.

**Noonan, K.** (1975). The 'Chicano' and bilingual education—a matter of exclusion. Paper presented at the Fourth Annual International Bilingual Bicultural Education Conference, Illinois, May 22–24, 1975.

**Norwood Committee** (1943). *Curriculum and Examinations in Secondary Schools*, H.M.S.O.

**Ohannessian, S.,** and **G. Ansre**. 'Some reflections on the uses of sociolinguistically oriented language surveys', in S. Ohannessian et al. (eds) *Language Surveys of Developing Nations* Arlington, Virginia, Center for Applied Linguistics.

**Oishi, Janyie,** and **Dorothy Kakimoto**. 'Pidgin and Pidgin Speakers', Term paper, Speech 164, University of California, Berkeley, 1967.

**Ornstein, Jacob** (1971). Language varieties along the U.S.–Mexican Border. In G. E. Perren and J. L. M. Trim, Applications of Linguistics, Cambridge.

**Ornstein, Jacob** (1974). 'The Sociolinguistic Studies on Southwest Bilingualism: A Status Report'. *Southwest Areal Linguistics*. San Diego: Institute for Cultural Pluralism. 11–34.

**Osterberg, Tore** (1964). *Bilingualism and the First School Language:*

*An Educational Problem Illustrated by Results from a Swedish Dialect Area.* Umean: Vasterbottens Trycheri AB.

**Park, Robert E.** (1930). Introduction to the Science of Sociology. Chicago. P.

**Parkin, D.** (1972). Chapters 5–8 in: *Language in Kenya*, ed. by W. H. Whiteley. Oxford University Press.

**Paulston, Christina B.** (1974). Linguistics and communicative competence. *TESOL Quarterly*, 8, 4, 347–362.

**Paulson, C. B.** (1975a). Ethnic relations and bilingual education: Accounting for contradictory data. *Working Papers on Bilingualism* 6, pp. 1–44.

**Paulston, C. B.** (1975b). *Questions concerning bilingual education.* Papers in Applied Linguistics, Bilingual Education Series, Arlington, Va., Center for Applied Linguistics.

**Penfield, W.** (1953). 'A consideration of the neuro-physiological mechanisms of speech and some educational consequences', *Proceedings of the American Academy of Arts and Sciences*, 82, 201–214.

**Penfield, Wilder** and **Lamar Roberts** (1959). *Speech and brain mechanisms.* Princeton: Princeton University Press. (Chapter on 'The Learning of Languages' reprinted in Michel 1967, 192–214).

**Penfield, W.** (1964). 'The uncommitted cortex: the child's changing brain', *Atlantic Monthly*, 214, 1, 77–81.

**Perez Sala, Paulino** (1973). *Interferencia Lingüística del Inglés en el Español Hablado en Puerto Rico.* Puerto Rico: Interamerican University.

**Perren, G. E.** and **J. L. M. Trim** (1971). Applications in Linguistics. Cambridge.

**Philips, S. U.** 'Participant structures and communicative competence', in C. Cazden, V. John, D. H. Hymes (eds.) *Functions of Language in the Classroom* London and New York: Teachers College Press, Columbia University. Also in R. D. Abrahams and R. C. Troike (eds) *Language and Cultural Diversity in American Education* Englewood Cliffs, N. J.: Prentice-Hall.

**Philips, Susan U.** (1970). Acquisition of rules for appropriate speech usage. In James Atalis (ed.), Bilingualism and Language Contact: Anthropological, Linguistic, Psychological and Sociological Aspects. *Monograph Series on Languages and Linguistics*, 23. Washtingon, D.C.

**Phillips, J. M.** (1975). Code-switching in bilingual classrooms, M.A. Thesis, California State University, Northridge.

**Pimsleur, Paul** (1966). Testing foreign language learning. In Albert Valdman (ed), *Trends in language teaching*. New York, McGraw-Hill Company.

**Plumer, Davenport** (1970). A summary of environmentalist views and some educational implications. In Frederick Williams, Language and Poverty. Chicago: Markham Press.

**Politzer, Robert** and **Louis Weiss** (1969). *Improving achievement in foreign language*. Philadelphia, The Center for Curriculum Development, Inc.

**Prator, Clifford** (1968). The British heresy in T.E.S.L. in J. Fishman, C. Ferguson and J. Das Gupta, Language Problems of Developing Nations. New York.

**Price, Eurwen**. 'Early Bilingualism', In *Towards Bilingualism*, edited by C. J. Dodson, et al., p. 34. Welsh Studies in Education, vol. 1, edited by Jack L. Williams, Cardiff: University of Wales Press, 1968.

**Pride, J. B.** 'The deficit-difference controversy', *Archivum Linguisticum*, April, 1974.

**Pride, J. B.** 'Bilingual education and the recognition of speech communities', in W. Viereck ed. Munchen: Wilhelm Fink *Sprache als soziales Verhalten*.

**Rainey, Mary**. 'Style-Switching in a Headstart Class'. Language-Behavior Laboratory Working Paper No. 16. Berkeley: University of California, 1969.

**Reinecke, John** (1969). Language and Dialect in Hawaii. Honolulu.

**Reissman, F.** (1962). *The Culturally Deprived Child*. New York, Harper and Row.

**Reisman, Karl** (1961). 'The English-based creole of Antigua', (Research Notes), *Caribbean Quarterly* 1(1).
(1965), 'The isle is full of noises! A study of creole in the speech patterns of Antigua, West Indies.' Ph.D. dissertation. Harvard University.

**Rice, F. A.** (ed) (1962). *Study of the Role of Second Languages in Asia, Africa, and Latin America*. Washington, D.C., Center for Applied Linguistics.

**Richards, Jack C.** (1971a). A non-contrastive approach to error analysis. English Language Teaching 24, 204–219.

**Richards, Jack C.** (1971b). Error analysis and second language strategies. Language Sciences 17.12–22.

**Richards, Jack C.** Some social aspects of language learning. TESOL Quarterly 6, 3, 1972.

**Richards, J.** 'Social factors, interlanguage, and language learning', Language Learning 22, 2, 1973.

**Robinson, W. P.** 'Social Factors and Language Development in Primary School Children'. In *Mechanisms in Child Language Development*, edited by Renira Huxley and Elizabeth Ingram. London: Academic Press, 1971.

**Ronjat, Jules** (1913). *Le développement du langage observé chez un*

Bibliography 235

*enfant bilingue.* Paris: H. Champion.

**Rosario, R.** *Vocabulario puertorriqueno.* Connecticut, 1965.

**Rosenthal, Marilyn** (1973). *The Acquisition of Child Awareness of Language: Age and Socio-Economic Class Correlates.* Unpublished Ph.D. dissertation, Georgetown University.

**Rosenthal, R.,** and **Lenore Jacobson** (1968). 'Teacher Expectations for the Disadvantaged', *Scientific American* 218:19–23.

**Rubin, J.** 'Bilingualism in Paraguay'. *Anthropological Linguistics*, 1961, 4, 52–58.

**Rubin, J.** 'What the "good language learner" can teach us', *TESOL Quarterly*, 9, 1, 1975.

**Russell, T.** (1868). *The Etymology of Jamaica Grammar by a Young Gentleman.* Kingston, MacDougall & Co.

**Samarin, William** (1962). Lingua francas, with special reference to Africa. In Frank A. Rice (ed), Study of the Role of Second Languages in Asia, Africa and Latin America. Washington.

**Samarin, William J.** (1971). Salient and substansive pidginization. In Dell Hymes (ed), *Pidginization and Creolization of Languages.* Cambridge.

**Sanchez, Rosaura** (1972). 'Nuestra Circunstancia Lingüística'. *El Grito.* Berkeley: Quinto Sol Publications.

1974, *A Generative Study of Two Spanish Dialects.* Unpublished Ph.D. dissertation, University of Texas at Austin.

**Saporta, Sol** (ed) (1961). *Psycholinguistics*, New York, Holt, Rinehart & Winston.

**Schools Council** (1968). *Young School Leavers*, Inquiry I. London: H.M.S.O.

**Schaedel, R.** (ed) (1969). *Research and Resources of Haiti.* New York, Research Institute for the Study of Man.

**Schmidt-Mackey, I.** 'Language Strategies of the Bilingual Family', in Conference on Child Language Chicago, November, 1971. Les Presses de l'Université Laval, Quebec.

**Schudardt, H.** (1882). *Kreolisch Studien*, 11 vols. Vienna.

**Schumann, J. H.** 'Affective factors and the problem of age in second language acquisition', *Language Learning*, 25, 2, 1975.

**Schumann, J. H.** 'Social distance as a factor in second language acquisition', *Language Learning*, 26, 1, 1976.

**Schumann, J. H.** 'The implications of interlanguage, pidgins and creoles for the study of adult second language acquisition', *TESOL Quarterly*, June, 1974.

**Scoles, I.** (1885). *Sketches of African and Indian Life in British Guiana*, Guiana, The Argosy Press.

**Seaman, David.** 'Modern Greek and American English in Contact: A sociolinguistic investigation of Greek-American bilingualism in Chicago'. Unpublished Ph.D. dissertation, Indiana University, 1965.

**Sebeok, Thomas** (ed) (1969). Linguistics in South Asia: Current Trends in Linguistics 5. The Hague: Mouton.

**Seligman, C. R., G. R. Tucker** and **W. E. Lambert**. 'The effects of speech style and other attributes toward pupils', *Language in Society* 1, 1, 1972.

**Selinker, Larry**. Interlanguage. International Review of Applied Linguistics 10, 3, 1972.

**Shore, M. S.** (1974). *The content analysis of 125 Title VII bilingual programs funded in 1960 and 1970.* New York, Bilingual Education Applied Research Unit, Project BEST, New York City Bilingual Consortium, Hunter College Div.

**Shultz, J.** (1975). Language use in bilingual classrooms. Paper presented at the Ninth Annual TESOL Convention, Los Angeles, March 4–9, 1975.

**Shuy, R. W.** 'Sociolinguistics and teacher attitudes in a southern school system', in D. M. Smith and R. W. Shuy (eds) *Sociolinguistics in Cross-Culture Analysis* Washington, D.C.: Georgetown University Press.

**Shuy, R. W.** (ed) (1964). *Social dialects and language learning.* Champaign, Illinois, NCTE.

**Shuy, R. W.** (1972). 'Strategies for implementing socilinguistic principles in the schools', in: Craig (ed), forthcoming.

**Shuy, Roger W., Joan C. Baratz** and **Walt Wolfram** (1969). *Sociolinguistic Factors in Speech Identification.* NIMH Final Report, Project No. MH 15048–01.

**Shuy, Roger W.** and **R. Fasold** (1972). Contemporary emphases in sociolinguistics. In: Monograph series on languages and linguistics. No. 24. 185–97. Washington, D.C., Georgetown University Press.

**Shuy, R. W., W. A. Wolfram** and **W. K. Riley** (1967), 'Linguistic correlates in social stratification', in: *Detroit Speech*, Final Report. Co-operative Research Project 6–1347, Office of Education.

**Shuy, Roger W., Walter A. Wolfram** and **William K. Riley** (1968). *Field Techniques in an Urban Language Study.* Washington, D.C.: Center for Applied Linguistics.

**Skinner, B. F.** (1957). *Verbal Behavior.* New York: Appleton-Century-Crofts.

**Sledd, James** (1969). 'Bi-dialectalism: The Linguistics of White Supremacy', English Journal 58:1307–29.

(1972), 'Doublespeak: Dialectology in the Service of Big Brother', *College English* 33:439–56.

**Sole, Yolanda** (1975). 'Sociolinguistic Perspectives on Texas Spanish and the Teaching of the Standard Language'. *Southwest Languages* *and Linguistics in Educational Perspective.* San Diego: Institute for Cultural Pluralism.

**Solomon, D.** (1966). 'The system of predication in the speech of Trinidad: a quantitative study of decreolization'. M.A. Thesis. Columbia University.

(1972), 'Form, content and the post-creole continuum', in: Craig (ed). 1974.

**Spears, R.** (1972). 'Pitch and intonation in Cayman English', in: Craig (ed), forthcoming.

**Spencer, J.** (1963). Language in Africa. Cambridge.

**Spencer, John** (1971). The English Language in West Africa. London: Longman.

**Spencer, John** (1971). West Africa and the English language. In John Spencer, *The English Language in West Africa.* London: Longman.

**Spolsky, B.** 'Attitudinal aspects of second language learning', *Language Learning,* 19, 3 and 4, 1969.

**Spolsky, B.** Review of W. E. Lambert and G. R. Tucker *Bilingual Education of Children,* TESOL Quarterly 7, 3, 1973.

**Stern, H. H.** (1974). What can we learn from the good language learner? Unpublished paper presented at the Ontario Modern Language Teachers' Association, April 19–20.

**Stern, H. H.** and **M. Swain** (1973). Notes on language learning in bilingual kindergarden classes. In G. Rondeau (ed) *Some aspects of Canadian applied linguistics,* Montreal, Quebec, Center Educatif et Culturel Inc.

**Stewart, W.** 'Functional Distribution of Creole and French in Haiti'. *Georgetown Monograph Series,* No. 15, 1962, 163–72.

**Stewart, William** (1962). An outline of linguistic typology for describing multilingualism. In Frank A. Rice (ed), Study of the Role of Second Languages in Asia, Africa and Latin America. Washington.

**Stewart, William** (1962). Creole languages in the Caribbean. In Frank A. Rice (ed), Study of the Role of Second Languages in Asia, Africa and Latin America. Washington.

**Stewart, W. A.** (ed) (1964). *Non-Standard Speech and the Teaching of English.* Washington, D.C.: Center for Applied Linguistics.

**Stewart, W. A.** (1967). 'Sociolinguistic factors in the history of American negro dialects', *The Florida FL Reporter* 5(2).

(1969), 'Negro dialect in the teaching of reading', in: Baratz and Shuy (eds), 1969.

**Stewart, W.** (1968). A sociolinguistic typology for describing national multilingualism. In: Readings in the sociology of language, ed. by J. A. Fishamn. 531–45. The Hague, Mouton.

**Stewart, William A.** (1969). 'The use of Negro Dialect in the Teaching of Reading', in *Teaching Black Children to Read*, ed. Joan C. Baratz and Roger W. Shuy. Washington, D.C.: Center for Applied Linguistics.

**Stolt, Birgit** (1969). Luther sprach 'mixtim vernacula lingua'. *Zeitschrift fnr deutsche Philologie* 88.432–435.

**Strevens, Peter** (1956). English overseas: choosing a model of pronunciation. *English Language Teaching* 10.123–131. Styles of Learning Among American Indians: An Outline for Research. Washington, 1968.

**Sumner, R.** and **F. W. Warburton** (1972). *Achievements in Secondary School*. Slough: NFER.

**Swain, M.** (1974). French immersion programs across Canada: Research findings. *The Canadian Modern Language Review*, 31, 117–129.

**Taylor, D.** (1945). 'Certain Carib morphological influences on creole', *International Journal of American Linguistics* 11 (3).

(1952), 'A note on the phoneme /r/ in Dominican creole', *Word* 8 (3).

(1955), 'Phonic Interference in Dominican Creole', *Word* 11.

(1961), 'Some Dominican creole descendants of the French definite article', in: *Conference on Creole Language Studies*, ed. by LePage. London, Macmillan.

(1963), 'Remarks on the lexicon of Dominican French creole', *Romance Philology* 16.

(1968), 'New languages for old in the West Indies', in: *Readings in the Sociology of Language*, ed. by J. A. Fishman. The Hague, Mouton.

**Taylor, Orlando L.** (1973). 'Teachers' Attitudes Toward Black and Nonstandard English as Measured by the Language Attitude Scale', in *Language Attitudes: Current Trends and Prospects*, ed. Roger W. Shuy and Ralph W. Fasold. Washington, D.C.: Georgetown University Press.

**Thomas, J. J.** (1869). *The Theory and Practice of Creole Grammar*. (Reprinted London, New Beacon Books. 1969).

**Thompson, R. W.** (1916). A note on some possible affinities between Creole dialects of the old world and those of the new.

**Torrey, Jane**. 'Teaching Standard English to Speakers of Other Dialects'. Second International Congress on Applied Linguistics, Cambridge, England, 1969.

**Triandis, H. D., W. D. Loh** and **Leslie Levin**. 'Race, Status, Quality of Spoken English, and Opinions about Civil Rights as Determinant of Interpersonal Attitudes'. *Journal of Personality and Social Psychology* 3 (1966): 468–72.

**Trotman, J.** (1973). 'The teaching of English in Guyana: A linguistic approach'. Mimeo. Faculty of Education, University of Guyana.

**Tucker, G. R.** and **A. d'Anglejan** (1974). New directions in second language teaching. Paper presented at the Inter-American Conference on Bilingual Education, Mexico City, Nov., 1974. (To appear in collected papers from the conference, Center for Applied Linguistics, Arlington, Va.).

**Tucker, G. R., W. E. Lambert** and **A. d'Anglejan** (1973). Are French immersion???

**Tucker, R.** and **W. Lambert**. 'White and Negro Listeners' Reactions to Various American-English Dialects'. *Social Forces* 47 (1969): 463–68.

**Twaddell, Freeman** (1967). *Teacher's manual le Francais: parler et lire*. New York, Holt, Rinehart and Winston, Inc.

(1973), Vocabulary expansion in the ESOL classroom. *TESOL Quarterly*, 7, 1, 61–78.

**Tyndall, B.** (1965). 'Some grammatical aspects of the written work of creolese-speaking school children in British Guiana'. M.A. Thesis. University of Manchester.

(1973), 'Reading habit and the written expression of secondary school first formers'. Mimeo. Faculty of Education, University of Guyana.

**UNESCO** (1953). *The Use of Vernacular Languages in Education*. Monographs on Fundamental Education, No. 8. Paris: UNESCO.

**UNESCO** (1965). *World Conference of Ministers of Education on the Eradication of Illiteracy: Final Report*. Paris: UNESCO.

**Ure, Jean** (1968). The mother-tongue and the other tongue. Ghana Teachers' Journal 60. 38–55.

**U.S. Commission on Civil Rights** (1972). *The excluded student: Educational practices affecting Mexican Americans in the Southwest*. Mexican American Education Study, Report III. Washington, D.C.: U.S. Government Printing Office.

**U.S. Commission on Civil Rights** (1972). Teachers and students: Differences in teacher interaction with Mexican American and Anglo students. Mexican American Education Study, ReportV.Washington, D.C. U.S. Government Printing Office.

**Valdes-Fallis, G.** (1972). Bilingual education: Early efforts supply cues to meeting current needs. Accent on ACTFL, Nov., 28–30.

**Valdman, A.** (1969). 'The language situation in Haiti', in: Schaedel (ed), 1969.

**van Name, J.** (1870). 'Contributions to Creole grammar', Transactions of the American Philological Association, 1. Boston.

**van Sertima, J.** (1897). 'Among the common people of British Guiana', *British Guiana Pamphlet*, No. 35.

(1905), *The Creole Tongues of British Guiana*. Berbice, British Guiana, The British Gazette Store.

**Venezky, Richard L.** (1970). 'Nonstandard Language and Reading', *Elementary English* 47: 334–45.

**Walsh, N. G.** (1967). Distinguishing types and varieties of English in Nigeria. Journal of the Nigerian English Studies Association 2. 47–55.

**Waterhouse, J.** 'Report on a Neighborhood Youth Corps Summer Language Program, July 1–August 2, 1968'. University of California, Berkeley. Mineographed.

**Wax, Murray, Rosalie Wax** and **Robert Dumont** (1964). Formal education in an American community. Social Problems 2, no. 4.

**Weber, Rose-Marie** (1969). 'Some Reservations on the Significance of Dialects in the Acquisition of Reading', *The Reading Specialist* 7: 37–40.

**Weinreich, Uriel** (1953). *Languages in contact: findings and problems*. New York. (Publications of the Linguistic Circle of New York, No. 1) Reprinted 1963, The Hague).

**Whinnon, Keith** (1971). Linguistic hybridization and the 'special case' of pidgins and creoles. In Dell Hymes (ed), Pidginization and Creolization of Languages. Cambridge.

**Whiteley, W. H.** Introduction to *Language Use and Social Change*, London: Oxford University Press.

**Wiggins, M. Eugene** (1972). 'The Cognitive Deficit-Difference Controversy as a Socio-Political Struggle'. Unpublished manuscript.

**Williams, F.** 'Some research notes on dialect attitudes and stereotypes'. In R. W. Shuy and R. W. Fasold (eds) *Language Attitudes: Current Trends and Prospects*. Georgetown University Press.

**Williams, Frederick** (1970). Language and Poverty. Chicago: Markham.

**Williams, F.** 'Psychological Correlates of Speech Characteristics: On Sounding Disadvantaged'. *Journal of Speech and Hearing Research*, in press.

**Williams, F.** and **Rita C. Naremore**. 'On the Functional Analysis of Social Class Differences in Modes of Speech'. *Speech Monographs* 36 (1969): 77–101.

**Willaims, Ronald** (1971). 'Race and the Word'. *Today's Speech* 19, No. 2:27–33.

**Wolff, Hans** (1959). 'Intelligibility and Inter-Ethnic Attitudes', *Anthropological Linguistics* 1, No. 3: 34–41.

**Wolff, H.** 'Intelligibility and inter-ethnic attitudes', in D. H. Hymes *Language in Culture and Society*. New York, Evanston & London: Harper & Row and Tokyo: John Weatherhill, Inc.

**Wolfram, W.** *Detroit Negro Speech*. Washington: Center for Applied Linguistics, 1969.

**Wolfram, Walt** and **Ralph W. Fasold** (1969). 'Toward Reading Materials for Speakers of Black English: Three Linguistically Appropriate Passages', in *Teaching Black Children to Read*, ed. Joan C. Baratz and Roger W. Shuy. Washington, D.C.: Center for Applied Linguistics.

**Wolfram, W.** and **R. W. Fasold**. *Social Dialects in American English* (Chapter 8) Englewood Cliffs, N.J.: Prentice-Hall.

**Wurm, S.** 'Language Policy, Language Engineering and Literacy: New Guinea and Australia', in *Current Trends in Linguistics* No. 8.

**Yeni-Komshian, Grace** (1965). Training Procedures for Developing Auditory Perception Skills in the Sound System of a Foreign Language. Unpublished doctoral dissertation: McGill University, Montreal.

# Index